Human Capital Leadership

An Experiential Approach

Stephanie J. Thomason, Ph.D.
The University of Tampa

Human Capital Leadership

Human Capital Leadership

The intention of this textbook is to provide an overview of the various functions of human resource management for courses that instruct this topic. "Human resource management" was once termed "personnel administration." Universities at the time offered courses in personnel administration. Today, businesses and universities use the term "human resource management," yet in my opinion, this is becoming outdated. A better title is human capital leadership, which is the overall theme of this textbook.

Rather than viewing our workforce as resources, I call attention to our workforce as capital. Our people are valuable and should be treated as investments, not as commodities or costs. Further, rather than merely managing our workforce, I call attention to leading. Managing employees is more transactional, while leading a workforce is more transformational. The latter fits in better with the overall theme of the book.

Human Capital Leadership: An Experiential Approach

Author: Stephanie J. Thomason

Copyright 2020 Stephanie J. Thomason

Published by Amazon Create Space Kindle Direct Publishing.

All rights reserved.

ISBN-9781699661918

* Version 1 License Notes

No part of this publication may be reproduced, stored in a retrieval system, or transmitted in any form or by any means, electronic, mechanical, photo-publishing, recording, or otherwise, without the prior written permission of the publisher.

Printed in the United States of America by Amazon Kindle Direct Publishing.

Human Capital Leadership

CONTENTS

Chapter 1: International Human Resource Management 1
QUESTIONS FOR REVIEW 23
APPLICATIONS 24
CASE STUDIES 28
Chapter 2: Legal Issues 34
QUESTIONS FOR REVIEW 53
APPLICATIONS 54
CASE STUDIES 59
Chapter 3: Job Analysis 65
QUESTIONS FOR REVIEW 76
APPLICATIONS 77
CASE STUDIES 78
Chapter 4: Planning and Recruitment 80
QUESTIONS FOR REVIEW 97
APPLICATION 98
CASE STUDIES 99
Chapter 5: Selection 101
QUESTIONS FOR REVIEW 118
APPLICATIONS 119
Chapter 6: Performance Management 127
QUESTIONS FOR REVIEW 140
APPLICATIONS 141
Chapter 7: Training and Development 148
QUESTIONS FOR REVIEW 157
APPLICATIONS 158

CASE STUDY	164
Chapter 8: Compensation	**165**
QUESTIONS FOR REVIEW	186
CASE STUDIES	188
Chapter 9: Benefits and Incentives	**191**
QUESTIONS FOR REVIEW	205
APPLICATIONS	206
CASE STUDIES	209
Chapter 10: Unions	**211**
QUESTIONS FOR REVIEW	227
APPLICATIONS	228
CASE STUDIES	229
Chapter 11: Health and Safety	**236**
QUESTIONS FOR REVIEW	251
APPLICATIONS	252
CASE STUDIES	255
Chapter 12: Servant Leadership and Ethics	**256**
QUESTIONS FOR REVIEW	271
APPLICATIONS	272
CASE STUDIES	275

Chapter 1: International Human Resource Management

Introduction

In China's fast-paced technology industry, being young has its perks. In fact, according to *Bloomberg BusinessWeek,* youth is often favored over experience with hiring managers preferring employees under thirty, while routinely dismissing applications and continuations of employment for those much older.[1] Robin Chan, an entrepreneur and angel investor in Chinese companies such as Xiaomi and Twitter commented, "Working in tech is like being a professional athlete. You work extremely hard from 20 to 40 years and hope you hit it big. After that, it's time to move on to something else and let someone younger try their hand." China has national laws prohibiting discrimination based on gender, disability, and religion, yet discrimination based on age is entirely legal. Furthermore, despite having gender protections, there is no equal pay protection for women and they earn (on average) 36 percent less than men. Companies like the Shenzhen Stock Exchange and JD.com routinely advertise for positions for employees "under 28." Some in China feel the policies have benefits. As stated by Liu Huai Yi, 33, "I don't buy the idea that after 35 you can't get a job. Someone is IT has to just keep learning to keep up." Forty-seven percent of China's population is over forty and that number is expected to rise to fifty-five percent by 2030, so pressure to consider older workers for positions may increase.

Laws and workplace hiring preferences vary substantially around the world, with less developed countries tending to have more lax laws and fewer restrictions, while more developed countries tend to have stricter laws and greater restrictions. In chapter 2, we will cover the laws in the United States, which do offer protections for workers who are forty or older. International human resource managers in organizations should be aware of the regulations, norms, and hiring preferences around the world when setting up global subsidiaries. China, with its 1.4-billion-person population, is considered an attractive location for foreign direct investment (and is the number one recipient of FDI) based on its educated middle and upper classes and its relatively low labor costs. India closely follows China, with its 1.3-billion-person-population, growing middle class and business-friendly environment.

Why is the middle class important? The vast majority of humanity was living on today's equivalent of $1 a day around 1800. The industrial revolution, growth of capitalism, and information revolution over the past two hundred years greatly changed the world. Prior to 1800, people were either rich or poor. The middle class was largely inexistent. Capitalism and the industrial revolution ushered in a new, influential middle class. Our middle class today has helped to improve the financial stability and security of billions throughout the world today.

Objectives:

After reading this chapter, you should be able to:

- Recognize the difference between human resource management and international human resource management.
- Identify recent human resource management trends.
- Discuss the challenges and remedies associated with international work assignments.
- Recognize the costs and benefits of the international modes of entry.
- Articulate the reasons business leaders select particular locations for their international subsidiaries.
- Discuss international HRM strategies.
- Identify and articulate the challenges associated with international assignments.
- Identify and articulate ways in which HRM managers can effectively address challenges in international assignments
- Recognize several international approaches to international staffing

Distinguishing International Human Resource Management

Human resource management is the organizational function related to attracting, recruiting, selecting, training, compensating, and retaining human talent. Human resource management further includes attention to unions, health and safety issues, and legal compliance in both domestic and international operations. Human resource managers oversee these functions, yet managers of other functions, such as accounting, finance, or marketing, are responsible for some of the same tasks that HR managers do. For example, an accounting manager may be actively involved in the hiring process of his subordinates, while a marketing manager may oversee on-the-job training. All decisions that affect an organization's workforce are a function of human resource management.

When organizations manage their workforces by valuing their employees as human capital, they can create and sustain competitive advantages by maximizing employee engagement. Zappos is an example of an organization that has maximized employee engagement by valuing its employees. According to Rebecca Henry, the former director of human resources for Zappos, Zappos has consciously decided on its corporate culture and how to reinforce and support its culture and ten core values through all human resources and management work systems.[2]

Zappos' ten core values include "deliver WOW through service," "pursue growth and learning," "be passionate and determined," and "create fun and a little weirdness." The company's job descriptions, on-the-job training, hiring process, and day-to-day work environment remind and reinforce Zappos' ten core values with employees, visitors, customers, and partners.[3]

As examples,[4] the hiring process at Zappos lasts four months and is similar to a courtship between Zappos' employees and job applicants, as they meet in a variety of social settings outside of Zappos' home office. Zappos has also developed a variety of behaviorally-based interview questions to illuminate a job applicant's congruence with Zappos' core values. Behaviorally-based interview questions ask applicants how they have handled various situations in the past, such as an irate customer. Applicants who are hired next spend time in Zappos' call center for three or four weeks. Once this on-the-job training is complete, they're offered $3,000 to leave. Yes, you read that correctly: they're paid to leave. Zappos would rather only the most committed stay.

According to the Gallup Organization (2017), 70 percent of the variance in culture can be attributed to team leaders and managers – and when managers provide meaningful feedback to employees, those employees are three and a half times more likely to be engaged. Furthermore, according to Gallup's *State of the Global Workplace Report,* 67 percent of global employees are not engaged and 18 percent are actively disengaged in the workplace, resulting in $7 trillion in lost productivity! Organizations should engage in practices to increase their percentages of highly engaged employees as these employees make an impact on organizations' bottom lines.

Some organizational leaders pay little attention to maximizing employee engagement, treating their employees as if they're mere expenses on a balance sheet and breeding a culture of fear. As an example, in February of 2017 former Uber employee Susan Fowler alleged that Uber's culture was one of sexism and sexual harassment. Her claims, coupled with investigations of alleged intellectual property theft and illegal interference with rival company Lyft led thirteen executives of Uber to resign, including its CEO.[5] As a second recent example, numerous sexual abuse claims against Harvey Weinstein of The Weinstein Group ignited public outrage, as many believed the leadership at The Weinstein Group was complicit in Weinstein's actions.[6] Apple subcontractor FoxConn is a third example, due to accusations of poor working and living conditions that led to a series of employee suicide attempts and suicides by jumping from the tops of buildings in its Shenzhen China location. FoxConn's response, which was to install safety nets to catch suicidal employees, was not viewed favorably in the eyes of the public. A better response would have been to address and correct the cause of the suicides by improving working and living conditions.

What are the demographics of the highly engaged employees? Employees in all types of jobs or levels or demographics may be engaged. One recent study found that despite the assertion of some that older employees are less engaged, the authors found that older employees are more engaged.[7] The authors posited that older workers' well-regulated emotions and strong commitments to their careers may contribute to the positive relationship between age and work engagement.

"High performance work systems" (HPWS) refer to practices that have been shown to significantly impact human resource performance and to result in greater employee satisfaction. Examples of these high impact practices include (1) giving realistic job previews; (2) using validated selection tools; (3) incorporating employee suggestion or innovation programs; (4) using competence or performance-based pay; (5) offering continuous mentoring, training and leadership development; (6) creating an egalitarian work environment; and (7) giving regular performance evaluations. Employees are more empowered and involved and have greater responsibilities in HPWS. HPWS practices are correlated with financial performance, productivity, cost control, and product and service quality.

International human resource management can be distinguished from domestic human resource management in that the former incorporates an attention to the socio-cultural, political, ethical, legal, and economic macro-level factors that contribute to an organization's success when operating across international borders.

Trends in Human Resource Management from Bridge

According to Bridge, the following trends are impacting or will be impacting human resource managers:[8]

1. Work-life integration and flexibility will move to the forefront.

2. Design thinking: How to train your dragon employees.
3. Training is not just for onboarding.
4. Rise of teams (collaboration versus competition).
5. Perceptions in the value of people analytics grow.
6. Employee engagement is a top priority.
7. Rise in gig and remote workers.

Work life integration and flexibility

Younger generations (Millennials and Generation Z) can be distinguished from Baby Boomers and Generation X in a few ways. They are more tech savvy, having been raised with the internet and mobile phones. They're socially conscious with a strong desire to do something meaningful. They're short on attention span and many are very proficient in multi-tasking. They desire flexibility in the workplace and appreciate options such as tele-commuting. Many want an even balance of time for family or friends with work. Many expect quick promotions within only a couple of years. They're also less loyal to their organizations. Over 90 percent have indicated they'll leave their organizations within three years. Some are "boomerang" employees who have no problem with leaving a company at one point and returning at another. Many are also frequent users of social media, so rather than prohibiting social media in the workplace (which may turn them off), some companies are figuring out ways to integrate and capitalize on it. Some use social media to attract talent from younger generations.

Design thinking

Design thinking refers developing people-centric ways to solve problems in the workplace. It is often defined as creative problem-solving. For example, if employees are getting stressed out over constant pings from emails or texts, managers should consider creative ways to mitigate their stress. They could start by analyzing their expectations on employees' email response times. Do they expect employees to respond within an hour? Within 8 hours? Within 24 hours? Do they expect responses when an employee isn't at work? Managers may suggest that employees set certain times to respond to emails rather than responding all day long as emails pour in. For example, an employee may decide to only open his emails at 9 a.m. and 3 p.m. each day. During the other times of the day, he could be more productive, finishing projects and being able to concentrate on the tasks in front of him. Managers may also consider holding off on sending emails in the off hours, unless absolutely necessary.

Training is not just for onboarding

35 percent of millennials consider high quality training as the most desirable quality of a workplace. High quality training is even higher than salary for this group! Onboarding (socialization processes) should not be the only type of training offered. Workers should be provided with continual opportunities for learning throughout their careers. Lunch and learn sessions, on-line training, mobile phone responsive training, and other forms should be offered to maximize employee engagement, professional growth, motivation, and skill sets.

Rise of teams

To maximize collaboration in the workplace, leaders may consider developing networks of teams of people rather than traditional office hierarchies. These teams may be charged to focus on business challenges, new opportunities, customer needs, product launches, product advancements, service offerings and more. These teams should be led by subject matter experts. Due to the global nature of the workforce, leaders may consider virtual teams where employees communicate with one another using electronic media. They can build networks where they learn from one another and gain cross-cultural insights.

People analytics

Analyzing data on workforces is quickly becoming a business necessity. Via people analytics, leaders can collect information about job candidates, identify industry trends, determine approaches to people management used by competitors, gauge the human resource climate, identify pools of top talent globally – and more. According to Deloitte, companies that use people analytics outperform their peers who don't in the areas of retention, employer branding, leadership capabilities, and the quality of hire.

Employee engagement

Since the younger generations are unlikely to remain in their workplaces for a long time, leaders should figure out ways to engage them while they're working for them. Highly engaged employees may be more committed to their organizations and less likely to leave. Workers want to be passionate about their careers and desire meaning and purpose. Leaders should consider structuring jobs or volunteer opportunities to imbue a sense of purpose, meaning and fulfillment in employees.

Rise in gig and remote workers

31 percent of U.S. employees are temporary employees, freelancers, independent contractors and/or part-time workers. Some don't desire a full-time job and instead prefer the flexibility of temporary gigs. These employees may therefore be more difficult to engage. Leaders may consider incorporating cloud-based learning management systems to store relevant training information and learning materials. These systems house the information virtually and allow easy, global access for employees. Those working on virtual teams may also use these systems to gather, collect, and store data.

In summary, human resource managers should always be scanning the marketplace to identify current trends and opportunities. In coming chapters, many of these trends will be explored in more depth.

International Modes of Entry

Exporting

Companies that choose to expand their operations abroad can do so via a variety of modes. The easiest, least risky and least costly mode is to simply export their products. *Exporting*, which is shipping products from one location to another, is therefore one of the most commonly used modes of entry. Though exporting is subject to transportation costs, tariffs, local customs and preferences, and market competition, its access to new markets often outweigh these risks.

Cross border trade agreements, such as **NAFTA**, can also mitigate costs. NAFTA, which is the North American Free Trade Agreement, is a trilateral agreement between the United States, Canada, and Mexico that eliminated tariffs and duties on exports between member countries. Since its inception in January of 1994, NAFTA has had its share of supporters and detractors who have pointed to either its positive economic impact or its transfer of jobs from the U.S. and Canada to lower-labor-cost Mexico.

In October of 2018, U.S. President Donald Trump renegotiated some of the terms of the agreement and renamed it to the **U.S.-Mexico-Canada Agreement**, or USMCA.[9] In the new agreement, rules of origin for the automobile industry were tightened. Now 75 percent of each vehicle must originate in the member countries, instead of only 62.5 percent. 40 percent of each vehicle must come from factories paying at least $16 per hour. Additionally, the intellectual property rights of U.S. pharmaceuticals were strengthened.

Contract Manufacturing

Companies sometimes choose to contract with suppliers to produce their products. This agreement is referred to as *contract manufacturing.* Contract manufacturing differs from licensing in that owners retain complete ownership of the product. For example, Nike, Mattel, Disney, Apple, Fisher Price, and Walmart often contract with low-cost suppliers in Asia to produce their products for prices much less expensive than they could realize in the United States, given higher labor prices in the latter. One challenge to this arrangement occurs when the contracted organizations (a.k.a. "sweatshops") engage in practices inconsistent with prevalent values in the home countries of the companies. For example, recent accusations of child labor, toxic chemical exposure, and suicides by SACOM against Sturdy Products, which is a company Disney has employed to produce its *Cars* toys, negatively impacted public perceptions of Disney.[10]

Licensing and Franchising

Licensing is an entry mode in which one company grants permission to another company to carry its intellectual property and to use its name. Examples of products or services licensed include brand names, trademarks, copyrights, patents, methods, and procedures. *Licensors* retain control of the brand itself, yet oftentimes they must monitor and train those carrying their products. Licensing can eliminate many of the expenses and much of the time involved in overseas expansions. A special form of licensing is *franchising.* Franchising usually grants the owner, or *franchisor,* the right to provide more ongoing support than in the typical licensing agreement.

Examples of businesses with franchises can be found in a variety of industries, such as the hospitality and fast food industries. Hyatt Hotels, Marriott International, McDonalds, Domino's Pizza, and KFC are examples of businesses that operate with international franchises. In both cases (licensing and franchising), licensees and franchisees pay fees to owners to carry their products or services. These relationships can benefit owners interested in expansion, yet they do not come without risks. Licensors and franchisors may not share the same values as their owners, as exemplified when licensees and franchisees engage in poor business practices. As examples, cleanliness standards in some fast food franchisees could be ignored, resulting in damage to the franchisor's brand name.

Cooperative Relationships

Strategic alliances and *joint ventures* are modes of entry in which organizations partner with one another to split costs and share knowledge. Joint ventures differ from strategic alliances in that they result in the formation of a new, separate entity to jointly produce a product or service.

The advantages of forming a joint venture include sharing of the costs and risks involved in producing a new product or service. Organizational leaders may want access to a particular technology or to additional capital. They may want to share risks, gain knowledge about a culture, reduce production costs or take advantage of tax breaks. Hong Kong exemplifies the latter. Lower corporate and personal income taxes in places such as Hong Kong, which is a special administrative region of China, are often attractive.[11] Pairing with a Hong Kong-based organization to form a new entity in Hong Kong could have relative tax advantages. Other "tax havens" (where taxes are relatively low) include Bermuda, the Bahamas, Panama, Lichtenstein, the Cayman Islands and Monaco.[12]

The disadvantages occur when the relationships sour as the two parties fail to come to terms on priorities, future investments, strategies, or other relevant matters. Multinational organizations often choose to form joint ventures in China to take advantage of local partners' knowledge and networks, or what the Chinese call *guanxi.* Pharmaceutical companies GlaxoSmithKline and Novartis partnered with smaller, local Chinese companies Shenzhen Neptunus Interlong BioTechnique Company and Zhejiang Tianyuan Bio-Pharmaceutical, respectively, capitalizing on local knowledge and resources. Yet the protection of intellectual property is a relatively new concept in China, so consultants such as McKinsey advise companies operating in China to either keep their critical intellectual property out of the joint venture, bring only older technology to China, leave blueprints in the home country, or to charge for intellectual property up front.[13]

Foreign Direct Investments

The most expensive and risky entry mode is to make a *foreign direct investment* in a *wholly owned subsidiary* by either a merger or acquisition of another existing company or through a greenfield investment and setting up its own operations. The advantage of foreign direct investments is that firms retain full control of their management and operations. The disadvantage relates to its relatively high costs and risks. As an example of the latter, consider Walmart's experience in Germany. Walmart acquired the Wertkauf and Interspar hypermarket store chains in Germany in 1997, yet due to a variety of strategic, cross-cultural, and logistical mishaps, the company ended up selling its 85 stores in 2006.[14]

International HRM Staffing

Staffing Approaches in International Assignments

Companies consider several strategies when managing their international subsidiaries. Companies that use an *ethnocentric* approach tend to be more centralized, more decisions are made in the home office, and foreign subsidiaries have little autonomy. Key positions in host country subsidiaries are staffed with *parent country nationals*, who are people from the home office.

Companies that use a *polycentric* approach tend to give their subsidiaries more autonomy and decision-making authority. Companies often consider this approach when there are significant cultural, legal, political, or economic systems between the home and host countries, so giving local managers more autonomy helps to navigate these systems more efficiently. Polycentric approaches are often used when the host countries are developed, so locals can be hired to staff positions from entry level to upper management levels. Companies with polycentric approaches often staff their foreign subsidiaries with *host country nationals* and their home offices with *parent country nationals.*

Companies that use a *geocentric* approach have the highest degree of integration between subsidiaries in the host countries and the home country office or offices. Key positions in companies using this approach tend to be filled by the person best suited for the position, regardless of his or her home country. In other words, either *parent country nationals* or *host country nationals* may be positioned in either the home or host offices in the home or host countries.

Some firms use a *regiocentric* approach in which they staff their locations with managers within their particular geographic regions. This approach is useful when regional expertise is needed, yet sometimes people with that expertise fail in having a more global perspective.

International Assignments

According to KPMG's Global Assignment Policies and Practices Survey, 83 percent of employers offer short-term assignments to employees (usually less than a year), while 97 percent offer longer assignments of between one and five years, and 61 percent offer permanent relocations.

Employees who go abroad to work in host countries' international subsidiaries are referred to as *expatriates.* When they return to their home countries, they're referred to as *repatriates.*

The Global Mobility Trends Survey annually identifies trends in international assignments. In 2017, 75 percent of respondents were male, 25 percent were female, and 68 percent were partnered or married. These trends are consistent with trends over the past decade as females are less likely to take on international assignments.

Why do companies send employees abroad?

According to the Society for Human Resource Management, companies often send employees abroad to: (1) satisfy needs in existing operations; (2) launch a new product or service; (3) transfer technology or company knowledge/culture to a location; (4) aid in employee development; and/or (5) analyze the international marketplace. Sending employees abroad is not an inexpensive option, as the costs for a three-year assignment can easily exceed $3 million.[15]

Assignment failures

Yet despite the prevalence of and need for international assignments, oftentimes the assignments fail. In fact, one recent report has indicated an astounding 42 percent failure rate in international assignments. [16] Reasons for failure include the spouses' inability to adjust, a feeling of being "out of sight and out of mind," inadequate preparation, and culture shock. Culture shock occurs when expatriates find difficulties in adjusting to a new way of life, a new set of attitudes or an unfamiliar culture. The spouses' and children may further find difficulties in securing visas to work or in finding the right schools. Such challenges may be particularly challenging in dual career families in which both spouses prefer to work outside of the home.

Successful assignments

Research from the Worldwide ERC Foundation has identified several attributes of successful expatriates: (1) intellectual capital, which relates to knowledge, skills, understanding, and cognitive complexity; (2) social capital, which relates to the ability to build trusting, social relationships with others; and (3) psychological capital, which relates to the ability to function successfully in the host country through acceptance of its culture and a desire to learn more about its culture.

Companies consider a wide variety of applicant traits when staffing their home and host country locations. These traits include potential expatriates' language skills, communication skills, technical skills, cross-cultural competencies and knowledge, openness to experience, interpersonal skills, global experience, family flexibility, and country-specific experience.

Cross-cultural Implications

Prior to sending employees abroad, companies should set expectations for the expatriate assignment and for repatriation. Many may consider involving former expatriates who have visited the host countries of the assignment in setting realistic job previews. Companies may further provide electronic or written materials that detail helpful information about the host countries. Issues to be addressed include securing visas, identifying educational institutions for spouses, significant others, or children, identifying appropriate housing, establishing benefits and incentives packages, providing language training, providing training in cultural norms and values, and identifying locations for obtaining electricity, water, groceries, and other relevant supplies, amenities, or necessities. Such practices will help to mitigate culture shock.

To mitigate expatriates' feelings of being "out of sight, out of mind," companies should consider establishing social networks and mentoring programs by pairing expatriates together and assigning mentors from the home office. They should also send periodic newsletters and updates to keep their employees abroad abreast on company occurrences, changes, and initiatives.

Extensive benefits and preparation in cultural and language training often aid in the adjustment of expatriates and their families and some adjust very well to their new environments. Many live in "expatriate bubbles" with other expatriates, placing their children in private international schools and reaping the awards of living in new and exciting vibrant cultures. For example, for those immersed in Europe, the close proximity of many cultures with fascinating histories may appeal to individuals open to new experiences.

Repatriation

People sometimes assume that when expatriates repatriate to the home country, everything will return to normal and be fine and they won't experience any difficulties. Yet some expatriates have reported difficulties when returning (repatriating) to their home countries. Children of expatriates may suffer from academic difficulties, while expatriates and their families may further suffer from alienation, stress, disorientation, depression and interpersonal difficulties.

Companies that do not gradually reduce the expatriate benefits in compensation packages may contribute to these difficulties as the reduction in benefits may be perceived as extreme. For example, repatriates who worked in societies in which household help was relatively inexpensive may experience some difficulties when they're suddenly cast into the positions of chief bottle washer, baby sitter, chef, chauffeur, and maid. Repatriates with children in private international schools may experience challenges when such schools are no longer funded, so they must either fund private schooling or place their children in public educational institutions. Repatriates in these situations often experience *reverse culture shock,* which is the shock one encounters when returning to the home country.

Furthermore, companies that do not place repatriates in positions that capitalize on their newly acquired cross-cultural experiences or knowledge may also alienate them. For example, a repatriate who had developed strong knowledge of the Russian culture and language may hope to incorporate this knowledge in his new role. Otherwise, he may feel his new skills are not appreciated and are being wasted.

If significant changes occurred in the home office while the expatriates were on assignment, repatriates may further suffer some difficulties. Changes in management, coworkers, cultures, or employment practices are examples. To mitigate these difficulties, companies should be sure to offer outreach, mentors, and support and discussion groups.

International Compensation

Companies adopt several approaches to compensating expatriates: (1) localization (or "market rate" or "going rate") in which employees are paid at the same rates as those living in the host countries are paid; (2) the balance sheet approach, in which employees are paid at the same rates as they would be paid in the home country in the host country; (3) the headquarters-based approach, in which employees are paid at the home country rate, regardless of location; and (4) the cafeteria-style approach, in which employees are given choices to customize their benefits to fit their own needs within the budget established by their organizations.

The localization approach makes the most sense when compensation levels between the home and host countries are relatively similar, such as when a U.S.-based employee works in England or Germany. The balance-sheet approach makes the most sense when an employee from a developed country with relatively high compensation levels works in a less developed country with much lower expected pay levels. For example, when a U.S.-based employee works in China, pay levels between the two countries vary significantly, so to "keep the employee whole," companies apply home country rates.

Furthermore, companies that send employees into more difficult or challenging environments often add a *foreign-service premium* to their compensation packages. The most difficult countries with the highest risk of danger to expatriates command the highest foreign-service premiums. Foreign-service premiums refer to extra sums of money.

Tax Implications

U.S. citizens who work abroad are subject to taxation in both the home and host country. According to the Society for Human Resource Management, companies can take several approaches to handle taxes. They can: (1) hold the employee responsible for taxes; (2) determine tax reimbursement on a case-by-case basis; (3) withhold U.S. taxes and pay foreign taxes; and (4) pay the difference between the taxes paid in the United States and those in the host country.

Legal Implications

U.S. citizens who travel abroad to work for U.S.-based organizations are legally protected by four major laws: (1) Title VII of the Civil Rights Act of 1964; (2) the Americans with Disabilities Act; (3) the Age Discrimination in Employment Act and (4) the Uniformed Services Employment and Reemployment Rights Act (USERRA). The latter act only covers veterans or reservists who are working for the federal government or a firm under U.S. control while the first three acts cover U.S. citizens who are employed by U.S.-based companies abroad or by companies controlled by U.S.-based companies abroad. Non-U.S. citizens are not covered by these laws, even if they work for a U.S.-based organization. They are generally covered by these laws when working on U.S. soil, however. Each of the laws includes an exemption in cases where compliance with the law would result in a violation of a law in the country in which it is located.

Non-Immigrant Visas

Expatriates travel for a variety of reasons and often require work permits in the host countries. Securing work permits may be challenging and for non-immigrants travelling to the United States, they may be expensive and time-consuming to secure. For non-immigrant expatriates who work in the United States, the following types of temporary permits are available:

- *B-1 Visitor for Business:* for individuals for business tourism, pleasure, or visiting, or a combination.
- *H1-B Temporary Workers:* for individuals in specialty occupations, such as in technical or other professional positions. This is the most commonly sought visa for professional workers. Specialty occupations include jobs such as computer programmers or accountants, which require specialized knowledge or a particular bachelor's degree.
- *H2-B Non-Agricultural or Seasonal/Intermittent Workers:* for workers to come to the United States to perform temporary or seasonal work.
- *J-1 Exchange Visitors:* for individuals approved to work in work and study-based exchange visitor programs.
- *TN Visa (NAFTA professional worker):* pursuant to the North American Free Trade Agreement, professional workers who are Canadian or Mexican citizens with a specialized degree, experience or licensing can apply for a TN Visa at either the port of entry (Canada) or at the U.S. embassy in Mexico. Citizens must maintain their home-country citizenship and must re-apply each year. The TN visa is awarded in one-year increments.
- *L-1 Intracompany Transferees:* for individuals with specialized knowledge relating to the organization's interests to transfer from an international location to the United States.

According to the Pew Research Center (2019), the top prospective employers of workers with H1-B visas are as follows:

Company	Approved Visas	Average Salary
Cognizant Tech Solutions	21,459	$84,303
Infosys	12,780	$84,344
Tata Consultancy Services	11,295	$71,819
Accenture	6,831	$79,416
Wipro	6,819	$73,937
IBM	3,569	$79,275
Microsoft	3,556	$126,096
HCL America	3,492	$83,980
Tech Mahindra Americas	3,344	$76,737
Deloitte Consulting	3,114	$102,558
Amazon	2,739	$115,257
Google	2,517	$131,882
Syntel Consulting	2,286	$67,145

Global Virtual Teams

Rather than transferring employees to different locations around the world, multinational organizations may establish global virtual teams so that individuals can stay in their home offices while communicating via technology with coworkers around the world. Advances in communications in the past few decades have made global communication a quick, easy, and inexpensive way to share information in real time. In response to the recent Coronavirus pandemic, this option has become very popular.

Cross-Cultural Values

Over the past century, hundreds of studies by multiple cross-cultural scholars have identified values prevalent within subcultures of countries, countries and regions. These scholars have determined that values and norms evolve in cultures over a long period of time. Determinants of cross-cultural values include religion, political and economic philosophies, social structures, education, and languages. Models of national cultures from a variety of scholars suggest cultures vary between one another along five themes: (1) power distribution and social stratification; (2) uncertainty avoidance and social control; (3) individual or group-level social relationships and preferences; (4) people's level of control or harmony with their environment; and (5) time management.[17]

Attention to likely variations between the home and host countries is useful to expatriates when building relationships with people in host countries. For example, people in Sweden tend to be more egalitarian with respect to their distribution of power between managers and subordinates. Expatriates in Sweden may therefore expect fewer formal interactions between supervisors and subordinates and less use of formal titles.

People in Japan, in contrast, tend to be more hierarchical and formal, and gender stratification between males and females has been identified by cross-cultural scholars such as Geert Hofstede. Expatriates in Japan may experience more formality between supervisors and subordinates and a greater appreciation for titles. They may further notice fewer women occupying higher level managerial positions.

People in China and India tend to be more collective than people in the United States, who favor individualism, so preferences to work within groups and to be evaluated for performance as a group are more prevalent in China and India than in a country such as the United States. People in the United States may instead be more appreciative of individualized attention and recognition. They may also prefer compensation systems and performance evaluations developed at the individual level.

The same differences relate to harmony with versus control of the environment. People in China tend to be more focused on harmony with the environment, while people in the United States are more focused on mastery over their environment. Expatriates may notice these preferences may impact the way space is organized in the workplace. People in Chinese cultures who have an appreciation for Feng Shui, which is a system that seeks to harmonize individuals with their environments, may have certain preferences for their office spaces. People who endorse Feng Shui believe that organizing furniture in certain ways in rooms increases the likelihood of promoting better relationships and relaxation.

Other Challenges in International Human Resource Management

As companies grow and expand in size, company leaders often consider ways to increase their market share. Sometimes they choose to expand operations internationally. When they do so, they consider both macro-level factors and micro-level factors. Macro-level factors include the political and economic systems within other countries with special attention on a country's political and economic stability, regional trade agreements, legal protections, taxes, and regulations. Socio-cultural factors are further important. Prevailing norms and values, religious beliefs, education systems, communication and transportation infrastructure, literacy rates, poverty rates, mortality rates, and human rights all contribute to the attractiveness of investments in particular countries.

As the old real estate adage goes: location, location, location. Location matters to resale value in real estate and to the potential for success in business. Companies that expand globally should do their due diligence when selecting locations abroad to ensure a strong cultural fit and a high potential for profitability, along with all of the aforementioned institutional variables.

Variations by Country

For example, Saudi Arabia is home to Islam's holiest sites and it is a highly conservative, absolute monarchy ruled according to Sharia law. In September of 2017, Saudi King Mohammad bin Salman bin Abdulaziz Al Saud gave women the right to drive cars, effective in June of 2018. One intention was to increase the presence of women in the workplace, since many women had to spend much of their salaries on drivers or had to be driven to work by male relatives.[18] Such restrictions inhibited the attractiveness of employment to Saudi women.

The laws in Singapore can also present challenges as they restrict practices considered commonplace in other countries.[19] The first-time penalty for selling chewing gum can be as high as $100,000 and can come with a two-year prison sentence. Annoying someone with a music instrument in a public place can result in a $1,000 fine. Flying a kite or playing a game that interferes with traffic can come with a fine of up to $5,000. Finally, if you're caught singing obscene song lyrics, you could be imprisoned for up to three months. Other offenses subject to stiff penalties include jaywalking, spitting, feeding pigeons, connecting to another's Wi-

Fi, walking around naked in one's home with the curtains open, and forgetting to flush the toilet.

German *labor laws* can further challenge companies with German subsidiaries. German labor laws strongly favor employees.[20] Employees who fall sick are entitled to receive 100 percent of their pay from their employers for the first six weeks of their sickness. Should they fall sick again and under certain circumstances, the six-week pay period can be triggered for more than once per year.

Sexual harassment protections vary substantially around the world too. In the United States, employees are protected from sexual harassment through Title VII of the Civil Rights Act of 1964. The #MeToo movement on social media and attention to numerous recent sexual harassment cases in the news media have attracted much attention to policies that companies can enforce to mitigate sexual harassment. Yet millions aren't covered by laws such as those in the United States. According to the World Policy Analysis Center at UCLA, in 68 other countries, including France, Italy, and nations in the Middle East and Latin America, employees have no protections when faced with a hostile work environment or an abusive supervisor or coworkers.[21]

Corruption varies substantially across cultures as well. Corruption is defined as the abuse of entrusted power for private gain. Since 1993, Transparency International has been collecting perceived levels of public corruption across the globe.[22] In 2017, the countries considered the least corrupt included New Zealand, Denmark, Finland, Norway, Switzerland and Singapore. The most corrupt included Somalia, South Sudan, Syria, Afghanistan, Yemen, and Sudan. The United States tied with Austria and Belgium for 16th place. Transparency International notes that activists and the media are critical to generating an awareness of corruption, yet each week, at least one journalist is killed in a country that is considered highly corrupt.

Porter's Five Forces

In 1980, Michael Porter published a book entitled, *"Competitive Strategy: Techniques for Analyzing Industries and Competitors,"* which is still well-regarded by business professionals today. Porter identified five forces to measure the intensity of competition in industry, along with an industry's attractiveness and profitability. These include (1) competition in the industry; (2) potential new entrants to the industry; (3) bargaining power of customers; (4) bargaining power of suppliers; and (5) the threat of substitute products.

For example, the Parisian café is considered the center of social life, along with a place to relax and refuel. Over 7,000 Parisian cafes serve customers, making competition relatively intense within this industry. This intensity may help to reduce some of the potential for new entrants, as switching costs between one café and another are relatively low. In other words, customers are not limited to only a couple of options when selecting a café in which to dine, and few (if any) financial constraints force the choice of one café over another, so the threat of substitute products is high.

Costco is a bulk membership retailer that specializes in an assortment of high quality, low-priced goods and services. Because Costco is a multi-billion-dollar global retailer with operations in eight countries, Costco can achieve what economists term *economies of scale* by negotiating low prices with suppliers to buy in bulk. Costco has much bargaining power as a customer.

Within the diamond industry for the past one hundred and fifty years, De Beers has been a global leader. De Beers controls around a third of the global market, giving the company much bargaining power as a supplier to wholesalers and retailers within the diamond industry.[23]

In summary, business leaders should consider a variety of macro-level and micro-level factors when determining where to locate operations abroad. Macro-level factors include a country's political, economic, legal, and socio-cultural institutions, while micro-level factors include the forces impacting industry competitive intensity, profitability, and industry attractiveness. Taken together, business leaders can identify locations with the highest probability of sustainable profitability.

Conclusion

When deciding to expand abroad, business leaders are faced with a variety of decisions, from an appropriate mode of entry given their resources and risk levels to appropriate staffing within their subsidiaries should they choose to expand abroad. Some of the many challenges they face relate to managing international assignments through attention to preparation, training, incentives, and compensation. Consideration of the legal, economic, regulatory, and socio-cultural characteristics of the societies in which global subsidiaries are located is additionally important.

Remaining nimble while keeping focus on the core competencies and strategies of organizations help to align their business strategies with their human resource management strategies.

QUESTIONS FOR REVIEW

1. What country-level factors do companies consider when establishing subsidiaries overseas?

2. What are the modes of entry that companies can use in their international operations?

3. Which modes of entry are the riskiest and most expensive?

4. What is the difference between a strategic alliance and a joint venture?

5. Identify three approaches to international compensation. Identify the situation in which each would be considered appropriate.

6. How does international human resource management differ from domestic human resource management?

7. What are some ethical issues international human resource managers face when overseeing overseas subsidiaries?

8. What are some of the challenges associated with expatriate assignments? What can an organization do to overcome the challenges you identified?

9. What are some of the challenges associated with repatriation? What can an organization do to overcome the challenges you identified?

10. What are current trends impacting human resource managers?

APPLICATIONS

1. Global Sexual Harassment

Go to the internet and conduct a survey of sexual harassment protections that employees have in other countries. Which countries have few protections against sexual harassment? Do sexual harassment protections correspond to the level of development in countries?

2. Trends in Expatriate Assignments

Go to the Global Mobility Trends Surveys at http://globalmobilitytrends.brookfieldgrs.com/. Identify current trends in expatriate and repatriate assignments. What challenges have international human resource managers identified over the past few years in such assignments and what have they done to remedy or address these challenges?

3. The Research-Practice Gap

Work in teams of two or three people to answer whether each of the following questions is true or false. This survey comes from a cross-cultural study of human resource practitioners.[24] Findings from that study indicated a significant gap between what is known in research based on empirical studies and what is practiced, particularly in the area of staffing.

1. Leadership training is ineffective because good leaders are born, not made.

2. The most important requirement for an effective leader is to have an outgoing, enthusiastic personality.

3. Once employees have mastered a task, they perform better when they are told to "do their best" than when they are given specific, difficult performance goals.

4. Companies with vision statements perform better than those without them.

5. Companies with very low rates of professionals' turnover are less profitable than those with moderate turnover rates.

6. If a company feels it must downsize employees, the most profitable way to do it is through targeted cuts rather than attrition.

7. In order to be evaluated favorably by line managers, the most important competency for HR managers is the ability to manage change.

8. On average, encouraging employees to participate in decision making is more effective for improving organizational performance than setting performance goals.

9. Most managers give employees lower performance appraisals than they objectively deserve.

10. Poor performers are generally more realistic about their performance than good performers are.

11. Teams with members from different functional areas are likely to reach better solutions to complex problems than teams from single areas.

12. Despite the popularity of drug testing, there is no clear evidence that applicants who score positive on drug tests are any less reliable or productive employees.

13. Most people over-evaluate how well they perform on the job.

14. Most errors in performance appraisals can be eliminated by providing training that describes the kinds of errors managers tend to make and suggesting ways to avoid them.

15. Lecture-based training is generally superior to other forms of training delivery.

16. Older adults learn more from training than younger adults.

17. Training for simple skills will be more effective if it is presented in one concentrated session than if it is presented in several sessions over time.

18. The most valid employment interviews are designed around each candidate's unique background.

19. Although people use many different terms to describe personalities, there are really only four basic dimensions of personality, as captured by the Myers-Briggs Type Indicator (MBTI).

20. On average, applicants who answer job advertisements are likely to have higher turnover than those referred by other employees.

21. Being very intelligent is actually a disadvantage for performing well on a low-skilled job.

22. There is very little difference among personality inventories in terms of how well they predict an applicant's likely job performance.

23. Although there are "integrity tests" that try to predict whether someone will steal, be absent, or otherwise take advantage of an employer, they don't work well in practice because so many people lie on them.

24. On average, conscientiousness is a better predictor of job performance than is intelligence.

25. Companies that screen job applicants for values have higher performance than those that screen for intelligence.

26. When pay must be reduced or frozen, there is little a company can do or say to reduce employee dissatisfaction and dysfunctional behaviors.

27. Most employees prefer to be paid on the basis of individual performance rather than on team or organizational performance.

28. Merit pay systems cause so many problems that companies without them tend to have higher performance than companies with them.

29. There is a positive relationship between the proportion of managers receiving organizationally based pay incentives and company profitability.

30. New companies have a better chance of surviving if all employees receive incentives based on organization-wide performance.

31. Talking about salary issues during performance appraisal tends to hurt morale and future performance.

32. Most employees prefer variable pay systems (e.g., incentive schemes, gain sharing, stock options) to fixed pay systems.

33. Surveys that directly ask employees how important pay is to them underestimate pay's true importance to employees. In other words, pay is more important to employees than they let on in surveys.

CASE STUDIES

1. Whom to Hire?

Brian Townsend has a common dilemma. He has just finished interviewing four candidates who expressed a strong interest in a regional store manager position in his organization. He is now considering the qualifications of each candidate, wondering which would be the best fit. Brian is the international human resources manager of the Oakland Bridge Shoe Company (OBSC), a large retail organization based in Miami, Florida. Its mission is to "change the world, one foot at a time through its products, people, and practices." OBSC employs around 15,000 workers in its fifteen U.S. and twenty international locations. The company is an equal opportunity employer and has a diverse workforce that adequately represents the population of the geographical area in which each store is located.

The advertisement for the job, which appeared in the local paper and on the company website, is as follows: "Highly energetic, youthful, and motivated regional store manager needed in Miami, Florida for the oversight of fourteen retail locations. Primary duties include the supervision of store managers with oversight of their purchasing, budgeting, accounting, and human resource practices. The qualifications for the position include a minimum of 3 years of managerial experience in a retail organization, the ability to speak fluently in Spanish and English, a willingness to travel extensively, and a four-year college degree in business from an accredited institution. Salary commensurate with experience."

Townsend wanted to hire the best candidate, so he planned to carefully review his interview notes. Highlights from his notes are listed below. In groups of 3 or 4 persons, evaluate each of the candidates and select your top person for the position. Which qualifications did you consider the most important? Which qualifications did you either not consider or consider the least important?

Candidates

Candidate 1: Casey Johnson. Casey is a bubbly 35-year-old who has recently been divorced. She is a white mother of three small children, two in daycare and one in the first grade. She graduated from the University of West Indies with a bachelor's degree in marketing 13 years ago and spent the first five years of her career after graduation working for one of

OBSC's top competitors. Over the past 8 years, she has risen through the ranks at OBSC, spending the last five years as the store manager of its Hialeah store location. Her downsides include that she has three small children, so she may need to take extra time off to care for them. She has also been overly emotional over the past few months. Casey scored high on "extroversion," "conscientiousness," and "neuroticism" on the company's personality test. She currently resides just north of Miami and speaks both English and Spanish. She is willing to travel, yet prefers no overnight stays.

Candidate 2: Joe Chang. Joe is a 23-year-old single Asian-American male with no small children who recently graduated from the University of Miami with a degree in business management. He included with his resume an unofficial copy of his transcript, which documented his high GPA and magna cum laude honor. Joe worked part-time during his college years as a salesman for a retail apparel organization. Two years ago, Joe received a promotion to supervise to eight workers. He is quick-witted, energetic and enthusiastic. He also smiles a lot and seems confident. He scored high on "extroversion," "openness to experience," and "conscientiousness" on the company's personality test. Joe currently resides about an hour from the HSBC office in Miami, yet is willing to relocate to be closer to the store. He only speaks English, but he assured Brian that he is a quick learner of languages, as he also speaks French fluently. He is willing to travel extensively.

Candidate 3: Bob Jackson. Bob is a 62-year-old black married male with two grown children. He received an MBA from the University of Chicago years ago and has spent the past fourteen years working in a retail merchandising organization as one of its Caribbean regional sales managers. Bob scored high on "extroversion" and low on "neuroticism" on the company's personality test. He and his wife reside in Sainte-Anne, Martinique, yet he is willing to relocate. He is also willing to travel extensively and is fluent in Spanish, Mandarin, and English.

Candidate 4: Kelly Silva. Kelly is a 42-year old married Brazilian with four children in middle and high school. She graduated from a large university in Brazil with a degree in marketing about 20 years ago. She has held numerous positions since graduating that have each lasted about 2 years. She has about 10 years of experience in retail sales from her work in 5 different organizations. Kelly is personable, well-dressed, and attractive. Her downside is that she refuses to work on Sundays due to her religion. Kelly scored high on "extroversion" and "openness to experience." Kelly currently resides in Miami and she speaks Portuguese, Spanish, and

English. She is willing to travel extensively.

2. Sweatshops

The United States Department of Labor defines a sweatshop as a factory that violates two or more labor laws pertaining to child labor, benefits, wages, or working hours. Oftentimes, workers in sweatshops face substantial exploitation, such as verbal or physical abuse, arbitrary discipline, and the absence of a living wage.[25] Products often produced in sweatshops include shoes, clothing, rugs, toys, chocolate, bananas, and coffee. In China, toy workers earn an average of 30 cents an hour, compared with an average of $11 in the United. States.[26]

In Pakistan, thousands of children between the ages of four and fourteen work as carpet weavers.[27] Handmade woolen carpets are labor intensive, yet are some of the largest export earners for countries such as India, Nepal, Pakistan, and Morocco, which typically export carpets to the United States and Europe.[28] Carpets "are made in factories in which children as young as four years of age, often chained to their looms, squat shoulders hunched, fourteen hours a day, six days a week, making beautifully intricate carpets by tying knots with fingers gnarled and callused from years of back-breaking labor."[29] They come from Pakistan's poorest families, often sold into servitude to put food on the family's table for periods lasting up to ten years. [30]

Goodweave, which is a human rights organization, has created an effective certification system for child labor-free rugs. "Since 1995, 11 million child labor-free carpets bearing the Goodweave label have been sold worldwide, and the number of 'carpet kids' has dropped from a million to 250,000."[31]

1. Identify the interests and motivations of relevant stakeholders to the Pakistan carpet industry.

2. Some argue that the alternatives for impoverished children, which include prostitution and working in agriculture, are more dangerous than the sweatshops. Evaluate this argument.

3. What can companies in the aforementioned industries do to ensure that the subsidiaries producing their products do not employ young children full-time?

4. Should the U.S. government force organizations in these industries to comply with non-governmental human rights organizations, such as Goodweave?

3. International Assignment Problems at Acme

Madison Clark was recently promoted to the position of the director of international human resources at Acme Corporation. Acme is a multinational corporation with subsidiaries in twenty countries, including France, Israel, Australia, Brazil, Russia, India and China. They sell a wide range of luxury consumer goods and are considered highly innovative and strategic. They hire employees who are also creative, innovative, ethical, and passionate and they pay them above the market rate and offer an extensive benefits package, onsite daycare, and a diverse set of educational training opportunities. Their goal is to attract and recruit the most talented human capital in the market. Currently, they employ 15,000 expatriates and have recently filled thousands of positions in the emerging markets of Dubai, South Africa, and India.

The previous director, Jackson Wheat, was very well-regarded at Acme. He left Acme to work for a competitor in a higher-level position. Madison was glad that the door to his position was opened to her and they promoted her instead of offering his position to an external candidate.

Acme sent expatriate managers from the U.S. to foreign subsidiaries to fill skills gaps, transfer Acme's culture to the local facilities, and to launch new endeavors. Expatriates were usually sent for a period of four years, but some were sent for shorter periods when the locals could be trained to fill their positions. Around 20 percent of the assignments ended prematurely. The main reason for these assignment failures was the spouses' inability to adjust to the new culture. Other reasons cited were culture shock, the feeling of being "out of sight and out of mind" and an inability to work well with the locals.

For 13 years, Jackson Wheat oversaw all aspects of the expatriate experience, including recruitment, selection, training, development, compensation and incentives. To recruit candidates, Jackson checked Acme's internal database first, filling positions with the most qualified applicants from anywhere on the globe. Those who had previously served as expatriates were the most likely to be successful in new expatriate roles. Jackson also looked for candidates with solid job performance records, strong technical expertise and, of course, a willingness to relocate internationally. About 85 percent of the expatriate population was male, 60 percent were married, and 50 percent were accompanied on assignments by their children.

The female expatriate population was negligible, considering Acme's large pool of promising female candidates. Those who accepted positions were often single or divorced and without children. Finding married females willing to relocate was rare.

Given the important role the expatriates served for Acme, the pay package was very generous. Typically, expatriates earned around $350,000 annually. They were also offered a cafeteria benefits plan in which they chose benefits that totaled $100,000 in value. Options included company cars, cross-cultural and language training, chauffeurs, housing differentials, cost of living allowances, domestic help, country club memberships, tuition for the international schooling of children, foreign-service premiums in hazardous locations, extended vacation time to meet local customs, and tax equalization.

Once the assignment was complete, the benefits package was replaced with the domestic package, which was not nearly so generous. Cross-cultural training and training on the local language was not offered to spouses or dependents, as they were considered to be unnecessary expenses.

Despite such extensive benefits and pay, many expatriates complained and turnover was high. Some said that they felt "out of sight, out of mind" while on assignment. This feeling was exacerbated on their return to the U.S., when they discovered that their workplaces had changed, sometimes dramatically. Sometimes they would return to find new subordinates and colleagues, new workplace policies and different managers. Many times they were placed in lateral positions that did not take advantage of their new skill sets and cross-cultural knowledge, which they acquired while on their international assignments. A formal repatriation program had not been established at Acme under Jackson's tenure. Madison wondered whether such a program would offer a good return on their investment.

When she took over the position, she was told that their program was flawed. For one, locals in some host countries were complaining that the pay of U.S. expatriate managers was exorbitant, given their own pay. Local managers in India and China were averaging around $9,000 a year, while expatriate managers were averaging $450,000 (including benefits). In many cases, locals felt equally qualified and questioned the policy of sending expatriates for extended periods of time.

1. What problems did you identify for expatriates and repatriates?

2. What solutions will adequately address these problems?

Chapter 2: Legal Issues

Introduction

At the age of twenty six, Christina Chen-Oster had secured a good position at Goldman Sachs, which epitomized Wall Street power and had a reputation of rewarding fierce loyalty with fat bonuses.[32] About seven months into her position selling convertible bonds, Chen-Oster was out one night celebrating the promotion of one of the men who had recruited her. The group made its way to a strip club, where she got bored and left. A male co-worker, who ranked beneath her, convinced her that he would walk her home. Yet outside of her apartment, he pinned her against the wall and kissed her and groped her and attempted to engage in a sexual act. He then convinced her to say nothing.

Two years later when she thought she was going to be moving across the country for another role at Goldman Sachs, she decided that it was time to speak up. Yet when she told her boss, her response was something like "Oh. That was you?" Her boss had helped the man seek therapy, yet he never tried to identify the woman whom he had attempted to assault. He advised her not to make a big deal out of it.

Her career next started to deteriorate as she noticed her job responsibilities were siphoned off and her performance reviews, which were once stellar, were assigned to distant colleagues who had no way to provide meaningful assessments. Her pay increased 27 percent, yet her alleged assailant's pay more than quadrupled and he was promoted to managing director – then partner. She went out for maternity leave twice and in late 2004, when she returned from maternity leave, she found that her team had been reorganized and she was assigned a desk near a group of women administrative assistants. "It was so clear. It was such a visceral, visual representation of how little Goldman cared about my career," she said. She quit in 2005.

She eventually hired a lawyer and became a part of a larger class action lawsuit of 2,300 current or former employees. In 2014, her side laid out their case after determining through statistical analysis that women were being paid 21 percent less than men after controlling for factors other than bias. The case is still lingering in the courts. In 2004, rival investment bank Morgan Stanley agreed to settle a sex discrimination case for $54 million, so the stakes could be high.

Objectives:

After reading this chapter, you should be able to:

- Identify and apply the three major sources of federal redress in the United States: Title VII of the Civil Rights Act of 1964, the Age Discrimination in Employment Act of 1967, and the Americans with Disabilities Act of 1990 and as amended in 2008.
- Identify other relevant laws impacting legal compliance, such as the Genetic Information Nondiscrimination Act and the Immigration Reform and Control Act.
- Define affirmative action and recognize factors impacting voluntary and involuntary affirmative action programs (e.g., reverse discrimination and manifest imbalance).
- Explain the business case for diversity in the context of a more diverse domestic and global workforce.
- Explain the importance of diversity awareness and compliance programs with specific attention to LGBT groups, generational differences, racial/ethnic diversity, cross-cultural diversity, language issues, pregnancy, and sexual harassment.
- Explain why workplace bullying and workplace ostracism are troublesome in the workplace.

Employment Discrimination

Imagine a time in which your boss tells you that he won't be promoting you since you're an older married Hispanic woman and your pay will be about thirty percent less than that of a male peer with the same skills, performance, and responsibilities. Prior to 1964 in the United States, this sort of occurrence would not have been considered unusual as there were no laws prohibiting employee discrimination as a function of race, gender, or age. Thankfully, with the landmark passage of **Title VII of the Civil Rights Act of 1964,** your boss cannot legally make such an employment decision. Title VII protects workers from discrimination based on their race, religion, color, national origin, and sex.

According to the Equal Employment Opportunity Commission,[33] it "shall be an unlawful employment practice for an employer (1) to fail or refuse to hire or to discharge any individual, or otherwise to discriminate against any individual with respect to his compensation, terms, conditions, or privileges of employment, because of such individual's race, color, religion, sex, or national origin; or (2) to limit, segregate, or classify his employees or applicants for employment in any way which would deprive or tend to deprive any individual of employment opportunities or otherwise adversely affect his status as an employee, because of such individual's race, color, religion, sex, or national origin."

Title VII applies to organizations with fifteen or more employees who work twenty or more weeks per year and who are involved in interstate commerce (due to the 10th Amendment in the Constitution in which states' rights are delineated). The law also generally applies to public and private educational institutions, state and local governments, labor organizations, and employment agencies.

Title VII was amended in 1991 by the **Civil Rights Act of 1991.**[34] This amendment corrected several omissions from the original 1964 Act. One change was to eliminate the employee practice on placing quotas for hiring and promotion of particular races/ethnic groups. Many organizations had placed hiring quotas based on employee race. Another change was to allow for jury trials and the awarding of compensatory and punitive damages by the courts. Compensatory damages are monetary damages that compensate injured parties for their losses, while punitive damages are monetary damages designed to punish an injuring party that has intentionally caused harm to another party. The Act further placed caps on the damages that could be awarded based on the number of employees in organizations, which ranged from $50,000 for organizations of 15 to 100 employees to $100,000 for organizations with 101 to 200 employees to $200,000 for organizations with 201 to 500 employees to $300,000 for organizations with 501 or more employees. Title VII and ADA coverage was further extended to American and American-controlled employers operating abroad.

Types of Discrimination

Title VII identified several types of workplace discrimination: adverse impact, disparate treatment, and pattern and practice. Title VII further identified situations in which one could judge whether discrimination was occurring or whether a particular employment decision, practice, or job requirement was a business necessity or a bona fide occupational qualification or exhibited job relatedness.

Bona fide occupational qualifications are requirements that employers are permitted to consider when making employment decisions in hiring and retention because the requirement is considered to be an essential job duty necessary for the operation of a particular business.

If a particular employment practice has an adverse impact on a protected group, the EEOC requires that the practice is a *business necessity* that is job-related for the position in question. A business necessity is a practice that is necessary for the safe and efficient operation of a business. For example, requiring good vision and hearing for school bus drivers may adversely impact people with related disabilities, yet the practice is a business necessity. *Job relatedness* exists when a test for employment is a legitimate practice based on business necessity. For example, school bus drivers may be required to pass a driving test to ensure safety on the road. Driving tests are related to better performance in bus driving.

Adverse (or disparate) impact refers to an employment practice that appears to be neutral, yet has an adverse impact or effect on members of a protected group. For example, in Dallas, firefighters are required to scale six-foot fences. This requirement has an adverse, or negative impact, on women, older people, and the physically handicapped, yet due to the large number of fences in Dallas, the requirement is considered a business necessity and a bona fide occupational qualification (BFOQ). The requirement that commercial airline pilots retire at the age of sixty has an adverse impact on those older than sixty, yet the requirement is considered a business necessity and bona fide occupational qualification for safety reasons.

How can a company determine whether adverse impact is occurring? They can use the *four-fifths (or 80 percent) rule.* The four-fifths rule is a selection rate that for any sex, race, or ethnic group that is less than four fifths of the group with the highest passing rate. For example, if 75 percent of Hispanic job applicants were promoted, 50 percent of white job applicants were promoted, and 62 percent of African American job applicants were promoted, employers would multiply the top passing rate (75 percent) by 80 percent to get the critical number of 60 percent. For there to be evidence of adverse impact, the passing rates of the lower scoring groups would need to be less than 60 percent. Since only 50 percent of white job applicants were promoted, white job applicants were adversely impacted.

In 2018, internet retailer Amazon launched a search for a second headquarters with specific attention to correcting a manifest imbalance in its own workplace by hiring more women and minorities.[35] A *manifest imbalance* occurs when representation of a protected group is well below that in the surrounding labor force. At Amazon, men make up 73 percent of its professional employees and 78 percent of its senior executives and managers. Of the ten people who report to Chief Executive Officer Jeff Bezos, all are white and only the head of human resources is female. "In the pageantry of choosing a city for a HQ2, it has been looking at gender and racial diversity in the workforce, according to people close in the process. Its executives have also met with local public school officials to gauge interest in possible partnerships in science, technology, engineering and mathematics

(STEM) fields. They're thinking about who's in their hiring pipeline, now and in the future."[36]

Disparate treatment differs from adverse impact in that disparate treatment is intentional. Individuals in similar situations are intentionally treated differently based on an individual's membership in a protected group. For example, if an employer intentionally established a job requirement that all applicants be six feet tall or more to minimize the number of women applicants, the employer is guilty of disparate treatment.

Pattern or practice discrimination occurs when a person or group engages in a number of actions over a significant period time that are intended to deny the rights provided by Title VII to protected groups.

Which Groups Are Protected Under Title VII?

Title VII of the Civil Rights Act of 1964 covers the following protected classes: race/ethnicity, religion, color, national origin, and sex. Note that coverage is extended to the majority group (white males) under Title VII, so if white males are being harassed or discriminated against, they can file a claim of *reverse discrimination* with the Equal Employment Opportunity Commission.

Race/Ethnicity. Race refers to a person's physical characteristics, such as skin, bone structure, eye color, and hair. *Ethnicity* refers to cultural factors, such as ancestry, nationality, regional culture, and language. *Color* is further included because people may vary in color within a race.

Religion is defined broadly by the EEOC as that which concerns the ultimate ideas about life, purpose, and death. Religion includes both traditional religions, such as Christianity, Judaism, Islam, Hinduism, and Buddhism as well as less traditional, new, or uncommon beliefs. Atheism and agnosticism are further protected under the religion category. Social, political, or economic philosophies are not included.

National Origin is defined as the country from which workers originated and with which they identify.

Sex refers to whether a person's biological and physical characteristics related to being either a male or female. The EEOC has recently interpreted this category to include *sexual orientation* and *gender identity,* yet the courts vary in accepting this interpretation. One example of this type of discrimination occurs when there is a *glass ceiling* in an organization, which means that women in the organization are prevented from advancing up the career ladder due to barriers imposed by men.

When people perceive that they are being discriminated against based on gender, they experience negative outcomes. A meta-analytic study[37] found correlations between perceptions of gender discrimination and job attitudes (procedural justice), physical health outcomes and behavior, job-based work outcomes (job performance), relationship-based work outcomes (exchanges between leaders and subordinates), and psychological health (anxiety). These correlations were (surprisingly) stronger in countries with more stringently enforced policies to promote gender equality. In other words, in countries considered high on the dimension of "gender egalitarianism," people focus more closely on *differences* between the genders, which seems to lead to greater perceptions of discrimination.

Sexual Harassment is also covered. It is unlawful to harass a person because of his or her sex. This type of harassment applies to harassment from the same sex, from females to males and from males to females. The EEOC defines harassment as "unwelcome sexual advances, requests for sexual favors, and other verbal or physical harassment of a sexual nature.

The harassment does not need to be of a sexual nature and can include offensive remarks that a reasonable person would consider to be offensive and contributing to a *hostile work environment.* Sexual harassment does not need to include a *quid pro quo,* which translates as "this for that." In other words, the person claiming harassment does not need to show that he or she was demoted, terminated, or an employment decision was made from the person harassing him or her. He or she only needs to show that a reasonable person would consider the harassment significant and pervasive, contributing to a hostile work environment.

There are two types of sexual harassment: either a quid pro quo type of harassment, where a benefit or punishment is made contingent on submitting to sexual harassment or a hostile work environment. In a hostile work environment, it is difficult for a person to work due to behavior that is sexual in nature from an individual or group working in that environment.

Employers can be held liable for the actions of their employees, so it is in an organization's best interest to have an affirmative defense against sexual harassment. An *affirmative defense* includes (1) developing a policy that defines sexual harassment; (2) communicating the policy to all employees; (3) developing a mechanism that ensures that people will speak out; (4) providing multiple avenues to report; (5) ensuring just cause procedures are followed when investigating the complaint; and (6) preparing to carry out disciplinary actions for violators.

Cases for plaintiffs are stronger when employees do not have an affirmative defense or when they knew about or should have known about the sexual harassment, yet they did nothing to stop it. Examples of such a situation occurred in Fox News, where a wave of sexual harassment claims against Chairman Roger Ailes and news correspondent Bill O'Reilly ultimately cost them their jobs and millions of dollars in settlements. In O'Reilly's case, Fox News settled with one claimant for $32 million dollars after acknowledging that they were aware of her allegations of repeated harassment and the sending of gay pornography and other sexually explicit material.[38]

The *Pregnancy Discrimination* Act of 1978 was an amendment to Title VII of the Civil Rights Act that prohibits sex discrimination based on pregnancy, childbirth, or related medical conditions. The Act specifically prohibits discrimination in any aspect of employment, including hiring, promoting, and compensating. Such claims can be expensive. At Chipotle, which is a Mexican restaurant, Doris Garcia Hernandez was forced by her manager to alert her coworkers anytime she needed to use the restroom so they could cover for her. The restaurant did not require the same of non-pregnant workers. Her supervisor also denied her access to drinking water during her four-hour shift and denied her request to leave early for a prenatal appointment. The jury awarded her $50,000 in compensatory damages and $500,000 in punitive damages.[39]

Workplace Bullying

Workplace bullying and sexual harassment often go hand-in-hand. Nike Inc. ousted a handful of male executives over bullying behavior in early 2018 following the famous #MeToo movement on social media.[40] "According to the former Nike employees, the lack of a fear of reprisal created an environment where male executives, many married, could pursue and have sexual relationships with subordinates and assistants – behavior Nike says it tries to prevent but doesn't prohibit."[41] Many times the careers of those involved were not impacted – and when there were repercussions, females faced consequences while males received little, if any, punishment.

Trouble often starts from the top in such cases and at Nike, 55-year old Nike brand president Trevor Edwards was trouble. His reputation of bullying and humiliating subordinates with insults and disparaging comments finally caught up with him when Nike dismissed him in early 2018.[42] Once a leader sets such a tone, people mirror his behavior. Several who mirrored his behavior have since left Nike.

A 2017 survey by Zogby Analytics that was commissioned by the Workplace Bullying Institute found that men comprised 70 percent of the bullies and 34 percent of the targets.[43] Nine percent of respondents indicated that they were currently being bullied; ten percent have been bullied; nineteen percent witnessed bullying; and 25 percent were aware of bullying at their workplace but had not experienced or witnessed it. Furthermore, surveys have found that bullying behaviors are four times more prevalent than legally actionable sexual harassment.[44] Workplace bullying is the only form of abuse that hasn't been addressed by law in the United States. That makes the U.S. a laggard when compared with Western Europe, Australia, and Canada.[45]

Workplace Ostracism

Remember the wallflowers at the Homecoming Dance or at the Prom? How did they feel when everyone else was asked to dance and they were left alone? What happens when someone is made to feel ostracized at work? The person is left out of activities and not invited to coworker parties.

Researchers call these occurrences workplace ostracism, which has devastating consequences. *Workplace ostracism* occurs when a person is excluded from the group or the individuals with whom he or she works. A recent meta-analytic study found that workplace ostracism has a negative impact on well-being, emotions, and self-perceptions.[46] It may make people feel badly about themselves and may lead to higher turnover, worse performance, and less organizational commitment. Males are more likely to be ostracized than females, which may correspond to their relational dispositions.

Workplace loneliness is another problem in organizations. Feeling lonely in the workplace leads to lower job performance and lonelier employees tend to have less affective commitment to their organizations and lower approachability.[47] Affective commitment refers to how much employees desire to stay with their organizations.

Americans with Disabilities Act

According to the U.S. Department of Justice Civil Rights Division, "Title I of the Americans with Disabilities Act of 1990 prohibits private employers, State and local governments, employment agencies and labor unions from discriminating against qualified individuals with disabilities in job application procedures, hiring, firing, advancement, compensation, job training, and other terms, conditions, and privileges of employment. The ADA covers employers with 15 or more employees, including State and local governments. It also applies to employment agencies and to labor organizations."[48] The ADA defines a person who has a disability as "a person who has a physical or mental impairment that substantially limits one or more major life activities, a person who has a history or record of such an impairment, or a person who is perceived by others as having such an impairment. The ADA does not specifically name all of the impairments that are covered."[49]

A study by the Center for Talent Innovation of 3,570 white collar workers found that thirty percent of them had a disability as defined in 2015 by the Americans with Disabilities Act.[50] The numbers did not vary across generation, race, and gender. In other words, people with disabilities represent a large talent pool, yet they often face discrimination, bias, exclusion, and career plateaus. The following conditions are automatically considered a disability by the ADA: cancer, HIV infection, multiple sclerosis, severe disfigurement (excluding tattoos or piercings), or visually impaired or partially visually impaired. Illegal use of drugs is excluded. Obesity alone is also excluded. In *Richardson v. The Chicago Transit Authority,* the court ruled that obesity alone is not a disability as it must be coupled with an underlying physiological disorder or condition. A physiological disorder is one that occurs when the organs of one's body malfunction, causing the disease. Asthma is a physiological disorder of the lungs. Glaucoma is a physiological disorder of the eyes.

Employers are asked to make a *reasonable accommodation* for people with disabilities, which is an accommodation that does not pose an *undue hardship* on an organization. This accommodation may vary depending on the size of the organization as a function of its resources. Small organizations with fewer financial resources would not be required to make the same financial commitment to creating an accommodation as large organizations. For example, if a 100-year old two-story building only contains a stairway and does not contain an elevator from the first to the second floor, an employee in an organization would not be able to get up the stairs. Smaller companies would likely not be required to add an elevator as the cost could pose an undue hardship. Offering the employee an office on the first floor would be a reasonable accommodation.

According to one recent study[51], employers have some concerns and questions about hiring job candidates with disabilities. The top five concerns are as follows: (1) They're worried about the cost of providing reasonable accommodations so workers can do their jobs; (2) they don't know how to handle the needs of disabled workers; (3) they're afraid they won't be able to discipline disabled workers due to the potential for a law; (4) they can't ask about a job applicant's disability because of a potential lawsuit; and (5) they can't ask about a job applicant's disability, which makes it hard to assess whether the person can do the job.

Service Animals

Henry Goldstein suffers from extreme anxiety, so he brings his service dog Cookie with him when he goes to restaurants.[52] In the summer of 2017, Goldstein and Cookie entered a restaurant called the Limon Jungle in New York. A restaurant employee approached him and asked him for Cookie's "papers," along with a bunch of other questions. Goldstein provided the dog's registration papers. Yet he felt humiliated, belittled, and discriminated against, so he and his dog left the Limon Jungle without having a meal. His dog is registered in New York's Department of Health. New York's Human Rights Law requires restaurants to accommodate guests with service dogs if they have registered with the Department of Health. Goldstein sued the Limon Jungle and a judge ruled that the Limon Jungle would need to pay Goldstein $14,000 and would need to pay additional city fines of $28,000. The judge wanted to send a signal so people start taking laws concerning service animals more seriously.

If you have noticed an increase in the number of service dogs in public places, your observations are accurate. Organizational leaders need to keep up with laws protecting people's rights to bring their service dogs with them in public places.

Age Discrimination in Employment Act

The Age Discrimination in Employment Act of 1967 prohibits discrimination of people who are forty years old or older. People younger than 40 area not protected, yet some states (Michigan, Minnesota, New Jersey, and Oregon) have laws protecting younger workers. It is not illegal to favor older workers over younger ones and the act does not have an upper limit on age. Workers are protected in any aspect of their employment, including pay, hiring, firing, promoting, and offering training programs. If a person claims age discrimination, he or she needs to show that age is the reason behind an adverse employment decision. Harassment is illegal when it is so frequent and severe that reasonable people would consider the environment to be hostile and offensive. The harasser could be the person's supervisor, coworker, someone who is not an employee of the employer, or a client or customer. Claims of age discrimination occur frequently with an aging workforce as people work later into their years.

Does this mean companies cannot require employees to retire at a particular age? The answer to this question is that if companies set retirement ages based on non-discriminatory reasons, such as safety reasons, then setting a retirement age is fine. For example, the mandatory retirement age of airline pilots is 65. The reaction times of pilots 65 or older are likely to be slower than for those younger.

Genetic Information Nondiscrimination Act

The Genetic Information Nondiscrimination Act of 2008 protects people from discrimination in employment and healthcare based on the misuse of genetic information. An example of an application of this Act is when an employer makes a hiring decision based on an employee's or applicant's predisposition to get a certain disease based on his DNA.

Immigration Reform and Control Act

The Immigration Reform and Control Act of 1986 criminalized the act or pattern or practice of knowingly hiring an "unauthorized alien." The Act further established financial and other penalties for those employing illegal immigrants under the theory that by limiting employment prospects for illegal immigrants, fewer illegal immigrants would come into the United States.

Generational Differences

Though there are no standard definitions for when a generation begins and ends, the following generations consist of people born between specified years. The *Silent Generation* is the generation born between 1925 and 1945; the *Baby Boomers* were born between 1946 and 1964; *Generation X* were born between 1965 and 1979; *Millennials (or Generation Y)* were born between 1980 and 1994; *Generation Z* were born between 1995 and 2012; and *Generation Alpha* were / will be born between 2013 and 2025.

Human resource managers often make a big deal out of generational variations, making the assumption that people born around the same time share similar experiences and form similar preferences and behaviors. Several differences that matter in the workplace are as follows: (1) management preferences; (2) team culture; and (3) motivations.

Variations by generations that matter are as follows.[53] Eight out of ten millennials prefer their bosses to act as coaches or mentors, while baby boomers prefer bosses to be ethical, consistent, fair and dependable. 55 percent of millennials consider team consensus to be important in making decisions, whereas only 39 percent of baby boomers consider it important. 61 percent of generation X employees consider team consensus important. The generations further vary widely in motivations. Older employees would consider choosing a new employer based on making more money and working in an innovative environment, while millennials strongly consider company values. All three of these working groups are interested in flexible schedules, tele-commuting options, and making an impact on their organizations or on society.

When trying to figure out differences between generations, consider the events within their generations that likely impacted them greatly. The Great Depression of the 1930s likely led many in the Silent Generation to be thrifty, always taking measures to enhance the financial security of themselves and their families. The Korean War and Vietnam likely had an impact on the Baby Boomers, leading to various opinions on warfare and freedom. The recent financial downfall in 2008 most likely has had an impact on the Millennials, as many may seek greater job and financial security. The Coronavirus pandemic of 2019 and 2020 is likely to severely impact workers of all generations for years to come.

Whistleblowing and Retaliation

What happens if an employee files a claim of discrimination based on his treatment in the workplace and the company retaliates by firing him? Is the employee legally protected? Yes. The Occupational Safety and Health Administration (OSHA) protects workers from discrimination based on whistleblowing and retaliation against employees who file discrimination, harassment, workers' compensation, or other related claims against their employers. They are further protected when they blow the whistle (or alert external parties) of health and safety violations or illegal activity within their organizations. Employees are protected from adverse actions against employees, which include terminations, discipline, blacklisting, overtime or promotion denials, reassignments, and harassment.

Corporate Board Representation

Over the past fifty years, women and minorities have made much progress in advancing in organizations, thanks to changing popular opinions and legislation against discrimination. Oftentimes in the past, people would consider higher level positions to be an "Old Boys Club," but today, we are seeing trends towards more diversification. According to the Alliance for Board Diversity and Deloitte in 2018, women held 22.5 percent of Fortune 500 board seats, while minority women held 4.6 percent. Caucasian men held 66 percent.

An author at Fortune Magazine studied the composition of corporate boards in Fortune 500 firms.[54] More than three dozen companies only have zero or one woman in directorships. Yet in a handful of organizations, women outnumber men. At General Motors, Bed, Bath & Beyond, Casey's General Stores, Viacom, CBS and Omnicom Group, women outnumber men in their boards of directors. At Ascena Retail Group, Best Buy, Navient, Progressive Corporation, Williams-Sonoma and Ulta Beauty, females have 50 percent representation. More than two dozen of corporate boards in Fortune 500 organizations are at the 40 percent mark.

But are there any benefits to diverse board representation? Yes. One study found that women CEOs are more likely than their male counterparts to champion diversity policies and practices. Yet the same study found that differences in other types of policies, such as community engagement initiatives, governance, or stronger product development were not evident.[55] Women and minorities may bring different perspectives to boards and may help to better appeal to diverse target markets. Perhaps this is one reason we're seeing increased female and minority representation in corporate boards of large organizations.

Social Media

Social media has become pervasive over the past decade. Millions in the United States have active social media accounts on platforms such as Instagram, Twitter, YouTube, and Facebook. Employers started requesting job candidates' social media account names and passwords to protect their trade secrets or other proprietary information. Schools also started requesting students' social media account names and passwords for monitoring and safety reasons. This invasion of privacy has driven most states to adopt laws against such requests. Social media discussions are covered under the first amendment on free speech. Currently, 26 states in the United States prohibit employers from requesting on-line names and passwords and 16 states prohibit educational institutions from making those requests.[56]

Conclusion

If employers and employees followed the Golden Rule, which is to treat others as they wish to be treated, claims of workplace discrimination, harassment, and mistreatment would be significantly lessened if not eliminated. Yet these claims persist. For example, in 2016, the Equal Employment Opportunity Commission resolved 97,443 charges and secured over $482 million for victims of discrimination in private, federal, state, and local government workplaces.[57] Accordingly, adopting programs and practices in the workplace that are designed to mitigate the potential for workplace discrimination, harassment, and litigation is important. This chapter identified several major sources of federal redress, Title VII of the Civil Rights Act, the Age Discrimination in Employment Act, and the Americans with Disabilities Act, along with other laws about which employers should be aware to ensure compliance.

Summary of Employment Laws

Law or doctrine	Groups subject to law (if not all employers)	Actual law or discrimination based on:	What constitutes a violation?	Exemptions
Title VII	Employers with more than 15 employees or government workers; except armed forces, private clubs, religious organizations, and places of employment connected to an Indian reservation. EEOC requires that employers with 100+ employees submit an annual EEO-1 form that identifies possible patterns of discrimination	Race, color, religion, national origin, sex. Federal employees are also protected from discrimination based on sexual orientation (1998), veteran status, sexual orientation, and gender identity (2014).	Hostile work environment. Adverse impact should be checked with the 4/5 rule. If adverse impact is present, the burden shifts to the employer to prove that the practice is valid and job-related. Then burden shifts back to plaintiff to present alternative practices	BFOQs, essence of the business; seniority systems; veteran's preference rights; national security reasons; job qualifications based on test scores, background, or experience.
Pregnancy Discrimination Act	Amendment to Title VII, same groups	Pregnancy, childbirth or related medical condition	Forbids employers to discharge, fail to hire, or otherwise discriminate	
Sexual harassment	Amendment to Title VII, same groups		Hostile work environment	
ADEA, Age Discrimination in Employment Act	Employers with 20+ employees, unions of 25 or more members, employment agencies, and federal, state, and local governments	Persons 40+	Must show (1) employee a member of protected group, (2) employee has ability to perform satisfactorily, (3) employee was not hired, promoted, or compensated or discharged, laid off, or forced to retire, and (4) the position was filled by a person younger than claimant	Practice is reasonable

Law or doctrine	Groups subject to law (if not all employers)	Actual law or discrimination based on:	What constitutes a violation?	Exemptions
ADA, Americans with Disabilities Act	Employers with 15+ employees or government workers	Person has a physical or mental impairment that substantially limits one or more major life activities (the impairment is not minor), has a record of such impairment, or is regarded as having an impairment. Included in the protected groups are severely obese people and persons with AIDS. The ADAAA (amendment 2008) expands the term of major life activities to include caring or oneself, performing manual tasks, eating, hearing, seeing, walking, sleeping, standing, lifting, bending, concentrating, learning, communicating, thinking, and working		Reasonable, accommodation, undue hardship

Summary of Important Court Cases

Albemarle Paper Company v. Moody - Clarified the job-relatedness defense, which required a careful job analysis to identify the knowledge, skills, and abilities necessary to perform the job or study correlating scores on a procedure with job performance.

Burlington Industries, Inc. v. Ellerth - - Sexual harassment cases do not require a causal link, or "quid pro quo" defense. An employee who refuses the unwelcome and threatening sexual advances of a supervisor, yet suffers no adverse, tangible job consequences, may recover against the employer without having to show that the employer is negligent or at fault for the supervisor's actions. The employer can still present an affirmative defense.

Connecticut v. Teal – At all steps in the multiple-hurdle staffing procedure, "job-relatedness" arguments must be applied.

DeStefano v. Ricci (2009) – The Supreme Court ruled that the exams used to promote firefighters were consistent with business necessity and there was no evidence that an equally valid, less discriminatory option was available, so discarding the exams after determining they resulted in disparate impact was illegal.

EEOC v. Waffle House – In an ADA enforcement action, a prior agreement between an employer and an employee to arbitrate employment-related disputes does not prevent the EEOC from pursuing victim-specific judicial relief. Examples include pursuing back pay, reinstatement, and damages.

Faragher v. City of Boca Raton – In sexual harassment claims, an employer can be held liable for the actions of its supervisors, yet the employer can also offer an affirmative defense.

Farley v. American Cast Iron Pipe (1997) – Employers can give themselves legal protection (an affirmative defense) by having a good harassment policy in place.

General Dynamics Land Systems vs. Cline – Employers can favor older workers over younger workers. The ADEA does not prohibit an employer from practicing 'reverse age discrimination.'

Griggs v. Duke Power – Employment practices or job qualifications must be job-related if they pose a disparate impact on protected groups.

Harris v. Forklift – In cases of sexual harassment, people do not have to provide evidence of psychological damage or psychological effects to constitute harassment. If a reasonable person would consider the harassment hostile or abusive, that is enough to constitute sexual harassment.

Johnson v. Santa Clara Transportation - Organizations may adopt voluntary programs to hire and advance equally qualified minorities and women to correct a "manifest imbalance" in their representation in various job categories, even when there is no proven evidence of past discrimination.

Mastie v. Great Lakes Steel Corp. - ADEA case requires evidence that age was a determinative factor in a human resource decision.

McDonnell Douglas v. Green – In cases in which disparate treatment is adversely impacting protected groups, plaintiffs must provide evidence.

Meritor Savings Bank v. Vinson - Any workplace activity or conduct that is "sufficiently severe or pervasive to alter the conditions of employment and create an abusive working environment" constitutes illegal sexual harassment.

Pan Am World Airways v. Diaz (1971) - Employers cannot argue for a bona fide occupational qualification based on customer preference.

Smith v. Jackson (2005) - employers must show an age-neutral "business necessity" for their actions.

United Steelworkers v. Weber – Companies may adopt affirmative action programs to remedy a "manifest racial imbalance" regardless of whether an employer had been guilty of discriminatory job practices in the past.

QUESTIONS FOR REVIEW

1. What is Title VII of the Civil Rights Act of 1964? Which groups are protected under Title VII? Which groups are exempt?

2. What is the Americans with Disabilities Act? When can employers request an exemption?

3. Is reverse discrimination protected under the Age Discrimination in Employment Act?

4. What is a bona fide occupational qualification? Identify several examples.

5. What considerations and/or accommodations should employers make under the Americans with Disabilities Act?

6. How does adverse impact differ from disparate treatment?

7. What is the current state of affairs with respect to Affirmative Action?

8. What is a manifest imbalance?

9. If groups are not protected at the federal level under one of the three major sources of federal redress, do they have other protections?

10. Does a "quid pro quo" (causal relationship) need to be established in cases of sexual harassment?

APPLICATIONS

1. Calculations of Adverse Impact

To determine whether adverse (or disparate) impact is present, plaintiffs must show that an employer's practices had a disparate impact on members of the protected group by showing that the employment procedures (e.g., tests, interviews, credentials) had a disproportionately negative effect on members of a protected group (Griggs v. Duke Power, 1971).

- The burden begins with the plaintiff, who needs to provide evidence of adverse or disparate impact (e.g., four-fifths rule). Evidence of adverse impact or disparate treatment applies at each step in the selection process (Connecticut v. Teal);
- The burden shifts to the employer, who must produce evidence of "business necessity" and/or "job relatedness" for the employment practice (Albemarle v. Moody);
- The burden shifts back to the plaintiff who must show that an alternative procedure is available that is equal to or better (more valid) than the employer's practice and has less adverse impact.

To calculate the presence of adverse impact, the 4/5 rule can be applied by multiplying 80 percent times the highest passing rate or employment rate.

Group 1 passing rate: 70 percent (x 80 percent = 56 percent; this is the critical level that others must reach).
Group 2 passing rate: 50 percent
Group 3 passing rate: 60 percent

Scenario A: John Hayes applied to be a pilot on Acme Airlines and was told that he was not qualified since he didn't have a four-year degree. He felt that this requirement may have an adverse impact on those within his minority demographic, so he consulted with the EEOC. Does John have a case under Title VII of the Civil Rights Act? What would you need to know?

Scenario B: Acme requires that all employees score at least 70 percent on an intelligence test to make it to the next step of the selection process. Below is the breakdown of the scores by gender.

Male passing rate (who scored 70 or higher): 80 percent
Female passing rate: 70 percent

White passing rate: 70 percent
Hispanic passing rate: 75 percent
American Indian passing rate: 52 percent
African American passing rate: 70 percent
Asian American passing rate: 80 percent

Is there evidence of adverse impact by gender? By ethnicity?
If there is evidence, what does Acme need to do to prove the legitimacy of using intelligence exams?

2. Pan American and the Flight Attendant

In 1972, John Sanchez applied for a position as a flight attendant on Pan American Airlines. Pan American hiring managers told him that since customers preferred female flight attendants, they did not want to hire him. Sanchez sued, claiming discrimination under Title VII of the Civil Rights Act of 1964. Was this gender discrimination? What would Pan American Airlines need to prove?

3. Dolphin Bar Job Application

Today's Date:_____

Name_____
Social Security:_____
Present Address_____
Phone _____
How long have you lived at the above address?_____
Previous address_____
How long there?_____
Positions applied for_____
Rate of pay expected?_____
Would you work full-time_____ part-time_____

Specify days you cannot work

Monday		am		pm
Tuesday		am		pm
Wednesday		am		pm
Thursday		am		pm
Friday		am		pm
Saturday		am		pm
Sunday		am		pm

Were you previously employed by us?_____ If yes, when?_____
List any friends or relatives working for us_____
If you application is considered favorable, on what date will you be available for work?_____
Person to be notified in case of accident or emergency

_____
(Name)   (Address)
        (Phone #)
Are there any other experiences, skills, or qualifications which you feel would especially fit you for work with the Company?_____
_____
_____
_____

Would you be willing to submit a polygraph test?_____
Date of Birth_____Sex: F_____ M_____ Height_____
Weight_____

Marital Status: Single_____ Engaged_____ Married_____
Separated_____ Divorced_____ Widowed_____
Date of Marriage_____
Dependents including you_____# of children _____
Children's ages _____
Does your wife/husband work?_____
If yes, what kind?_____
Do you own your own home? _____ Pay rent?_____
Do you have a car available for your own use?_____
Do you have any physical defects?_____
If yes, describe _____
Have you had a major illness in the past 5 years?_____
If yes, describe_____
Have you received compensation for injuries?_____
If yes, describe_____
Have you been convicted of a crime in the past ten years?_____
If yes, describe _____

MILITARY SERVICE RECORD

Were you in the Armed Forces? Yes_____ No_____
If yes, what
branch?_____
Dates if duty: From _____To_____
Rank at discharge_____
Circle last year completed
Elementary School 5 6 7 8
High School   1 2 3 4
College   1 2 3 4

EDUCATION
Describe any training or education
_____

PLEASE LIST ALL PRESENT & PAST EMPLOYMENT, BEGINNING WITH YOUR MOST RECENT

_____
_____
_____

Have you ever been bonded?_____If yes, on what jobs?_____

May we contact the employers listed above?_____
If not, by #, which ones do you wish us not to contact?_____

The facts set forth in my application for employment are true and complete. I understand that if employed, false statements on this application shall be considered sufficient cause for dismissal. You are hereby authorized to make any investigation of my personal history and financial and credit record through any investigative or credit agencies or bureaus of your choice.

_____
Signature of Applicant

CASE STUDIES

1. Sarasota Deputy Files Claim of Disability Discrimination

In his twelve years at the Sarasota Police Department, Theodore Bowles advanced through the ranks. He was often commended for his leadership skills and by 2008 was serving as the team leader of a SWAT unit.

Yet Bowles was an admitted alcoholic who had been struggling with alcoholism since his pre-teen years. In several off-duty instances, Bowles had black-outs. In one case in an AppleBee's Restaurant, two female servers accused him of battery while he was under the influence of alcohol. Bowles noted that he never showed up to work while under the influence, yet several times he failed to report to duty, due to what he told his supervisors were bad hangovers.

According to court documents, it was widely known throughout the Sarasota County Sheriff's Office that Bowles suffered from alcoholism to such an extent that it substantially impaired and limited his ability to perform one or more of his major life activities.

Bowles was removed from his assignment on the SWAT team, pending his referral to an Employee Assistance Program. But despite his repeated requests to start the program, he was never admitted. After the Applebee's incident, he was fired for violating the sheriff's general orders relating to off-duty use of alcohol and for violations of the law during the incident in the restaurant.

Bowles sued for lost wages, attorney's fees, and other financial compensation. He requested that the sheriff's office provide a "reasonable accommodation to deputy sheriffs suffering from alcoholism."

Should the sheriff's office have provided the "reasonable accommodation"? Is alcoholism a disability as defined by the Americans with Disabilities Act? [58]

2. Press Machinist at Sarasota Herald-Tribune Files Disability Discrimination Claim

While working as a press machinist for the Sarasota Herald-Tribune, Rick Sangum, a press machinist, was diagnosed with hepatitis C. He began a series of medical treatments and requested that his supervisor accommodate the timing of the treatments by allowing him to continue on his 7:30 a.m. to 3:30 p.m. shift. Another worker with more seniority in the organization had requested the earlier shift, however, so the Sarasota Herald-Tribune asked Sangum to move to the later shift of 8:30 a.m. to 4:30 p.m. The supervisor indicated that he needed a machinist on duty later in the day and the one with seniority wanted the earlier shift.

Sangum eventually went out on leave. When he was ready return to his press machinist position, his doctor told him that he would be limited in pushing, pulling, lifting, walking, sitting, and climbing. The paper refused to let him return, even on light duty. Managers indicated that they couldn't modify his position. Ray became depressed and his condition deteriorated. Eventually the paper terminated him, since he couldn't work.

Sangum sued under federal and state laws, claiming that the Sarasota Herald-Tribune failed to reasonably accommodate him. Does Sangum have a strong case under the Americans with Disabilities Act?[59]

3. Paraplegic Mold Polisher Files Disability Discrimination Case

Tim Hardy, a paraplegic, was hired in 1986 as a mold polisher at Babson Industries. For 17 years, Hardy earned commendable performance evaluations for his work, though sometimes he was a minute or two late to work due to his mobility issues.

On rare occasions, he was tardier. Sometimes his tardiness was because he lost bowel control on his way to work and had to return home to change his clothes. Other times he was tardy due to his disability, such as having to wait in his vehicle during heavy rains for the rain to stop since it was difficult to operate both an umbrella and his wheel chair. Sometimes he was "late" because his company permitted only five minutes for all employees to clock in to avoid overtime and he was almost always at the end of the line due to his wheelchair.

In 2003, Babson hired an employee benefits specialist who created a "no fault" attendance policy. Under the policy, each absence counted as one occurrence and a tardy was a one-half occurrence. Employees who were late for any reason received a one-half occurrence, even when the occurrence was used for a planned event such as going to the doctor. Employees who had nine occurrences were terminated. Hardy was terminated.

Hardy noted that he was given reasonable accommodations in his first sixteen years at Babson, so he sued under the Americans with Disabilities Act. He also noted that he had always made up the time he lost by clocking in late. Do you agree with Babson's decision? Why or why not?[60]

4. Part-time Librarian Sues for Religious Accommodation

Connie Tate, a 54-year-old former junior high school math teacher, had been faithfully attending the Lutheran church where she and her husband were married 34 years ago. She also worked part time for the local public library. The library insisted she work on Sundays, yet laboring on the Sabbath was against her firmly held religious beliefs. The library thus terminated her, refusing to make a religious accommodation. Connie sued under Title VII of the Civil Rights Act of 1964. Did Connie Tate win? [61]

5. What Would a Reasonable Person Decide?

In sexual harassment cases, a quid pro quo (causal relationship) does not need to be established. To establish a case of sexual harassment, the courts use a reasonable person assessment. If a "reasonable person" would consider the situation sexual harassment, then the burden shifts to the accused to make appropriate sanctions and to demonstrate evidence of an affirmative defense, which is a well-communicated policy.

A) Kelly has held the position of an assistant purchasing manager for over a year. While meeting with her married boss, he asks, "Hey Kelly, you have to try the new restaurant downtown. What do you say that you and I finish this work up early and head on down for a couple of drinks and dinner? My treat." Is this sexual harassment?

B) Samantha has always been a smart dresser, often preferring suits and slacks to skirts. When she does decide to wear a skirt, her male supervisor always comments, "You look very nice today." Is this sexual harassment?

C) Robert was recently called into his boss' office to discuss a raise. His boss, Celeste, is the HR manager. She offers him an impressive $5,000 raise, yet there is a catch: she asks him for a favor in return. "I'm thinking you and I should take a quiet trip together this weekend. If you take this trip with me, I'll make sure that you get the $5,000 raise you deserve." Robert reviewed the HRM policy on sexual harassment and noticed that the policy requires that he report the harassment to his immediate supervisor (Celeste), so he chose not to report the incident. Can the company be liable in this incident?

6. Legal Affirmative Action or Reverse Discrimination?

Acme Trucking is an organization based in the United States that employs just over 1,000 workers in a number of administrative and delivery positions. Recently Acme announced a job opening for the position of truck driver. The qualifications for the position include 3 years of experience as a truck driver, a valid driver's license for large transport, and a score of over 70 on an intelligence exam. Currently, none of Acme's 438 drivers are female.

Two candidates emerged from the list of applicants with the appropriate qualifications: Suzie Jameson and Jim Johnson. Suzie spent the past 6 years working as a truck driver for a competitor, possessed the correct driver's license, and scored 71 on the Intelligence Exam. Jim has also spent 6 years working as a truck driver for another competitor, possessed the correct driver's license, and scored 78 on the Intelligence. Exam. After a series of interviews, Acme managers recommended that Jim be hired. They noted that Suzie was a "rabble-rousing, skirt-wearing" applicant who wouldn't fit in. Acme's HR Manager decided to hire Suzie, based on the company's voluntary Affirmative Action policy. Jim sued, claiming reverse discrimination.[62]

Who won?

7. Is Obesity Alone a Disability?

Mark Richardson was working as a bus driver for the Chicago Transit Authority (CTA). Between 2005 and 2009, his weight rose from 350 pounds to 566 pounds. In February 2010, he contracted the flu and missed work. When he returned, a third-party medical provider determined that he had uncontrolled hypertension so the CTA prohibited him from returning to work until he controlled his blood pressure. They transferred him to "Area 605," which is a temporary place where CTA employees who are considered medical unfit go until they can perform the essential function of their jobs.

In September of 2010, Richardson's blood pressure was under control and the CTA considered him physically fit and able to return back to work. Yet their bus seats were too small for Richardson as they were designed to accommodate people who weigh no more than 400 pounds. The CTA noted that Richardson could drive all of the CTA buses in a safe and trusted manner, yet he could not make the hand-over-hand turns that needed to be made occasionally. He also used both of his feet on the gas and brake pedals. Further, he rested his leg near the door handle. The CTA therefore cited safety concerns and returned him to Area 605.

After two years of inactive status and his failure to submit documentation to extend his time in Area 605, Richardson was terminated in February of 2012. Richardson sued the CTA, claiming that they violated the Americans with Disabilities Act by refusing to allow him to return to work because they considered him to be too obese to work as a bus driver.

Who won the case?

Chapter 3: Job Analysis

Introduction

Steve Jobs once said "it doesn't make sense to hire smart people and tell them what to do; we hire smart people so they can tell us what to do." Such a statement resonated with Chris Myers, founder and CEO of BodeTree who decided to chuck traditional job descriptions in favor of giving all employees the same job description: "Figure out what needs to be done and do it."[63] While this approach could work well in smaller start-up organizations, human resource managers advocate conducting job analyses and creating job descriptions for a number of reasons. Job descriptions help to set appropriate expectations. They provide a systematic, detailed summary of the tasks, duties, and responsibilities of a job. They can be used to determine compensation, appraise employee performance, and determine whether job candidates have the qualifications to do the jobs.

Objectives:

After reading this chapter, you should be able to:

- Distinguish between job descriptions and job qualifications.
- Explain the advantages of conducting a job analysis.
- Identify and apply commonly used job analysis methods.
- Identify ways to enhance job satisfaction, job enrichment, and job enlargement in organizations.

Job Analysis

The Society for Human Resource Management defines job analysis as "the process of studying jobs to gather, analyze, synthesize and report information about job responsibilities and requirements and the conditions under which work is performed." A job analysis forms the foundation upon which all of the other practices of human resource management are built. These are: planning, staffing, training, performance management, health and safety, employee relations, compensation and benefits, incentives, and legal compliance.

A job analysis has two components: *job descriptions* and *job qualifications.* Job descriptions are defined as a broad, general and written statement that covers the title of the job, the tasks involved in the job and the job's working conditions. Job qualifications are defined as what is required of the person to work effectively on the job. These are the KASOCS: knowledge, abilities, skills, and other characteristics. Other characteristics could include education, experience, attitudes and personality.

For example, according to the O*Net from the United States Bureau of Labor Statistics (onetonline.org), the job of a human resource manager involves the following tasks: serve as a link between management and employees by handing questions, interpreting and administering contracts, and helping to resolve work-related problems; advise managers on policy matters; analyze and modify compensation and benefits; perform difficult staffing duties, firing employees, and administering disciplinary procedures; and represent the organization at personnel-related hearings and investigations. The qualifications include knowledge of human resources, law and government, and education and training; the abilities of oral comprehension and expression, written comprehension, deductive reasoning and speech clarity; the skills of active listening, speaking, judgment and decision making, and reading comprehension; and the other characteristics (or work context) of integrity, self-control, leadership, dependability and cooperation.

Benefits of Job Analysis

By investing the time to analyze jobs, human resource managers reap numerous benefits. The goals of a job analysis include legal compliance, worker mobility and succession, planning, efficiency and safety. The products of a job analysis include job descriptions, job classifications, job evaluations, design/restructuring, job specifications, performance appraisals, and worker training. Detailed next are several benefits to legal compliance in selection and promotions, competitive pay scales, and valid performance evaluations.

According to the Economic Research Institute,[64] the following information should be included when conducting a job analysis:

- Identification information: organization, name, location, industry and job title
- Working conditions and physical requirements
- Environmental conditions (e.g., work outside, dirty or noisy conditions, explosions or chemicals present)
- Education, background, experience and training (speaking, writing, mathematical, reasoning, and decision-making)
- The extent to which the job deals with data, information, and ideas
- How the incumbent interacts with people. Does the incumbent act as a supervisor? How does he or she receive instruction?

Legal Compliance

Developing job descriptions and qualifications helps companies to comply with employment laws in the United States by (1) establishing job-relatedness; (2) identifying bona fide occupational qualifications; and (3) understanding what constitutes reasonable accommodations. For example, among the qualifications for the position of a truck driver are near and far vision. Truck drivers need to be able to see the road ahead of them and off into the distance. Does that requirement adversely impact people who are vision-impaired? Yes. But the requirements are bona fide occupational qualifications and they are related to the essential duties of the position. Is there a reasonable accommodation that a company could make for the visually impaired to drive trucks? No. At present, the only accommodation would be to hire another driver, which would not be financially reasonable.

Job qualifications must be job-related, according to the United States Supreme Court. In the landmark case *Connecticut vs. Teal,* the Supreme Court determined that if a qualification has an adverse impact on a protected group at any step of the selection process, the company requiring the qualification must provide evidence that it relates to performance on the job. Winnie Teal had applied for a promotion in the State of Connecticut's Department of Income Maintenance, yet she was denied early on in the selection process due to the fact she did not earn a passing score on a written examination. In fact, only 54.17 percent of candidates who identified themselves as black passed the exam, while 79.54 percent of white candidates passed.[65] Using the 80 percent rule, the passing rate of blacks should have been at 63.6 percent, so adverse impact is indicated. Connecticut was unable to demonstrate whether people who earned passing scores on the exam performed any better than those who did not, so the requirement was not job-related.

A second case decided by the Supreme Court that has an impact on job analysis is *Albermarle vs. Moody*. In this case, the Court required work analysis for demonstrating the *job relatedness* of selection systems after prima facie evidence (assumed to be true unless proven otherwise). Lawsuits by women based on the physical job requirements of firefighters and policemen have been decided based on whether the physical job requirements were related to the positions. For example, firefighters need to be physically agile and capable of managing a heavy water hose. This requirement has an adverse impact on some women, the disabled, and the elderly. Yet because physical agility and heavy lifting are essential functions of fire-fighting, the requirements are considered bona fide occupational qualifications. Older workers have also contested mandatory retirement ages. For example, Greyhound Bus has a mandatory retirement age of 55. Because workers older than 55 have slower reflexes than their younger counterparts that may impact bus safety, this requirement is considered a bona fide occupational qualification.

KASOCS and the tasks needed to complete jobs are legally defensible when the job analysis (1) uses a representative sample of job incumbents to gather data; (2) is in written form; and (3) specifies the level of competency for entry level work.

Competitive Pay Scales

Conducting a job analysis can further benefit organizations in setting pay scales. Human resource managers can choose to lag behind the market, lead the market in pay, or meet the market in pay. Many choose to meet the market, advertising the salaries they offer as "competitive." Ensuring pay is competitive with market pricing benefits organizations in employee recruitment, motivation, and retention. Analyzing market pay helps to establish external equity, so oftentimes human resource managers consult websites such as salary.com, glassdoor.com, or the O*Net to determine competitive base pay levels for the positions they're analyzing. Human resource managers also consider internal equity by gauging the internal worth of jobs relative to other jobs in the organization, alignment with the organization's strategy, contribution to the organization's bottom line, level of financial responsibility, level of supervisory responsibility, level of decision-making and accountability, and other factors important to business operations.

Valid Performance Appraisals

When evaluating the performance of employees, managers can consider their relevant duties and tasks and whether employees successfully achieve their duties and tasks in a timely and efficient manner. If they discover employee shortcomings, they can assess whether employees have the relevant qualifications to successfully perform and whether additional training is needed. If they discover strong performance, they can consider whether to offer promotions or pay raises.

Methods of Job Analysis

Human resource managers employ a variety of methods to conduct a job analysis. These include (1) observing an employee's performance on the job; (2) performing the job; (3) interviewing job incumbents; (4) requiring job incumbents to log a diary of their activities and responsibilities; (5) surveying background records, such as the O*Net; (6) asking job incumbents to complete questionnaires, such as the Position Analysis Questionnaire or the Management Position Analysis Questionnaire along with open-ended unstructured questions; and (7) collecting critical incidents.

The most useful work analysis methods include the Position Analysis Questionnaire, the Management Position Description Questionnaire, the Critical Incident Technique, the Job Diagnostic Survey of the Job Characteristics Model, the Job Compatibility Survey, the O*Net, competency modeling, and the Work Design Questionnaire.

Position Analysis Questionnaire

The Position Analysis Questionnaire (PAQ) is a structured questionnaire that provides a quantified assessment of jobs. According to the Economic Research Institute, "the PAQ consists of 187 items related to job activities or work situation. There are an additional 8 items related to the type of compensation received by the job incumbents. The PAQ items are organized into six divisions: Information Input, Mental Processes, Work Output, Relationships with Other Persons, Job Context, and Other Job Characteristics. These divisions provide a frame of reference for thinking about the major aspects of virtually any job. Familiarity with the overall structure of the PAQ will enable the analyst to obtain a very thorough analysis of a job. The analyst must recognize, however, that job incumbents seldom share this conceptual structure. Therefore, it is important that the analyst become adept at organizing the data obtained from the job analysis in a fashion both consistent with the PAQ and comprehensible to the job incumbents."[66] The advantage of the PAQ is it provides information on job relatedness of various job specifications, such as the Myers Briggs Personality profile and the general mental ability scores of successful job incumbents in various positions.

Management Position Description Questionnaire

The Management Position Description Questionnaire (MPDQ) is similar to the PAQ, yet it applies to management positions. The MPDQ collects a written statement of the duties, responsibilities, and requirements of jobs. The MPDQ provides 208 elements related to managerial positions in thirteen categories.

Critical Incident Technique

Critical incidents provide specific, observable, behaviorally-focused examples of exceptionally good behavior or exceptionally poor behavior in a particular work context. Critical incidents always exclude traits or judgmental inferences. For example, one critical incident in a customer service position could be when an irate customer comes into a store and berates the customer service employee. The employee punched the customer in the face. This is an example of exceptionally poor behavior – and it does not include a description of the personality traits of the employee (such as mean, angry, or deviant).

Job Compatibility Survey

The Job Compatibility Survey (JCS) collects job applicant preferences about all aspects of a job that are considered to be related to job incumbent performance, absences, job satisfaction and turnover. The assumption is that the greater compatibility with an applicant's preferences and the characteristics of the job, the more likely the applicant will stay on the job and perform well. The JCS works best for entry-level, low wage jobs, such as those held by theatre workers.[67]

Competency Modeling

Instead of focusing on sets of different tasks relevant to each job in an organization, some companies focus on competencies relevant to all jobs within an organization. Certain competencies may be predictive of performance of all jobs, such as qualitative analysis, quantitative analysis, interpersonal skills, decision-making, problem-solving, critical thinking, integrity, emotional resilience, innovation, creativity, oral communication, and written communication. Competency models are commonly used in organizations in the assessment of both hard and soft skills relevant to performance. They form the foundation of human resource management functions such as recruitment and selection, training and development, and performance management.

Job Design

The next step after job analysis is to conduct a job design. Job design is related to the specification of tasks, duties, and responsibilities for the achievement of specified organizational objectives. Designing jobs to maximize employee satisfaction, engagement, and motivation is important to organizations in capitalizing on their human capital.

Job Diagnostic Survey

The Job Diagnostic Survey (JDS) of the Job Characteristics Model is an instrument for the diagnosis of jobs and evaluation of job design (or redesign) programs. The JDS assesses the (1) objective characteristics of jobs and whether they enhance job incumbents' internal motivations and job satisfaction; (2) the personal affective reactions of job incumbents to their jobs; and (3) the readiness of job incumbents to respond to the newly "enriched" jobs.

Hackman and Oldham (1974)[68] identified core job dimensions and indicated that they predicted critical psychological states, which impacted personal and work outcomes. The core job dimensions of skill variety, task identity (i.e., the job has a complete and identifiable beginning and end) and task significance predicted the experienced meaningfulness of work. Autonomy (freedom to make decisions about one's job) predicted the experienced responsibility of work outcomes. Feedback predicted knowledge of the actual results of work activities. All of these core job dimensions and critical psychological states have an impact on high internal work motivation, high quality work performance, high satisfaction with the work and low turnover and low absenteeism.

Work Design Questionnaire

The *Work Design Questionnaire* by Frederick P. Morgeson[69] has identified aspects of jobs that have results in greater job satisfaction. Below are the job dimensions along with examples of the items used to measure each job dimension. The strongest predictors of job satisfaction are autonomy and social support.

Job dimension	Example of Item
Autonomy	The job allows me to make my own decisions about how to schedule my work
Task variety	The job involves doing a number of different things
Task significance	The results of my work are likely to significantly impact the lives of others
Task identity	The job involves completing a piece of work that has an obvious beginning and an end
Feedback from the job	The job itself provides feedback on my performance
Information processing	The job requires me to monitor a great deal of information
Problem-solving	The job requires me to be creative
Skill variety	The job requires a variety of skills
Specialization	The job requires very specialized knowledge and skills
Social support	People I work with are friendly
Interdependence	Other jobs depend directly on my job
Interaction outside of the organization	The job involves a great deal of interaction outside of my organization
Feedback	I receive feedback on my performance from other people in my organization, such as my manager or coworkers

Work context is further important. Work context includes ergonomics (such as comfortable seating), physical demands, work conditions, and equipment use. The two top sources of employee satisfaction from the Work Design Questionnaire are autonomy and social support.

Organization Design

Company leaders should further ensure the organization is designed to maximize strengths and mitigate weaknesses. To accomplish this task, leaders often examine the core competencies in the organization, or what they do well, where they have a competitive advantage, and what their purpose is. Organization design is a process in which dysfunctional aspects of work flow, procedures, systems, and structures are identified and realigned to correspond better to organizational strategies and goals.

In 2015, *Forbes Magazine*[70] identified ten steps to effective organization design:

1. Declare amnesty from the past: What is the organization's purpose? What sets the organization apart from its competition?

2. Design with the "DNA": Establish a framework based on the building blocks in the organization.

3. Fix the structure last, not first.

4. Make the most of top talent.

5. Focus on what you can control.

6. Promote accountability.

7. Benchmark sparingly, if at all. Benchmarking against competitors can be helpful in optimizing design or uncovering issues in need of attention, but it may result in a failure to capitalize on a company's distinct advantages.

8. Let the "lines and boxes" fit your company's purpose. Consider spans of control: How many people report directly to any given manager? Also consider layers: How far removed is the manager from the CEO?

9. Accentuate the informal: norms, commitments, mindsets, and networks.

10. Build on strengths.

Workflow Analysis

The first step towards business process success is to conduct a workflow analysis. A **workflow analysis** reviews all of the processes in an organization and then makes recommendations to streamline manual business processes to improve efficiency. Step one is to identify the staff in a department, along with job descriptions and positions. Step two is to identify strategies and priorities. Step three is to identify the current tasks performed in the department. The fourth step is to identify tasks that need to be performed or should be performed, but are not currently assigned to a particular position. The fifth step is to identify department priorities over the next five years to establish future tasks and strategies, along with technology or personnel needs. The final step is to separate tasks by job description and to develop new job descriptions that incorporate the results from the prior steps.

Equal Pay Act and Comparable Worth

The concept of comparable worth states that men and women should be paid equally for jobs of comparable worth to their organizations. For example, if an employer determined that a marketing assistant in an organization contributes value equivalent to that of an accounting assistant, both employees should be paid equally. The *Equal Pay Act* (as amended in 2010) indicates that men and women should be paid equally for equal work (skill, effort, responsibility, working conditions or any other job-related factor) under the same establishment (location). Pay differentials are permitted when based on job-related factors such as seniority, merit (performance), quality or quantity of production, education, experience, or any other job-related factor – other than sex.

Conclusion

To effectively structure human resources within organizations, HR managers should conduct job analyses in which they determine appropriate job descriptions and job qualifications. They can later use these tools to achieve compliance, establish pay ranges and levels, manage performance, consider training needs and opportunities, identify workforce needs, identify and select employees for training, development, and promotions, and more. Furthermore, job analyses can be used to enhance employee satisfaction, engagement, and productivity when jobs are structured to maximize all three, benefiting the company's bottom line.

QUESTIONS FOR REVIEW

1. What are KASOCs?

2. What is the difference between a job description and a job qualification?

3. What is an advantage of using a position analysis questionnaire?

4. What sorts of jobs can be analyzed using the job compatibility questionnaire?

5. What are the advantages and drawbacks of conducting an extensive job analysis?

6. What methods can be used to conduct a job analysis?

7. To determine whether a particular job qualification was necessary or effective for a particular job, what would be the best approach?

8. In addition to compensation, what can managers to do to enrich jobs?

9. What is the Job Characteristics Model?

10. What are the strongest predictors of job satisfaction?

APPLICATIONS

1. Qualifications for a Variety of Job Titles

Develop a list of qualifications for the following positions. Consider the knowledge, abilities, skills, and other relevant characteristics such as education, personality, and experience that should be required for the positions. The positions are: (a) cashier, (b) pharmaceutical sales representative, (c) lawyer, (d) chief executive officer of a Fortune 500 organization, and (e) bank teller. Using the Hay plan for job evaluation (know-how, problem-solving, and accountability) in which scores of 1 represent low levels of the three characteristics and scores of 10 represent high levels of the three characteristics, rank each of the positions.

2. Using the O*Net

Go to the Onetonline.org and search for the job descriptions and qualifications for a position in which you are interested. Do your qualifications match those typically required for the position? Discuss.

CASE STUDIES

1. A Degree for Grocery Store Cashiers?

Madison Clement has just become the store manager at Omni Grocery Store. She oversees fifty store employees who work in a variety of positions, from stock room assemblers to butchers and bakers to cashiers and baggers.

After reviewing the qualifications of the staff at the store, Madison notices that many do not have college degrees. Of particular concern is that none of the cashiers have college degrees. Madison analyzes the job requirements for cashiers, which specify that they have "basic English skills, math skills, and customer service skills." They further need to be able to "identify various types of produce." The average pay for cashiers at the store is $9.28 per hour, or $19,310 annually.

Through anonymous surveys, she has also discovered that many of the cashiers in the positions at the store complain of boredom. Long, eight-hour days standing at the cash register drag on for many whose primary duties include (1) collecting payments from customers for groceries; (2) issuing receipts, refunds, change, or credits to customers; (3) greeting customers entering the store; (4) assisting customers by providing information and resolving complaints; and (5) identifying the prices of groceries.

Madison decides that Omni Grocery Store needs to make some changes. She feels that if the cashiers were more educated, they would be more engaged workers. Therefore, she issues a new requirement that requires that all newly hired cashiers possess four-year college degrees. Is this a good decision? What else can Madison do to reduce boredom in the cashier position?

2. Sanders and the Power Company

In 1970, Willie Sanders filed a lawsuit against Greene Power on behalf of himself and several fellow African-American employees. He asserted that Greene Power's policy of requiring an intelligence test and a high school degree for all but the lowest level positions at Greene Power adversely impacted him and others in his minority group. In particular, Willie Sanders was unable to secure a position as a janitor because the position required that he pass an intelligence test and possess a high school degree.

1. Should Greene Power eliminate this requirement for the janitor position?[71]

2. What are the considerations in this case?

Chapter 4: Planning and Recruitment

Introduction

In April of 2017, U.S. President Donald Trump established and shared an executive order entitled "Buy American and Hire American." This order states the following: "In order to create higher wages and employment rates for workers in the United States, and to protect their economic interests, it shall be the policy of the executive branch to rigorously enforce and administer the laws governing entry into the United States of workers from abroad, including section 212(a) (5) of the Immigration and Nationality Act (8 U.S.C. 1182(a)(5))."[72] This order has had a significant impact on the hiring of international job applicants, as the complications and costs involved in sponsoring applicant visas have decreased their attractiveness to employers who are under no obligation to hire international applicants or secure H1B visas that permit them to work in the United States. This act exemplifies how legal, regulatory, and other environmental conditions or events in the marketplace can impact human resource management planning and hiring processes. Human resource managers who

Objectives:

After reading this chapter, you should be able to:

- Recognize the importance of environmental scanning in human resource planning.
- Recognize the benefits of using a balanced scorecard.
- Identify the means by which organizational managers forecast and reconcile via a gap analysis of supply and demand.
- Analyze and interpret HRM metrics.
- Explain the advantages and disadvantages of internal and external recruitment and hiring.
- Recognize alternatives to downsizing.

Scanning the Environment

During economic upturns and downturns, employment rates vary. During upturns, more people tend to be employed, so there are lower unemployment rates, while during downturns, fewer people are employed and unemployment rates are higher. When the supply of qualified job candidates is higher (**loose labor markets**), organizations have more latitude in establishing their compensation packages. In **tight labor markets**, the supply of qualified job candidates is more limited, so organizations may need to increase their compensation and benefits offerings to attract people from a more limited pool.

Gas prices in the United States peaked during an economic recession in the summer of 2008 when the price for a gallon of gas averaged $4.11. The implications of high gas prices rippled throughout the economy, even impacting HRM planning. Those involved in the transportation industry (airlines, railroads, trucking) and in the manufacture of automobiles considered ways to capitalize on more fuel-efficient modes of delivery. For example, changing consumer tastes may have led some automobile manufacturers to shift production from facilities producing gas guzzling trucks and sports utility vehicles to those producing compact hybrid automobiles. The Coronavirus of 2019 and 2020 has led to the dismissals or displacements of millions of employees in restaurants, hotels, bars, and other service businesses. Such unforeseen pandemics can devastate people and economies.

Rising gas prices or the Coronavirus are two examples of many where a factor in the environment may have an impact on staffing in organizations. The importance of scanning the environment for legal, regulatory, and environmental factors that may impact an organization's workforce cannot be underestimated. Organizations that have failed to take into account important changes in the environment have often failed to perpetuate themselves. Examples abound, including Kodak, which at one point had controlled 90 percent of the U.S. film market and was one of the world's most valuable brands. Kodak invented the first digital camera in 1975, yet did not market the camera as the company retained its initial focus on its film products. Other companies jumped in and began selling digital cameras, so by the time Kodak shifted its views, it was too late, resulting in bankruptcy.[73]

Staffing global companies also requires scanning of the global marketplace. Companies from the United States frequently outsource or set up offshore operations in India, since India has the second largest population in the world with a growing middle class and friendly business climate. The economic slump reported in 2019 in India in its rural areas (where 70 percent of the population reside) can have far-reaching implications.[74] In August of 2019, passenger car sales were down by 41 percent from the previous year, which is the biggest decline on record. "Consumption is the backbone of the Indian economy, making up about 60 percent of gross domestic product. So as sales of everything from Maruti Suzuki compacts to gold jewelry have tailed off, so has GDP growth. The unemployment rate is already at a 45-year high of 6.1 percent, and if the [struggling] auto industry is any guide, it's headed higher."[75]

While these examples point to negative trends, numerous examples of positive trends are present as well. HR managers who are in companies that market caffeinated products may want to pay attention to current trends in new developments of caffeinated products on the market. *Forbes Magazine* often publishes its "30 under 30 Energizers" list. On this list are young entrepreneurs who've struck it rich with creative products. In 2019, the list included five different "caffeinated" energizers.[76] Jim, Jake, and Jordan DeCicco cofounded Kitu Life, which is a ketogenetic-diet-inspired organic "super coffee" with high protein, no lactose, much caffeine, and no sugar. Amy and Peter Rothstein (cofounders of Dona Chai) invented chai-tea concentrates for non-coffee fans, which they wholesale to coffeehouses in the U.S., Canada and Japan. Graham and Max Fortgang (cofounders of Matchabar) invented green-tea matcha energy drinks, which contain the caffeine equivalent of a 12-ounce can of Red Bull. Henry Hu, founder of Café X, started a three-store coffee chain with fully robotic barista arms that are capable of making three coffee concoctions in under a minute. Finally, Ryan Chen, cofounder of Neuro, invented a line of caffeinated chewing gum and mints.

Employer Attractiveness

Innovative organizations are attractive to job seekers. Job seekers also consider other factors. Accordingly, organizations should position themselves to reach the best human capital by attending to factors that enhance their attractiveness. These factors include an organization's level of innovativeness, organizational culture, social responsibility, professional ethics, reputation, image, brand name, learning and development offerings, training environment, compensation and benefits packages, performance appraisal systems, product or service offerings, and organizational successes.

&Pizza is a fast-casual chain positioned to become the most progressive fast-food employers in the United States.[77] &Pizza uses the ampersand in its name to communicate its core values of inclusivity and unity – and around 100 of its 750 employees sport tattoos of ampersand logos as signs of support for the company's values.[78] &Pizza sells healthy and unique pizzas with toppings such as pineapple, salami, pickled red onions, spicy chickpeas and arugula. The company also pays well above the market. The average pay at &Pizza is $14, which dwarfs the industry average of $9.84.[79] &Pizza's strategy has appealed to job candidates, which is evidenced by a store opening in Washington that drew a whopping 1,000 job applications![80]

Balanced Scorecard

The best human resource managers are those who plan strategically. To plan strategically, many use the balanced scorecard. The balanced scorecard is a strategic planning system in which organizational managers connect the dots between big picture elements such as an organization's vision, mission, and goals with operational elements, such as objectives (continuous improvement activities) and measures or performance indicators. Balanced scorecards are used extensively in public and private firms, whether for-profit or nonprofit. Harvard Business Review editors consider the balanced scorecard to be one of the most influential business ideas in recent times.

Benefits of the balanced scorecard[81] include (1) the enhancement of communication between top leaders in organizations and lower level hiring managers; (2) the alignment of daily operations with organizational visions, missions, strategies and goals; (3) the measurement and assessment of progress toward strategic targets and (4) the prioritization of projects, products, and services.

Zappos is a highly successful organization that began as an on-line shoe retailer, yet has expanded into a variety of products. Its focus on customers and employees is exemplified in its goals to deliver both WOW and happiness. Such a focus seems revolutionary to some organizations that have strived to imitate Zappos' success. "Zappos' Insights" is an outgrowth of this interest. Through Zappos' Insights, Zappos offers training to other organizations interested in achieving strong, healthy company cultures. The company highlights (1) the importance of defining values; (2) committing to the values; and (3) hiring for culture fit. In this way, Zappos has achieved a balanced scorecard, aligning its business strategy of innovation in customer service with its HRM strategy of hiring job applicants who are interested in delivering WOW and happiness.

Forecasting Demand

A variety of factors impact the need for human resources in an organization. These may be external, including factors such as employment trends, tight or loose labor markets or economic conditions. In times of high unemployment when the economy is experiencing high inflation or recessions, the supply of job candidates may be greater (loose labor market), while in times of low unemployment and more ideal economic conditions, the supply may be fewer (tight labor market). Internal factors include productivity, sales expansion and growth, absenteeism, and turnover. Managers may use qualitative or quantitative methods of forecasting demand.

Qualitative Methods

Nominal Group Technique

The nominal group technique is a structured small group discussion method in which a group of individuals get together and brainstorm answers to open-ended questions. When used to determine workforce needs, the questions would be related to factors impacting the required size of the workforce and resources needed.

In the College of Business at the University of Tampa, for example, the Executive Council (of the dean, associate dean, and chairs) meets periodically to discuss the number of faculty needed in each of the departments in the future academic year.

Delphi Technique

The Delphi technique is also structured and involves the collation of opinions from a group of experts by an intermediary. This method avoids the use of face-to-face interactions to reduce potential biases that such interactions could produce.

In the College of Business at the University of Tampa, the associate dean may serve as the intermediary between the department chairs and the dean to determine hiring needs for the coming semester. She or he may use electronic mail as a means to share and transmit information.

Quantitative Methods

Trend Analysis

Trend analysis refers to the analysis of historical data to make future staffing predictions. For example, if over the past five years sales increased steadily requiring an additional fifty workers per year, the trend indicated that in the coming year, the organization will require an additional fifty workers. Trend analysis focuses on the *past* to predict needs for the future.

Ratio Analysis

Ratio analysis refers to the use of causal factors to create predictions in staffing. Ratio analysis involves the calculation of a *ratio* between a business variable (such as sales) with the number of employees needed to achieve that metric. For example, if the production of 5,000 widgets requires 5 workers, the ratio is 5,000/5. If the projections based on new contracts indicate new production levels of 10,000 widgets, the ratio will be double the original ratio of 5,000/5, so the ratio will be 10,000/10 workers.

Regression Analysis

Regression analysis refers to the use of an "if – then" (future, hypothetical) analysis. If sales increase by $100,000 then the firm will need three extra staff persons. If sales decrease by $100,000, then the firm will not need three people in its staff in those positions.

Forecasting Supply

Markov Analysis

A Markov analysis involves the creation of a matrix to estimate the average rate of historical movement from one position to another. In the chart below, 85 percent of managers remain in their positions, while 15 percent leave. 70 percent of assistant managers remain in their positions, while 5 percent become line workers, 15 percent become managers and 10 percent leave.

	Exit	Manager	Assistant Manager	Line worker
Manager	.15	.85	0	0
Assistant Manager	.10	.15	.70	.05
Line worker	.20	0	.15	.65

Succession Analysis

Human resource planners determine internal supply by estimating the following factors: promotions, transfers, voluntary turnover, terminations, and retirements.

Gap Analysis

Once HR planners have forecasted supply and demand, they can consider whether a gap exists between the two. In situations in which the supply of applicants exceeds demand, planners are positioned well to identify strong candidates for their positions. In situations in which the demand exceeds the supply, planners are not positioned well. They must consider ways to reduce the gap between demand and supply by increasing advertising, offering more competitive pay packages, or recruiting from additional sources.

Today's Marketplace

Ever since the great recession of 2008, the unemployment rate in the United States has steadily declined. The unemployment rate in 2019 was only 3.5 percent, which is considered very low. When the unemployment rate is low, the labor supply is considered tight. Fewer people are on the job market, so recruiters need to employ creative strategies to attract top talent.[82]

One strategy is to maximize flexibility. The younger generations of employees consider flex time appealing. Unlike Generations X and the Baby Boomers, many do not want to work the typical 9 to 5 schedules.

A second strategy is to hire outside of a traditional job market. Instead of only hiring college graduates with degrees in business, recruiters may consider hiring people with competencies in communication, writing, critical thinking and problem-solving that may be found in students of other majors. Recruiters may also consider hiring from groups who may have been overlooked: the elderly, the disabled, the high school students, or those with felony records who have been rehabilitated. Attention to the severity of the particular felony would be important though – and how recently the felony occurred.

A third strategy is to incentivize employees to refer people they think would do a good job in the workplace. HR leaders may offer gift cards to employees who refer others after the others have been hired and have remained in the organization for a specified period of time.

A fourth strategy is to market and promote the organization on social media. Given that millions are "plugged in" to social media, promoting on that platform may reap positive rewards.

Budgeting and HRM Metrics

HRM metrics help HR managers to gather relevant data on factors such as efficiency, productivity, satisfaction, and retention. HRM metrics can be used to analyze the "story" in an organization. For example, one might consider voluntary turnover. Voluntary turnover occurs when an employee voluntarily chooses to exit an organization. In general, low turnover is good and high turnover is bad.

Yet the story behind each is important. The metrics on turnover should be coupled with an analysis of "why" the turnover is either low, medium, or high. Is turnover low or high in the company's industry? Turnover can be a sign of a very healthy, very unhealthy, or changing industry. In the high-tech industry, jobs are fast-paced and challenging, pay is relatively high, and the demand for certain types of workers is very high, making turnover high. In the brick-and-mortar retail industry, jobs may be seasonal and the pay is generally low, so turnover is high. The turnover of a retail salesperson (19.3 percent), food service professional (17.6 percent) and hospitality professional (17 percent) are relatively high.

If turnover is high, one needs to ask some questions. Are employees dissatisfied with some aspects of their positions? Are there trends in dissatisfaction? For example, are employees in particular departments dissatisfied with their managers? Are they dissatisfied with their pay or benefits packages or working hours? Managers should seek out the answers to questions such as these.

Turnover and Retention

LinkedIn surveyed over 500 million of its users to determine turnover rates in the following industries.[83] The rates are as follows:

1. Restaurants: 17.2 percent
2. Sporting goods: 14.8 percent
3. Technology (software): 13.2 percent
4. Retail and consumer products: 13 percent
5. Media and entertainment: 11.4 percent
6. Professional services: 11.4 percent
7. Government/education/non-profit: 11.2 percent
8. Financial services and insurance: 10.8 percent
9. Telecommunications: 10.8 percent

Technology is relatively high – and some jobs within technology have even higher turnover rates. Consider user experience designers. LinkedIn reports the turnover rate for this highly desirable occupation is 23.3 percent.

Types of Turnover

Turnover can also be involuntary. Involuntary turnover occurs when an employer terminates (or fires) an employee. Voluntary turnover can have two forms: functional or dysfunctional. Functional turnover occurs when a low performing employee chooses to exit an organization – and the organization is not negatively impacted. Dysfunctional turnover occurs when medium or high performers choose to exit, which negatively impacts the organization.

SHRM Metrics

The Society for Human Resource Management has identified important HRM metrics, many of which are defined and listed in the table below.[84]

Metric	Formula
Return on investment: the return on the company's investment in a new program or activity.	((Anticipated benefits – total development cost of program)/total development cost of program) X 100
HR expense to revenue ratio	Total HR expenses / revenue
Revenue per FTE (full time employee)	Revenue / number of FTEs
Productivity	Revenue / labor hours
Time to productivity	Total days elapsed from the date each position was filled to the date each new person achieved satisfactory productivity / number of positions filled
Turnover rate	(Number of separations during a time period / actual number of employees during the time period) X 100
Cost per hire	Total costs related to all external hires / number of external hires
Retention	Number of employees in the selected group at the designated time / number of employees in that selected group originally
Absenteeism	(Total number of absence days /

	Workdays) X 100
Yield or selection ratio	Percentage of persons moving to the next stage / number of persons at prior stage Example: 100 resumes received; 50 found acceptable = 50 percent yield.
Offer rate	(Total number of candidates offered / number of candidates interviewed) X 100

Workforce Analytics

Human resource professionals are increasingly seeking to identify, hire, promote, and retain top talent by fully understanding the productivity and output of their top talent. Human resource managers have increasingly turned to workforce analytics to better gauge their talent and to assess how their human capital impacts their bottom lines.

According to Mark Huselid,[85] "Workforce Analytics refers to the processes involved with understanding, quantifying, managing, and improving the role of talent in the execution of strategy and the creation of value. It includes not only a focus on metrics (e.g., what do we need to measure about our workforce?), but also analytics (e.g., how do we manage and improve the metrics we deem to be critical for business success?)"

3-Step Process to Workforce Analytics

Alec Levenson proposes a 3-step process to workforce analytics.[86] In the first step, consultants or human resource managers would analyze the competitive environment of the organization through interviews with senior leaders. This examination would include a consideration of the strengths, weaknesses, opportunities and threats (SWOT) of the organization and its core competencies.

The second step relates to enterprise analytics. Consultants or human resource managers would analyze whether the team design, organization design and culture help to execute the organization's strategy. Does the organization have a positive culture and climate? Are people engaged and do they feel supported by their subordinates, peers and superiors?

The third step is to look at the role, individual, or process levels. Are people engaged and committed at the individual levels? Is Bob in the sewing room committed? How about Mark in accounting? The third step is only needed if there is a failure at some point in the second step. For example, if the culture in one department has a demotivating effect on workers, an analysis of worker's output, satisfaction, and engagement within each of an organization's departments may be valuable.

LinkedIn Talent Insights

According to a survey by LinkedIn, 22 percent of U.S. organizations use human resource analytics tools to identify, recruit, and select top talent. 11 percent have created specific HR analytics roles. The U.K. Corporate Research Forum in 2017 found that for organizations with 10,000 or more employees, that number increases to 69 percent. Organizational leaders are increasingly turning to HRM software programs to analyze their workforces internally and pools of available talent externally.

Which business sectors have adopted HR analytics? According to LinkedIn, the financial industry is the biggest adopter, followed by technology/software, oil and energy, healthcare and pharmaceuticals, technology/hardware and retail and consumer products.

Are you on LinkedIn? Has anyone ever endorsed some of your skills on LinkedIn? LinkedIn has a tremendous dataset with over 500 million people, which lists their jobs, industries, skills, locations, levels, and demographics. LinkedIn identifies and provides information about talent all over the world using a platform called Talent Insights.

LinkedIn has found that HR analytics are most commonly used in compensation/benefits and performance/productivity. Other uses include human capital development, talent acquisition and culture and diversity strategy. In the past, private organizations often kept compensation and benefits information about their workforces a secret. Not anymore. Many organizations are starting to be more transparent with their compensation so they use HR analytics tools to benchmark their pay packages against those of their competitors.

Hiring managers often use LinkedIn Talent Insights for the following purposes: (1) hiring strategy; (2) employer branding; (3) competitive intelligence; (4) geolocation decisions; and (5) workforce planning. *Hiring strategy* involves creating a recruiting strategy and setting expectations with hiring managers. *Employer branding* involves identifying target audiences, informing campaigns designed to generate brand appeal and awareness, and allocating a branding budget. *Competitive intelligence* refers to gaining insights about the industry leaders and peer companies. *Geolocation decisions* help managers to understand how the talent market and competition vary by region to support location decisions. *Workforce planning* refers to crafting data-driven plans for talent acquisition, development and retention.

LinkedIn Talent Insights generate "Talent Pool Reports" that provide the number of people who have the particular skills needed for a position in a certain geographic area. For example, if a hiring manager were looking for a senior software engineer in the San Francisco Bay area with experience in Java, SAP, Linux, and more, the Talent Pool Report would generate a list of people in that area with the skills needed. If the hiring manager found that very few candidates had the particular skills needed, he or she may widen the talent pool net by reducing the number of required skills. If the manager found that a large supply of candidates had a certain set of skills, he or she may narrow the list by adding skills.

LinkedIn Talent Insights can help to answer many important questions. Where do people with the strongest skills in particular fields come from? Where do they choose to work? Which educational qualifications or degrees matter? Which schools are the best? Which parts of the country or globe have stronger pools of talent? Where are the most diverse candidates? What is the average tenure in a competitor's organization?

Advantages and Disadvantages of Internal Recruitment and Hiring

Hiring from inside of the organization is advantageous to organizations in a number of ways. Hiring from within is considered a high-performance work system characteristic as it motivates employees and establishes the sense that upward advancement is possible within their organizations. This may engender greater employee loyalty and commitment. The costs and time to fill positions are lower than when hiring externally since advertising, recruiting candidates, and identifying candidates is not needed for internal applicants. Furthermore, hiring managers have an objective and accurate assessment of internal applicants' performance as their performance records are accessible. The training time is further reduced since internal hires do not require organizational orientations as they are familiar with the mission, vision, goals, and products and services of their organizations. The disadvantages to hiring from within include the vacancies created in the positions they have left that need to be filled and the potential of stifling diversity.

Advantages and Disadvantages of External Recruitment and Hiring

Hiring externally offers the potential to create more diversity and the potential to capitalize on new skill sets and knowledge. External hires who fill positions that they have already occupied (such as a university provost leaving one university and becoming a provost in another) do not need training in their new positions, though they will require training on the expectations of their new organizations. The disadvantages include higher costs and time to fill positions (over internal hires) and the need to train new hires in company orientations. Furthermore, internal employees may feel as if they were "passed over" when external applicants are awarded positions they desired. This feeling may demotivate them, generating a lack of commitment to their organizations.

Key Findings from the SHRM

A 2017 report by the Society for Human Resource Management (SHRM) released a number of key findings from data collected in 2016.[87] Recruitment costs, including background checks, third-party agency fees, and advertising costs were 15 percent of all HR-related expenses. 22 percent of organizations used automated prescreening to review job applications, which was down from 37 percent in 2015. The average-cost-per-hire was $4,425 in 2016. 23 percent of organizations measure the quality of the hire. 28 percent use 360-degree performance evaluations. 17 percent of newly hired employees left within six months of their first date, which was down from 26 percent in 2015. 26 percent left within a year, which was down from 29 percent in 2015. These findings underscore the importance of identifying the right talent in the first place!

Recruitment Sources

Internal Recruitment Sources

Internal employees may be interested in shifting into different positions in their organizations, whether via transfers to new locations or new lateral positions, promotions to higher level positions, or demotions to lower level positions. HR managers may only recruit from within their organizations to staff positions in a **closed targeted recruitment** or they may open the position to both external and internal applicants in an **open targeted recruitment.** They may further give priority to interested internal applicants who have been at their organizations longer, favoring seniority.

External Recruitment Sources

When advertising for positions to the external labor market, HR managers may place advertisements in local, regional, national, or international news or trade publications. They may employ job placement agencies or labor contractors to assist them in identifying qualified candidates. HR managers often host community or university job fairs where they meet directly with interested job candidates to share information about their organizations and open positions. Some may even keep in touch with university professors and administrators, hoping this group will refer their "star students" to them when positions open. One of the least expensive means of external recruitment is to rely on word-of-mouth advertisements in which internal employees or external applicants share information about job openings with one another in informal ways.

One popular means of external recruitment is the **job referral.** Job referrals occur when internal employees refer their friends, relatives, or acquaintances to the open positions. Sometimes organizations offer employees incentives for referrals who remain working for the organization for a set period of time since referrals are more likely to remain in an organization for longer periods of time than their counterparts. The benefit from relying on referrals is internal employees are most likely to refer people in whom they have confidence in their abilities and performance. Employees are unlikely to refer acquaintances whom they believe would not do a good job, lest their reputations may be adversely impacted. Applicants who have been referred to an organization may also be more likely to have received a **realistic job preview** from the internal employee on the good, the bad, and the ugly issues that they may encounter in their new positions. Such information is helpful in the screening process and may increase likelihood of a longer tenure, since only applicants willing to continue in the application process after receiving the realistic job preview would remain. One disadvantage of job referrals is the potential to stifle diversity if the pool of internal employees tends to be imbalanced in ethnicity or gender and the referrals match the imbalance.

HR managers can evaluate the quality of their sources by examining the quality or quantity of productivity of workers who came to the organization by various means. For example, if the top employees in a department were all sourced at a university job fair, it is likely that the organization's managers would be interested in investing in future university job fairs.

Because organizations want the "cream of the crop," or best human capital, identifying the sources of the best capital is important. Also important is to establish and convey a strong employment brand and company culture through advertising in various outlets and on the company website.

Downsizing

In some situations, HRM planners may determine that the size of their workforces and payroll costs are too large given their forecasts. In these cases, HRM planners have choices. Some choose to "downsize," which is to reduce the size of workforces by laying off employees temporarily, terminating employees, not replacing employees who exit (attrition), or offering severance packages that may entice employees to leave on their own. Some organizational managers refer to these programs as "right-sizing," which implies the size of the workforce prior to reductions was not right, so the move to reduce size was the right decision.

Despite expectations to improve the financial situation of a company by downsizing, there is no consistent relationship between downsizing and firm financial performance. Sometimes financial performance is stronger, while other times performance is weaker. Factors that negatively impact performance include changes in incumbents' attitudes towards their organizations, decreases in productivity, increases in theft and absenteeism, and higher rates of voluntary turnover. Reduced payroll may positively impact financial performance, yet if this benefit is offset by the aforementioned factors, companies may perform worse than expected.

If given the choice between downsizing via the sale of assets (targeted cuts) or downsizing via reducing employment, research has found that the former leads to a greater return on assets while the latter can be detrimental to the return on assets.[88]

To mitigate negative outcomes, planners may consider offering *outplacement counseling*. When counseling, managers offer suggestions for future employment or education based on the skill sets and interests of employees. They may further offer to assist in training employees to increase their skill sets or with placing them in other organizations.

Alternatives to Downsizing

HRM planners may offer other alternatives to downsizing to reduce payroll costs. These include job sharing, telecommuting, reducing or freezing the salaries or hourly rates of employees, hiring temporary employees, or hiring part-time employees. Job sharing refers to a situation in which two part-time employees "share" a full-time position by working at different days and times in that position. For example, one employee may work on

Mondays, Wednesdays and Fridays while the second employee may work on Tuesdays and Thursdays. Payroll costs are cheaper for two part-time employees because full-time benefits such as health insurance, vacation time, and life insurance may not be offered to part-timers. Telecommuting refers to working virtually from one's home. This approach reduces the costs of overhead related to the space filled within the organization by the employee in the form of a cubicle, office and/or desk.

Telecommuting has become increasingly popular. In 1980, only 2.3 percent of workers telecommuted, while today estimates suggest over three million in the United States call their homes their permanent offices.[89] According to the Telework Research Network, those figures are projected to grow by 63 percent over the next few years. Younger employees often desire to buck the traditional 9 – 5 trends of the older generations and many of them consider telecommuting an attractive benefit.

Employees enjoy telecommuting due to its flexibility, travel time and gas savings. Employers like telecommuting due to its "green" impact on the environment (based on lower fuel expenditures) and less office space required. However, telecommuting has some drawbacks. Employers fear less control over employee activities if they don't have a way to monitor productivity. They further may feel that telecommuting will do nothing to earn commitment from their employees through face-to-face activities within the company's culture.

Conclusion

Scanning the environment to inform HR decisions is a critical first step in the planning process. This step is followed by forecasting and reconciling gaps in human resource supply and demand. Organizations face a number of decisions during the planning process, such as the source of their recruitment (internal or external) and whether downsizing or alternatives to downsizing are needed given forecasted situations. The best decisions are those informed by planners who thoughtfully consider and take into account both the employees' and the employers' short-term and long-term interests.

QUESTIONS FOR REVIEW

1. What are the advantages and disadvantages of internal and external recruiting?

2. When would trend analysis be used in HRM? When would regression be used?

3. What is the relationship between downsizing and firm financial performance?

4. What are several alternatives to downsizing?

5. What is the difference between functional and dysfunctional turnover?

6. Why would it be wise to use HR analytics, such as the LinkedIn Talent Insights tool?

7. How would you calculate productivity?

8. What are the benefits and drawbacks of telecommuting?

9. Why should human resource managers scan the global environment?

10. What is a gap analysis?

APPLICATIONS

1. The Recruitment Paradox

Chinese universities produce 2.5 million graduates annually, including 30,000 doctorates and 650,000 engineers.[90] Despite such whopping numbers and China's population of over a billion people, China is short of talent, which is due to the global demand for talent in China. Thousands of organizations have chosen China as the location of their subsidiaries.[91] This supply shortage is also attributable to other reasons, such as government restrictions on mobility, housing shortages, a shrinking workforce due to the long tenure of the one-child policy, and the desire of many in the upper class to relocate to other countries.[92]

What recruitment strategies should organizations with Chinese subsidiaries use to ensure that they attract top talent in China?

2. Anything Goes

In most organizations, discrimination against minorities and protected group members is considered illegal. Unfortunately, however, discrimination still occurs. According to Thomas Zhang, 'anything goes' in China.[93] Zhang says that most banks in China require that job candidates have prior internship experience and top-level university education. But those requirements only scratch the surface. What owners and managers in the finance industry don't put on paper is their strong preferences for males. If they must hire females, they prefer married females with children, since such females are less likely to take maternity leave.

What can organizations with subsidiaries in the finance industry in China do to ensure that persistent discrimination is eliminated?

CASE STUDIES

1. Attracting Top Talent

Being considered "attractive" to job hunters benefits organizations seeking to attract and retain top talent. Organizations with an abundance of top talent have a competitive advantage over their peers.[94] Organizational attractiveness is defined as the "envisioned benefits that a potential employee sees in working for a specific organization."[95] Over the past couple of decades, consultants and academics alike have published numerous articles about the resources required to be attractive and benefits derived by being attractive to job seekers.[96]

Despite such advantages, many organizations, both large and small, are considered unattractive to job seekers for a variety of reasons. Job seekers may be turned off by unpopular, outmoded, or unethical product lines or perceptions of low pay and benefits.

In 2013, Rick Ungar distinguished the quarterly sales of Costco and Wal-Mart, which are two large U.S.-based retailers. His analysis indicated that Costco was growing at a healthy 8 percent per year, while Wal-Mart was growing at an anemic 1.2 percent rate, despite an identical economy. He says, "Here's a crazy thought – might it have something to do with the fact that Costco pays nearly all of its employees a decent living (well in excess of the minimum wage) while Wal-Mart continues to pay its workers as if their employees don't actually need to eat more than once a week, living in an enclosed space and, on occasion, take their kids to see a doctor?"

Wal-Mart reduced the number of employees in its stores by 1.4 percent as it simultaneously increased its store count by thirteen percent.[97] Staffing reductions have led to the piling up of merchandise in stock rooms as fewer employees are present to handle such needs.

Crummy, low-wage jobs at companies like Wal-Mart and McDonalds lead to crummy service, while higher-wage jobs at companies like Costco and Trader Joe's lead to outstanding service.[98] It's proof that you get what you pay for.

Yet hope is in the air for low-wage job incumbents. Some organizations considered less attractive to job seekers have been taking measures lately to raise the wages of their lowest paid workers. In 2015, both McDonalds and Wal-Mart announced wage increases of 10 percent and to a minimum of $10 for low-wage employees, respectively.[99]

1. Aside from pay and product lines, what other factors are likely to attract employees to organizations?

2. What benefits do organizations gain from being considered attractive to job seekers?

3. Identify other organizations with which you are familiar. What are the characteristics of those most and least attractive?

2. A Good Fit?

Acme Corporation is a nonprofit organization with about ten thousand employees, which has its headquarters in Denver, Colorado. The organization is focused on the triple bottom line of people, profits, and planet and it supports multiple environmental causes to "save the planet." You have just been hired as the lead human resource director and your job is to identify the right people for positions in Acme. Their values will need to "fit" Acme's values. How will you align your HRM planning, recruitment, and selection to identify the right types of people?

Chapter 5: Selection

Introduction

"We've actually passed on a lot of really smart, talented people that we know can make an immediate impact on our top or bottom line, but if they're not good for the company culture, we won't hire them for that reason alone," says Tony Hsieh.[100] As the CEO of Zappos, Tony Hseih has focused much of his attention to Zappos' company culture, which is focused on sharing happiness, having fun, and being a little weird. Zappos is a billion-dollar on-line shoe and merchandise retailer, which is considered one of Fortune 500's top 100 companies to work for. To work at Zappos, applicants must first pass a social test where they meet with several Zappos employees at a company or department event. They must also pass a nice test. To determine whether applicants are good people, hiring managers gather information on how the candidates treated people they met throughout the day of their interviews. These may include administrative staff in waiting rooms, shuttle bus drivers, and others not actually involved in the interview process. A third test is the service test in which applicants man phones for the first four weeks of training to deliver Zappos' WOW! Finally, after candidates pass Zappos' training, they are offered $3,000 to leave Zappos. Hsieh figures that those who choose to take the money would not have been a good fit for their organization. Cultural fit means everything to Zappos' image, vision, mission, and goals. They hire for fit more than anything else.[101]

Objectives:

After reading this chapter, you should be able to:

- Identify and differentiate initial and contingent assessment methods.
- Recognize non-cognitive assessment methods.
- Differentiate employees, contractors, and temporary workers.
- Understand measurement concepts, such as reliability, validity, and utility of selection tools.
- Identify types of selection decisions and job offers.
- Recognize the relationships between the Five Factor Model of Personality, other personality and ethical traits, leadership, performance, and other employment outcomes.

Hiring the Right People

An old adage in business is to hire for attitude and train for skills. When companies advertise for positions, hiring managers are often faced with a multitude of candidates who have the required knowledge, skills, and abilities but the wrong attitudes or personality to fit in with their companies' cultures. To narrow down the pool of applicants, hiring managers employ a variety of validated selection methods, such as structured interviews, weighted application blanks and personality tests. Validated methods are those that have been correlated positively with performance. In other words, candidates who possess a particular personality trait (such as a high level of conscientiousness) captured in a personality test are more likely to succeed and perform well than candidates who do not possess that trait. Finding the right employees in organizations can lead to higher productivity and more organizational success.

Why is hiring the right people important? One study has found that between 60 – 75 percent of all employees have indicated that their immediate supervisors are the worst aspect of their jobs.[102] Some leaders behave in destructive ways, whether towards their subordinates and/or towards their organizations.[103]

Toxic leaders may engage in bullying and abusive practices that generate fear among employees. One recent study of a corporate psychopath highlighted the way that such practices can result in negative employee behaviors, such as aimlessness and a lack of direction.[104] Corporate psychopaths have little conscience, yet can be "highly manipulative individuals who charm their way into senior positions that are in reality above their ability and qualifications."[105] Former Enron executive Jeffrey Skilling exemplified corporate psychopathy during his tenure at Enron.[106] Accordingly, human resource leaders are encouraged to screen applicants for psychopathy.[107] Human resource leaders screen for other employee characteristics too by using a variety of initial and contingent assessment tools.

Initial Assessment Methods

To initiate the hiring process, hiring managers create a **position description** where they list the job title, tasks, and minimum or preferred qualifications of job applicants. They may advertise the position in a variety of ways, from local newspapers to signs to postings on the internet. Once the position is advertised, hiring managers' next task is to review the job applications, cover letters and resumes of interested candidates. A **resume** is a document where job applicants present biographical information, including their background, employment experience, career interests, and skills. Job applicants often include of list of references, which is a list of people with whom they have worked in the past. Job applicants send resumes to potential employees with **cover letters**, which convey information about a job candidate that is relevant to the position in which they are interested. A job applicant will often share her interest in a particular position and why she considers herself a good fit for the position. Many employers require that job applicants complete a **job application,** which helps to structure responses from job candidates. Job applications should ask employees about their background, education, employment experiences, and other relevant qualifications. Oftentimes, employers use **weighted job applications**, which is to say that they place a heavier weight on items that correlate most strongly with successful job performance. Applications should also be screened by human resource managers to ensure legal compliance.

Legal Compliance in Job Applications

The United States Civil Service Commission, the EEOC, the U.S. Department of Justice and the U.S. Department of Labor jointly adopted the **Uniform Guidelines on Employee Selection Procedures (UGESP)** in 1978. The purpose of the UGESP is to "establish uniform standards for the use of selection procedures by employers and to address adverse impact, validation, and record-keeping requirements. The Uniform Guidelines document a uniform federal position in the area of prohibiting discrimination in employment practices on the basis of race, color, religion, sex, or national origin. The Uniform Guidelines outline the requirements necessary for employers to defend their employment decisions based on overall selection processes and specific selection procedures."[108]

Job applications in U.S. firms should not include questions related to applicants' status in protected groups unless such qualifications are considered bona fide occupational qualifications. As examples, interviewers should refrain from questions about job applicants' marital status, number of children or pregnancy status, since such questions are likely unrelated to performance on the job. Due to the Genetic Information Nondiscrimination Act (GINA), employers are prohibited from asking about or collecting genetic information from job applicants. Employers can instead ask whether the applicants are legally permitted to work in the United States and whether applicants are eighteen or older. Questions concerning military service or veteran status are also acceptable, as employers may give applicants who have served or are serving in the military preferential status.

Measurement Concepts

All selection tools should demonstrate reliability and validity. **Reliability** refers to consistency of scoring. For example, one form of reliability is test-retest reliability. If an individual takes an intelligence test today and a second intelligence test a week from today without any additional preparation, her scores should be very similar. If they are very similar, the test is considered reliable. Coefficients closest to 1.0 are considered the most reliable. **Validity (predictive)** refers to whether a selection tool is predictive of job performance or some other relevant criterion. For example, validated intelligence tests are those that predict job performance in such a way that higher scores on the tests correlate positively to higher scores in performance evaluations. The opposite would be true for lower scores. The best selection tools have coefficients above .50. How much about an outcome does a .50 validity coefficient predict? One would square the score (or multiply the coefficient by itself) to determine the prediction. A validity coefficient of .50 would therefore predict 25 percent of job performance. Selection tools that are relatively inexpensive to administer or deliver with high levels of validity are considered to be high in **utility.**

Utility

As you will note from the table below, work sample tests, general mental ability tests (such as IQ tests) and structured employment interviews have the highest validity. **Work sample tests** require that applicants perform a work-related task or tasks and their performance is assessed by an evaluator. For example, if a welder is given a work sample test, he would likely be given the tools to perform a welding task. **General mental tests**, such as the Wonderlic test, are usually either computer-based or pencil and paper tests of verbal, math, and spatial abilities. Like work sample tests, structured employment interviews require the presence of an evaluator – the interviewer. Since work sample tests and structured employment interviews require the presence of another worker's time (and pay during that time), these have lower utility than general mental ability tests because they cost more money and time. General mental ability tests are low cost and high in validity, so they have the highest utility.

Validity of Various Selection Tools in Predicting Overall Job Performance[109]

Work sample tests	.54
General mental ability tests	.51
Structured employment interviews	.51
Peer ratings	.49
Job knowledge tests	.48
Job tryout procedures *	.44
Integrity tests (honesty)	.41
Unstructured employment interviews	.38
Assessment centers **	.37
Biographical data	.35
Conscientiousness	.27 - .31
Reference checks	.26
Job experience (years)	.18
Years of education	.10
Interests	.10
Graphology (handwriting analysis)	.02
Age	.01

* Job tryouts procedures are used when an applicant is hired with minimal screening. The person has a trial period in which her performance is assessed and her evaluators determine whether she is capable of satisfactorily performing the job.

** Assessment centers use multiple assessors and multiple techniques, such as role play exercises and in-box exercises to produce judgments on an applicant's performance or competencies.

Reference and Background Checks

HR managers also require that job applicants list several **references** of people they can contact to gather information about the potential performance of the job applicants and to confirm the validity of the applicants' work histories. Typically, these people are previous employers, yet they could also be the applicants' teachers or professors or other professionals in the community with whom they have interacted.

They also conduct **background** checks on the criminal, credit, or driving histories of job candidates. The latter would be collected when the position requires driving, such as for a pizza delivery person, a truck driver, or a bus driver. Employers conduct criminal background checks to be sure applicants do not have histories of crimes that would impede their ability to perform. HR managers should ask for details on any convicted felonies or misdemeanors as some could be much less serious than others. For example, a person convicted of public intoxication in Key West, Florida during Fantasy Fest three decades prior while in college would be much less of a threat than one convicted of manslaughter or rape charges in more recent times. HR managers may also only ask about *convictions,* not merely arrests, as arrests do not always result in convictions and such inquiries could adversely impact protected groups. Some employers conduct credit checks to determine the reliability of job candidates, yet these have been challenged in some states, such as Illinois, when not deemed related to performance on the job. To mitigate the potential for legal challenges, employers should only conduct credit checks in positions in which financial knowledge or banking or credit transactions are an essential function of the job.

Interviews

Once managers have identified their most qualified candidates from a pool of applicants, the next step in the hiring process is to conduct interviews. Interviews are the most common selection test. Oftentimes, managers will interview by phone or via an on-line visual means such as Skype or Zoom to reduce the pool of qualified applicants who will be brought in for face-to-face interviews. The questions interviewers ask may be in a variety of forms.

They have a choice of **structured, semi-structured**, or **unstructured interviews**. Structured interviews, in which interviewees are asked the same set of pre-planned specific job-related questions are the most valid. Semi-structured interviews are slightly less valid, yet they are still a good approach to collecting information on job candidates. Semi-structured interviews contain some structured and some unstructured questions. Unstructured questions are those geared to the unique interests and backgrounds of each candidate. While still valid, these are less valid than structured or semi-structured interviews. To increase the validity of unstructured interviews, human resource managers may consider adding interviewers. Using multiple interviewers helps by decreasing the potential for any personal biases of a single rater. The benefit of the structured and semi-structured interview approaches is interviewers can compare "apples to apples" when they ask each of the job candidates the same set of questions. Common questions include "Why do you want to work for us?" "Where do you see yourself in three years?" "What would your boss say are your strengths or weaknesses?"

Interviewers may also ask **situational** or **behavioral** interview questions. Situational questions are those in which candidates are asked how they *would* handle a particular situation if it arose, while behavioral questions are those in which candidates are asked how they *have handled* a particular situation in the past. For example, one might ask how a bank teller would handle an irate customer (situational) versus how they have handled irate customers in the past (behavioral). Behavioral interviews are the more valid of the two choices. In other words, they have a stronger correlation to performance.

When weighting the importance of either emotional intelligence or cognitive abilities (intelligence quotient), employers often consider emotional intelligence to be more important. **Emotional intelligence** is the ability to be aware of, express, or control one's emotions and to handle interpersonal relationships judiciously. Below are several interview questions that employers may use to assess a job candidate's emotional intelligence:

1. Can you give me an example of a time when you faced an ethical dilemma at work? How did you handle it? What resulted?
2. How would you resolve a dispute between two colleagues?
3. Can you give me an example of a time when you were criticized by someone at work? How did you handle it? What resulted?
4. Can you give me an example of a time when you had a conflict with a superior or supervisor? How did you handle it? What resulted?

Cognitive Assessment Methods

HR managers often administer intelligence tests or job knowledge tests to determine the general mental abilities of job applicants. Such tests examine how people reason, make sense of their environments, demonstrate verbal, spatial, or mathematical abilities, think critically, or solve problems. Intelligence tests have predictive validity *across all jobs*, so many managers utilize them in the selection process as a relatively low-cost, high validity (high utility) means of identifying the strongest applicants. At issue, however, is they may adversely impact African-American and Hispanic protected groups, so it is best that employers who collect cognitive assessments consider supplementing them with other selection tools that do not result in adverse impact to minimize the potential for litigation.

Litigation can sometimes lead to varying results. As a first example, in the Supreme Court case *Ricci* vs. *DeStefano* (2009), the city of New Haven Connecticut's firefighters certified and validated a cognitive ability test to identify appropriate candidates for promotions to lieutenants or captains, yet results were racially disproportionate. The city decided toss out the exams, resulting in a Title VII lawsuit from white applicants and claims of reverse discrimination.

The court ruled against the city, stating that "innocent non-minorities, solely because of their race," should "shoulder the burden of advancing employment opportunities for minority candidates." The court asserted that a Court decision in favor of DeStefano would amount to a sanction of employers' abilities to discriminate against whites, as long as they assert 'unfounded, good faith' fear of Title VII lawsuits from blacks."[110]

As a second example, a federal judge determined that New York City firefighter exams between 1999 and 2007 were biased against blacks and Hispanics. The tests had discriminatory effects that had little relationship to the job of a firefighter. Accordingly, the tests were eliminated.[111]

The difference between the first and second example is whether the test had been validated. In other words, tests that are predictive of job performance are legally defensible, while those that are not predictive are not.

Non-Cognitive Assessment Methods

Personality Assessments

Cognitive ability tests explain a portion of job incumbent performance, yet they do not fully explain performance. Other attitudinal factors additionally offer an explanation. For example, universities require that undergraduate students submit their ACT, SAT, or TOEFL scores because the scores have a positive correlation to academic performance. In other words, high ACT scores are likely to correspond to high grade point averages and low ACT scores are likely to correspond to low grade point averages. Yet as all students can attest, high cognitive ability test scores do not explain the performance of all students. Some "under-achievers" with high test scores may be unmotivated to perform well in their college courses, while the opposite may be true of "over-achievers." Accordingly, it is wise for managers to collect additional data on job candidates to have a better assessment of potential performance.

Among these variables are personality assessments, such as the **Five Factor Model of Personality (FFM).**[112] The FFM is a validated personality instrument in the prediction of job performance that assesses levels of the following five personality domains: agreeableness (.13), conscientiousness (.27), openness to experience (.07), emotional stability (.13), and extraversion (.15).[113] Conscientiousness was included in another meta-analysis, which found a slightly different validity coefficient of .31.[114]

People who are agreeable are warm, polite, empathetic, and cooperative. They contrast the less agreeable (skeptical) people who are more critical and antagonistic. People who are conscientious are dutiful, orderly, task-focused, and achievement-striving. Their less conscientious counterparts have opposing characteristics and a weak work ethic. People who are extraverted are sociable, while their introverted counterparts are the opposite. Extraverts derive their energy when surrounded by people while introverts derive energy when alone. Emotionally stable individuals are emotionally resilient, while their neurotic counterparts are worrisome, anxious, and depressed. Open individuals have a broad range of interests, preferring novelty to the routine and are interested in creativity, art, and beauty. Their less open counterparts prefer the tried and true and tend to be more conservative and to prefer less change. Of the five factors, conscientiousness is the most valid predictor of performance across all jobs, followed by extraversion and emotional stability. Agreeableness corresponds positively to jobs involving teamwork, while extraversion corresponds to jobs in which there are many social interactions, such as sales positions. People who are open to experience are more likely than their counterparts to work successfully as expatriates abroad.

A meta-analytic study[115] indicated that the five factors correlated to leadership as follows: neuroticism (-.24), extraversion (.31), agreeableness (.08), conscientiousness (.28), and openness to experience (.24). The greater the correlation, the stronger the relationship between the personality factor and leadership. Overall, the five factors correlated with leadership at .48. Note that although extraversion is the strongest correlate of leadership, researchers have identified examples of some highly effective leaders who are introverts.[116]

Personality also corresponds to job satisfaction. A meta-analytic study correlated the five factors to job satisfaction as follows: neuroticism (-.29), extraversion (.29), openness to experience (.02), agreeableness (.17) and conscientiousness (.26).[117]

Another dimension that offers incremental validity over the FFM is called **core self-evaluations.** In other words, by including both the FFM and core self-evaluations in the prediction of job performance, one is able to make a more valid prediction. Core self-evaluations is a broad, higher order personality domain with the following four traits: **self-esteem**, which is the value one places in oneself as a person, **self-efficacy**, which is a confidence evaluation of how well one can perform across a variety of situations, **neuroticism**, which is the tendency to focus on the negative aspects in one's life, and **locus of control**, which refers the control a person feels he has over the events in his life.[118]

Integrity tests can further be useful. They are used to test individual's honesty, work ethic, and dependability. Previous research has found that integrity testing has substantial validity in the prediction of overall job performance and counterproductive work behaviors (e.g., absenteeism, theft, violence on the job, rule-breaking, disciplinary problems, and theft).[119]

RedBalloon founder Naomi Simson says the following eleven questions help to test people's integrity.[120]

1. As a famous athlete, you are offered a $500,000 endorsement to promote a product that you dislike and would NEVER use. Do you endorse it?
2. You are working on a project along with several other companies and you notice that one of the companies is doing shoddy, dangerous work. If you report the company, the entire project may be shut down and you will lose 20 percent of your revenues for the year. Do you report the problem?
3. The taxi driver gives you a blank receipt as he drops you off. You are on an expense account. Do you write in the exact correct amount?
4. You're golfing with an important client who thinks that golf skills are as important as business skills. Your ball has a bad lie, but you can move it to a better position without being seen. Do you?
5. You're backing into a tight parking space in the work car park and you accidentally dent someone's car. Nobody has seen you. Do you leave a note taking responsibility?

6. A colleague wants to copy and swap some music CDs. You know it's illegal. Do you do it?
7. You know you are attractive and so does your prospective customer. Do you lightly flirt to get a major new account for your business?
8. A good friend has been unemployed for several months. They ask you to write a reference for a job that you don't think they're well qualified for. Do you agree?
9. You see some great content for a presentation, you know it is copyright – do you use it in your work presentation to make you look good?
10. Your budgets are tight, you procure some business services, the vendor forgets to invoice you… six months go by. Do you remind them to send the invoice?
11. You are offered tickets to a rock concert with a potential supplier that is currently tendering for a big contract. It is your favorite band and you really want to see them – and tickets have been sold out for months. You know it will not influence your contribution to the tender process. Do you go?

The Dark Triad

HR managers may further be interested in gathering information to predict other less attractive personality characteristics, such as **psychological entitlement** and the **Dark Triad of narcissism, Machiavellianism,** and **psychopathy.** People who have high levels of psychological entitlement tend to feel deserving of various outcomes, such as high performance evaluations, despite unequal levels of inputs (i.e., lower performance). Narcissists are people who feel superior to others and who seek admiration and special treatment. People with high levels of Machiavellianism often manipulate others, using deceit and lies. Psychopaths are apathetic, callous, cold, and insensitive. They also tend to be frustrated and to lose their temper more. A meta-analysis indicated (1) that psychopathy and Machiavellianism were correlated with reductions of the quality of job performance and (2) counterproductive work behaviors are associated with all three domains of the Dark Triad.[121]

In a survey of 680 students from universities in Croatia,[122] researchers discovered that prosocial behaviors are inversely related to the traits of the Dark Triad. In other words, higher scores on the Dark Triad traits resulted in less prosocial (or anti-social) behavior. Machiavellianism topped the list with the strongest negative relationship to prosocial behavior, followed by psychopathy and narcissism. In a meta-analysis of 310 independent samples from 215 sources, another study[123] identified relationships between the Dark Triad and the Five Factor Model of Personality.

Conscientiousness and Agreeableness were negatively correlated with Machiavellianism. Neuroticism was positively correlated with Machiavellianism. Narcissism was significant and positively correlated with Openness to Experience, Conscientiousness, and Extraversion. Psychopathy was negatively associated with Conscientiousness and Agreeableness. Other studies have also linked negative outcomes with the Dark Triad, such as cheating on exams and self-deceptive biases.[124]

Machiavellianism in the workplace may be "fully prompted" when an organization's bottom line mentality is consistent with a Machiavellian employee's bottom line mentality. If an organization focuses on profit over people and planet (i.e., focuses on the "bottom line" over the "triple bottom line"), a Machiavellian employee may align their own self-interested, manipulative, distrustful, and controlling nature with the goals of the organization.[125]

Situational judgment tests measure an individual's behavior and attitudes toward certain work-related scenarios. An example may be to describe a situation in a retail store in which an irate customer shows up in the store and starts yelling at a clerk about a shipment that failed to arrive on time. A variety of responses are offered and the job candidate is asked to identify the best option. These could be to apologize to the customer, listen to the customer's complaint, or call the shipping company to determine why the shipment is late. Because the latter is pro-active and likely to best diffuse the situation, the third option is the best choice.

Interest inventories assess job candidates' likes and dislikes with respect to work and leisure activities, people, and characteristics. Do you like going to the beach? In your spare time, would you prefer to paint a room or build a bookshelf? Do you enjoy reading and writing? What is your favorite academic subject? There are no right or wrong answers. The first interest inventories came about in 1927 when E.K. Strong determined that people who share the same occupation often share the same interests. Strong used the "Strong Interest Inventory" to help people choose suitable careers.[126] The Strong Interest Inventory assesses a person's personality type, work-related values, and aptitudes.

Contingent Assessment Methods

Once the screening and interview process has been completed and managers have identified the best applicants for the job, contingent assessments are administered, such as drug testing for the presence of illegal drugs via hair or urine analyses or medical exams. The latter would be used when particular physical characteristics are required for the job, such as 20/20 vision for an airline pilot.

The Surprising Factor: Birth Order

People's personalities are impacted by numerous factors, both relating to nature (inherited traits) and nurture (based on experiences). One well-studied factor that people may not consider is birth order. In certain types of jobs, one's birth order may correspond with how a person is likely to act under particular situations. Research has found that later-born individuals take bigger strategic or financial risks,[127] are more likely to switch jobs,[128] and have a greater risk of post-traumatic stress disorder.[129]

Employment Relationships

Various employment relationships are used in the workplace. "Employees" are people who work for organizations for agreed upon wages or a salary, usually at the non-management level. **Independent contractors** are considered as such if the payer has the right to control or direct only the result of the work, not *what* will be done or *how* the contractor will complete the work. The distinction is important in the United States as the employer must withhold income taxes and withhold taxes for Social Security and Medicare for employees. Employees may also be temporary workers, holding the positions for a limited time period. For example, shopping malls often staff retail outlets with temporary workers over the busy Christmas holiday season in December.

The National Labor Relations Board (NLRB) recently determined that Uber drivers are independent contractors. They applied a "common-law agency test" and weighted the factors of (1) control and (2) the relationship between the amount of fares collected and the company's compensation.

According to the NLRB, Uber "drivers [have] virtually complete control of their cars, work schedules, and log-in locations, together with their freedom to work for competitors of Uber, providing them with significant entrepreneurial opportunity. On any given day, at any free moment, UberX drivers could decide how best to serve their economic objectives: by fulfilling ride requests through the App, working for a competing rideshare service, or pursuing a different venture altogether."

This determination was a victory for Uber and others considered to be "virtual marketplace" companies. Service providers working for such companies are ineligible for minimum wages, overtime pay, and tax deductions due to their independent contractor status. Their rights to file labor complaints, seek protections from the federal government, and to unionize are also restricted.

Selection Decisions

"**At-will**" is a term used in the United States that states that an employee can be dismissed for any reason from work by the employer without having to establish "just cause" for the termination and without warning, reason, or an explanation, so long as the dismissal was not illegal or in retaliation. At-will further means that an employer can change the conditions of employment without warning. Forty-nine of the U.S. states are considered "at-will" states. The exception is Montana.

Employers must also ensure that job applicants have the proper legal documentation and authorization to work in the United States. The U.S. Citizenship and Immigration Services provides "Employment Authorization Documents" to individuals who are not considered lawful permanent residents or do not have a nonimmigrant visa that authorizes them to work for a specific employer.

Selection Decisions

Oftentimes, multiple applicants may be highly qualified, so hiring managers must determine which applicants are the most qualified. They may rank the applicants in order of preference, giving higher rankings to those considered to be a better fit for their organizations. To screen for person-organization fit, managers may ask questions designed to capture whether an individual's values and goals are consistent with those of the organization.

Job Offers

Once hiring managers have determined their top candidates, the next step is to extend a **job offer**. The manager may make a verbal offer either in person or by phone or email. This offer is often followed by a written job offer, which details the job description, salary/wages and benefits, paid time off, reporting structure and other relevant details. The job offer may be conditional, subject to passing a reference check, background check, medical exams, or drug testing. The candidate may accept the offer, reject the offer, or make a counter offer.

Onboarding

Onboarding, which is also known as organizational socialization, refers to the process of integrating new employees into the culture of the organization. New employees will learn of the company's values, mission, vision and goals, along with its products and services. They'll often hear stories of the "heroes" or founders of their organizations as a means to share information on the type of culture they should expect.

Great Place to Work[130] featured three examples of companies with strong onboarding programs:

Accor Hotels

"One of the essential elements of AccorHotels UK and Ireland's induction process that enables new employees to 'step into customers' shoes and experience the service culture of the brand they are working for is by having dinner, enjoying a drink at the bar and spending a night in the hotel (free of charge) in order to experience it as a guest. In the morning, their manager joins them after breakfast to discuss their experience. Every new starter working in an AccorHotels hotel goes through this experience alongside their family and friends."

The Sovini Group

"As part of the induction, all new staff at Sovini Group take a bus tour around the local area to gain an understanding of the neighborhoods and communities that they will work in. They meet frontline staff and residents and witness some of their work in the local community, helping to bring the work of their staff into context."

UK Fast

"One of new starters' favorite parts of their induction is a trip to Mount Snowdon. They have a hotel in North Wales and its tradition that every person who joins the UKFast team will tackle the 'Snowdon trip' within their first few months of their UKFast journey. The trip includes climbing Mount Snowdon, building and racing rafts around the lake, cooking and cleaning the hotel and playing games. They have found that there is something special about the energy that is generated on these trips and people often come back feeling like they can take on anything! If you can climb a mountain, what else can you achieve?"

Conclusion

Identifying and selecting the best human capital can benefit an organization's bottom line, as workers who are considered a "good fit" are often more satisfied and therefore more likely to perform better. Hiring managers can employ a variety of selection tools, from intelligence tests to personality tests to interviews. Once they've identified the best applicants for the position, managers extend job offers and begin the onboarding process.

QUESTIONS FOR REVIEW

1. What's the difference between validity and reliability?

2. Which factor in the Five Factor Model of personality is the most predictive of work performance? Which is the most predictive of leadership?

3. Are intelligence tests likely to predict performance across all jobs?

4. When does a company engage in onboarding? What is onboarding?

5. What can companies do to improve the validity of unstructured interviews?

6. What is the "Dark Triad" in personality?

7. Which type of interview has more validity – structured or unstructured? Why?

8. Which type of interview has more validity – behavioral or situational? Why?

9. Give an example of a selection tool that has high utility (high validity/low cost).

10. Give an example of a selection tool that has low utility (low validity/high cost).

APPLICATIONS

1. Resume Exchange and Mock Interview

Prior to coming to class, update your resume and print out two copies: one for yourself and one for your interviewer. Once in class, get into groups of two or three people. Exchange information about the types of jobs that you would prefer upon graduation if you were on the job market. Conduct a mock interview, each putting yourself into the role of either interviewer or interviewee. The interviewer should ask the following questions, while the interviewee should prepare his/her answers to the following "top ten" interview questions.

1. Why do you want to work for us?

2. Give us an example of a situation where you didn't meet your goals or expectations.

3. Give us an example of a situation where you faced conflict or difficult communication problems.

4. Where do you see yourself in 3 / 5 / 10 years?

5. What would your current manager say are your strengths?

6. What would your current manager say are your weaknesses?

7. Why should we give you this job?

8. Give us an example of when you have worked under an unreasonable deadline or have been faced with a huge challenge. How did you overcome the challenge?

9. Do you prefer working in a team or on your own?

10. What is the first thing you would change, if you were to start working here?

2. The Five Factor Model of Personality[131]

The following statements concern your perception about yourself in a variety of situations. Your task is to indicate the strength of your agreement with each statement, utilizing a scale in which 1 denotes strong disagreement, 5 denotes strong agreement, and 2, 3, and 4 represent intermediate judgments. There are no "right" or "wrong" answers, so select the number that most closely reflects you on each statement. Take your time and consider each statement carefully. Once you have completed all questions, compile your answers.

I see myself as someone who...

1 = strongly disagree
2 = somewhat disagree
3 = neither agree nor disagree
4 = somewhat agree
5 = strongly agree

1. is talkative E1 _____
2. tends to find fault with others A1 (reverse) _____
3. does a thorough job C1 _____
4. is depressed, blue N1 _____
5. is original, comes up with new ideas O1 _____
6. is reserved E2 (reverse) _____
7. is helpful and unselfish with others A2 _____
8. can be somewhat careless C2 (reverse) _____
9. is relaxed, handles stress well N2 (reverse) _____
10. is curious about many different things O2 _____
11. is full of energy E3 _____
12. starts quarrels with others A3 (reverse) _____
13. is a reliable worker C3 _____
14. can be tense N3 _____
15. is ingenious, a deep thinker O3 _____
16. generates a lot of enthusiasm E4 _____
17. has a forgiving nature A4 _____
18. tends to be disorganized C4 (reverse) _____
19. worries a lot N4 _____
20. has an active imagination O4 _____
21. tends to be quiet E5 (reverse) _____
22. is generally trusting A5 _____
23. tends to be lazy C5 (reverse) _____
24. is emotionally stable, not easily upset N5 (reverse) _____
25. is inventive O5 _____

26. has an assertive personality E6 _____
27. can be cold and aloof A6 _____
28. perseveres until the job is done C6 _____
29. can be moody N6 _____
30. values artistic, aesthetic experiences O6 _____
31. is sometimes shy, inhibited E7 (reverse) _____
32. is considerate and kind to almost everyone A7 _____
33. does things efficiently C7 _____
34. remains calm in tense situations N7 (reverse) _____
35. prefers work that is routine O7 (reverse) _____
36. is outgoing, sociable E8 _____
37. is sometimes rude to others A8 (reverse) _____
38. makes plans and follows through with them C8 _____
39. gets nervous easily N8 _____
40. likes to reflect, play with ideas O8 _____
41. has few artistic interests O9 (reverse) _____
42. likes to cooperate with others A9 _____
43. is easily distracted C9 (reverse) _____
44. is sophisticated in art, music or literature O10 _____

Assignment:

Reverse score the items that are marked with "reverse," so that 5 = 1; 4 = 2; 3 = 3; 2 = 4 and 1 = 5. Now add your total scores for each of the following dimensions, as indicated by the letter value at the end of each of the above statements.

Conscientiousness: _____

Extraversion: _____

Agreeableness: _____

Neuroticism: _____

Openness to experience: _____

The top scores for the domains are as follows: C = 45; E = 40; A = 45; N = 40; O = 50. People with higher scores closer to the top values rank highly on these dimensions, while those who have very low scores on the values rank very low on the dimensions.

3. The Dark Triad of Personality: Short Form[132]

Rank yourself using the following anchors: 1 = strongly disagree; 2 = disagree; 3 = neither agree nor disagree; 4 = agree; and 5 = strongly agree.

Machiavellianism Subscale

1. It's not wise to tell your secrets.

2. Generally speaking, people won't work hard unless they have to.

3. Whatever it takes, you must get the important people on your side.

4. Avoid direct conflict with others because they may be useful in the future.

5. It's wise to keep track of information that you can use against people later.

6. You should wait for the right time to get back at people.

7. There are things you should hide from other people because they don't need to know.

8. Make sure your plans benefit you, not others.

9. Most people can be manipulated.

Narcissism Subscale

1. People see me as a natural leader.

2. I hate being the center of attention. (R)

3. Many group activities tend to be dull without me.

4. I know that I am special because everyone keeps telling me so.

5. I like to get acquainted with important people.

6. I feel embarrassed if someone compliments me. (R)

7. I have been compared to famous people.

8. I am an average person. (R)

9. I insist on getting the respect I deserve.

Psychopathy Subscale

1. I like to get revenge on authorities.

2. I avoid dangerous situations. (R)

3. Payback needs to be quick and nasty.

4. People often say I'm out of control.

5. It's true that I can be mean to others.

6. People who mess with me always regret it.

7. I have never gotten into trouble with the law. (R)

8. I like to pick on losers.

9. I'll say anything to get what I want.

Reverse score any items marked with an R. Then compute your mean score on each of the scales. The mean score for college students on each scale is 3.1 for Machiavellianism, 2.8 for Narcissism and 2.4 for Psychopathy.

CASE STUDY

1. Kristi Chen's Successful Work Team

Kristi Chen has been leading a very successful work team that conducts research to solve scientific problems. Since her team has been so successful, the company's CEO asked her to nominate one member of the team to serve as the head of a new team that will work on other scientific problems. The other individuals in the new team have already been selected and represent a variety of research specializations.

Some believe that the best person for the promotion is Craig Baines. Craig graduated from the Harvard School of Business and holds a second degree in engineering from one of the best engineering schools in the United States. He has been an informal team leader and has contributed substantially to a number of successful product innovations. If Kristi chooses Craig for the promotion, some would miss him, but this move would be very good for his career.

A second possibility is the son of the CEO, Robert Anderson. Robert is a graduate of engineering from a regionally-recognized university and is also a contributor of valuable ideas to the team, yet he has been sort of a pain. He complains often and frequently reminds others of the fact that he is the CEO's son. The team wouldn't miss him much if chosen to head up the new work team.

1. Should Kristi choose Craig or Robert to serve as the head of the new team?

2. What are the short-run and long-run implications of each choice?

2. Who Is the Most Qualified?

Antelope Company is a medium-sized manufacturing facility with just over 500 employees located just outside of Chicago in Aurora, Illinois. Craig Reed is the regional vice president manager who oversees the Aurora plant. He is looking for a new plant manager to oversee his unionized plant. The five top candidates have emerged from over a hundred applicants and their qualifications are listed below. Craig also collected psychological assessments of each of the candidates on their abilities to manage stressful situations, handle conflict, and be creative in unusual situations. They are all qualified, but as Craig says, "Who is the MOST qualified?"

Go to the O*Net to identify the tasks, skills, abilities, and knowledge required for a plant manager. Then identify the top candidate.

1. Eve Keneinan is a 45-year old married female with two teenage children. She is currently employed at one of Antelope's top competitors as a plant manager and has been in her position for the past 13 years. Her organization is also unionized. She has a Ph.D. in industrial and organizational psychology. She scored 140 on an IQ exam. Eve scored a 100 on her ability to manage stressful situations, and 110 on her ability to handle conflict. She scored 115 on her ability to be creative.

2. Jack Burton is a 30-year old single male with no small children. He is currently employed at Antelope as the assistant plant manager. He has been in that role for six years and has received strong performance evaluations in each year since he started. He has worked closely with the plant manager who recently departed. He has a four-year college degree in business management. He scored 105 on an IQ exam. Jack scored a 120 on his ability to manage stressful situations, and 108 on his ability to handle conflict. He scored 99 on his ability to be creative.

3. Tony Murphy is a 50-year old divorced male with no dependents. He is currently unemployed, but six months ago and for the past 22 years, he worked as a plant manager for another of Antelope's competitors. His organization was not unionized. He has a high school education. He scored 88 on an IQ exam. Tony scored a 90 on his ability to manage stressful situations, and 80 on his ability to handle conflict. He scored 120 on his ability to be creative.

4. Mike Knight is a 65-year old married male with no dependents. He is currently a regional plant manager for one of Antelope's competitors, yet he desires to step down into a role with less pressure and stress. Bob has an MBA from Harvard. He scored 135 on an IQ exam. Bob scored a 95 on

his ability to manage stressful situations, and 92 on his ability to handle conflict. He scored 101 on his ability to be creative.

5. Tom Talon is a 44-year old single male with no dependents. He is currently an assistant plant manager at Antelope's Philadelphia plant who desires to live in the Chicago area. He has a four-year degree in accounting. His performance evaluations have been very good over the past five years in his role as an assistant plant manager. Prior to that, his evaluations were decent when he was in lower level positions. He scored 113 on an IQ exam. Tom scored a 102 on his ability to manage stressful situations, and 97 on his ability to handle conflict. He scored 110 on his ability to be creative.

Which candidate is the best candidate for the position?

Chapter 6: Performance Management

Introduction

Australian-based software company Atlassian analyzed their traditional performance review model in detail, looking for ways to enhance the performance of their employees.[133] They analyzed the positives and negatives associated with various aspects of the reviews they were using to develop a model that better motivated employees. They ended up with a lightweight, continuous model in which managers met more frequently with subordinates for feedback and coaching. Other progressive companies have been doing the same, replacing their traditional annual performance appraisals with more frequent coaching and feedback sessions.

Objectives:

After reading this chapter, you should be able to:

- Define performance management and performance appraisals
- Identify ways to overcome the biases associated with performance appraisals
- Distinguish the formats typically used to evaluate performance
- Identify approaches to mitigate litigation potential in performance evaluations
- Explain the value of valid and reliable performance appraisals

What is Performance Management?

Performance management has been defined as "a continuous process of identifying, measuring, and developing the performance of individuals and teams and aligning performance with the strategic objectives of an organization."[134] Under the umbrella of performance management are performance appraisal systems, which are often conducted annually in a formal way. The purposes of performance management are to fairly and objectively (1) set expectations; (2) monitor employee performance; (3) develop and improve employees; (4) reward and compensate employees; (5) plan for future needs, training, and staffing. The **performance criteria** used to assess performance may include communication skills, interpersonal skills, attendance, attitude and cooperation, initiative, integrity, productivity (quantity and quality), and timeliness.

Approaches to Measuring Performance

Performance appraisal systems have been defined as the "systematic description of an employee's strengths and weaknesses."[135]

Organizational managers use a variety of means to assess the performance of their employees. They may use formal top-down annual evaluations where supervisors evaluate their subordinates, or they may use 360-degree evaluations in which more than one evaluator is included. The evaluators may be supervisors, subordinates, peers, customers, or other relevant parties in positions to evaluate performance. A greater number of evaluators has the potential to reduce bias since more opinions are collected. Oftentimes, people submit their own self-evaluations in the review process to share information with evaluators on their performance. For example, university faculty often submit their own assessments of teaching, service and scholarship. The latter could include peer-reviewed journal articles, conference attendance, and textbooks published. People tend to over-estimate their own performance, however. Meta-analytic studies have found that self-ratings have higher means than peer or supervisory ratings.[136]

Researchers have offered several prescriptions for effective performance management and appraisal.[137] Evaluators should (1) strive for as much precision in defining and measuring performance dimensions as is possible; (2) link performance dimensions to internal and external customer requirements; (3) use multiple raters; and (4) incorporate the measurement of situational constraints. By following these prescriptions, managers can reduce the potential for litigation, which can result from overly subjective and biased performance appraisals.

Two general types of rating formats are typically used: **absolute** and **relative**.[138] Absolute formats require raters to rate individuals against a standard, while relative formats require raters to rate individuals against each other. For example, in an absolute format, a rater may use a five-point scale anchored by 1 as poor performance based on certain criteria and 5 as excellent performance based on particular criteria. Ratees should be informed of what constitutes each of the five standards so they can perform to achieve excellence. In a relative format, raters may be told that only 20 percent of ratees can fall into the "A" category of excellent performance, followed by 70 percent in the "B" category of solid performance and 10 percent in the "C" category. This approach is often called **forced distribution, stacked, rank and yank** or **differentiation** systems.

Relative Rating Scales

Forced Distribution Systems

Jack Welch labeled forced distribution systems as differentiation, as he felt that terms such as "rank and yank" have negative connotations. Welch is the former CEO of General Electric and he offers a good example on such systems. Between 1981 and 2001, Welch established a 20/70/10 "vitality curve" to identify the "top 20 percent" of "A" employees, "vital 70 percent" of "B" employees and "bottom 10 percent" of "C" employees.[139] Employees who fell into the latter category two years in a row were terminated. Using this program, General Electric's value increased by $300 billion,[140] which perhaps contributed to the adoption of forced distribution systems in other organizations, such as Microsoft, Intel, Goldman Sachs, and Cisco.

Two meta-analytic studies analyzed the differences between the two formats, finding that relative formats had greater correlations with sales volume, perceptual speed, quantitative ability, general mental ability, production quantity, and spatial/mechanical ability.[141] Relative systems further have been found to mitigate **leniency bias,** which occurs when managers inflate the performance evaluations of their subordinates to appease them. In other words, subordinates may deserve low scores in performance, yet they receive high scores instead. Consider leniency in the college classroom. If a professor gave all students A grades, those performing at low levels would not be motivated to improve their performance, while those performing at high levels would be motivated to reduce their productivity. Why should they work hard when low performers are earning the same grades as they are?

Though relative systems have demonstrated some positive outcomes, many managers and subordinates do not like them. Some feel that the systems are unfair, dysfunctional, or overly competitive, and harmful to company cultures. Pitting employees against one another can reduce their desire to practice citizenship behaviors voluntarily. Research has found that when employees are explicitly pitted against one another, social comparisons result, leading to escalated levels of competition and unethical behaviors to promote one's own self-interests.[142] They may not want to help one another for fear that the person being helped will raise his scores against the helper's. For these reasons and more, some organizations have dropped the systems, including General Electric, Microsoft, Amazon and Adobe. Furthermore, recent research has indicated that the individuals with low levels of conscientiousness and greater levels of psychological entitlement find relative systems to be attractive, suggesting that such systems may be attracting lower performers.[143] Despite such challenges to forced distribution systems, estimates indicate that twenty-one percent of Fortune 500 and mid-size organizations continue to use them.[144]

Ranking

A second relative approach to evaluate performance is for raters to rank employees against one another. In relatively small groups, this approach may be effective in recognizing and rewarding high relative achievers, along with their counterparts. An example would be if a department manager ranked his ten subordinates from 1 (highest performer) to 10 (lowest performer). Each of her ten subordinates would know where they stood in the ranking and could adjust their performance accordingly and if needed. Two disadvantages of the **ranking** approach are that it can be unwieldy in larger groups and the assumption that the distance between each of the ranks is equal. For example, if the top three employers are star performers, while the fourth through tenth fall far behind, the gap in rankings between one, two, and three is small, while the gap between the third and fourth rankings is wide.

Paired Comparison

A third approach is the **paired comparison**, which is applied when raters pair groups of employees and evaluate them against one another. For example, in a group of five employees, raters may compare one to two, one to three, one to four, and one to five. Then raters will compare two to three, two to four, and two to five. This process is continued until all have been compared. Then the raters tally the options to identify the one with the highest rankings.

Paired Comparison Chart

Option	1	2	3	4	5
1					
2					
3					
4					
5					

Absolute Rating Scales

Graphic Rating Scales (BARS)

In **graphic rating scales**, managers identify traits or behaviors that are important to effective performance and employees are evaluated based on these traits or behaviors. Below is an example of a graphic rating scale.

Graphic rating scale

	Poor	Fairly good	Good	Very good	Excellent
Interpersonal skills		X			
Communication skills			X		
Productivity				X	
Job knowledge			X		
Attendance					X

Raters who use graphic rating scales should be trained on what constitutes each of the anchors. In other words, what makes the attendance of the employee above excellent? No absences over a year? One or two absences? Each anchor needs descriptors to ensure fairness across various raters and ratees in an organization.

Behaviorally-anchored Rating Scale (BARS)

Instead of listing the anchors with a range from poor to excellent, raters may list the specific behaviors that correspond to effective performance. Behaviorally-anchored rating scales (BARS) compare an individual's performance against specific examples of behavior that are anchored to numerical ratings. The table below presents an example of a BARS. Raters must identify the most appropriate description for each employee evaluated.

BARS

Name of employee:
Name of behavior: Technical skills
5. _____ This employee performs a full range of technical skills and can be expected to perform in an outstanding manner.   4._____   3._____ This employee performs a medium range of technical skills and can be expected to perform satisfactorily.   2._____   1._____ This employee performs a very limited range of technical skills and can be expected to perform poorly.

Forced Choice

Another absolute approach used by managers is the **forced choice** format. In this approach, raters are forced to make a choice of the descriptors that best describe an employee's performance within a larger group of options. For example, in a college classroom, students could be asked to identify the two most appropriate descriptors of their professor.

1. Actively engages students in the classroom.
2. Describes the course objectives prior to each class.
3. Projects in a confident way.
4. Makes sure that all learners are accommodated, whether slower or quicker.

Items one and four best describe professor performance, while the second and third items are less descriptive of good performance in the college classroom. Because raters may be unaware of which descriptors correspond most closely to performance, they may be more likely to respond honestly (without trying to bias results to give intentionally favorable or unfavorable ratings).

Rater Errors in Performance Management

At times, performance management systems are plagued with cognitive biases. The following are the most common biases in performance appraisals.

Leniency/Severity

Leniency occurs when raters inflate ratings to give higher ratings than ratees objectively deserve. Severity is the opposite problem, which occurs when raters give lower scores than ratees objectively deserve. Leniency is much more common than severity,[145] which is also known as stringency. Leniency poses a significant problem when detected in performance appraisals. Managers who are uncomfortable giving honest feedback to their subordinates my inflate their ratings to higher levels than their subordinates objectively deserve. Research has found that raters who have low levels of assertiveness (which is a trait within the extraversion dimension), low levels of conscientiousness and high levels of agreeableness are the most lenient raters.[146]

Halo/Horns

Halo and horn biases occur when raters allow one trait, either good (halo) or bad (horns) to overshadow other traits. If a college dean at a "R1 (research) university" is impressed with a faculty member's research, he may elevate his otherwise lower ratings of the faculty member's teaching or service to the university. This exemplifies the halo bias. If a college dean at the same university is unimpressed with a faculty member's research, he may lower the scores of the faculty in other dimensions of performance, such as teaching or service. This exemplifies the horns bias.

Central Tendency

Central tendency occurs when raters tend to give ratees ratings in the middle of a scale, regardless of where ratees' performance objectively falls on the scale. For example, if a rater gave most of his ratees scores of three on a five-point scale, regardless of performance on the high or low ends of the scale, the rater is committing central tendency bias.

Representativeness (Stereotyping)

Representativeness occurs when people overgeneralize attributes associated with the members of a social group. This is also known as stereotyping. Researchers have argued that using stereotypes is a cognitive shortcut where people try to conserve cognitive resources by taking shortcuts and categorizing people. For example, if a rater determined that "All Asians work hard," so she assigned her Asian employees more difficult projects and evaluated them either more or less favorably than they objectively deserve, the rater would be guilty of stereotyping.

First Impression Error

First impression error occurs when raters allow their first impressions of ratees to outweigh other relevant indicators of job performance.

Resistance to Change

Training managers to identify biases may help to reduce biases, but one should note that most performance appraisal errors are extremely resistant to change.[147] Managers may be well aware that they're making errors when evaluating the performance of subordinates, yet they may continue to make the errors for personal or social reasons.[148]

Interrater Reliability and Validity in Performance Management

Legally defensible performance appraisals are those that mitigate the potential for bias by ensuring the evaluations are both **reliable** and **valid.** Reliability in performance appraisals occurs when strong inter-rater agreement exists. For example, if a supervisor's ratings of a subordinate are consistent with those of his peers or subordinates, results indicate strong interrater reliability. Valid performance appraisals are those that are objective assessments of actual performance. If a supervisor gives an employee a five on a five-point scale (indicating excellent performance), the ratee's performance should be considered excellent when assessed against objective criteria.

Ensuring validity and reliability are two ways raters' evaluations are legally defensible. Additional means include (1) ensuring ratees have a way to appeal their evaluations; (2) employing multiple raters in the process (360-degree evaluations); (3) including all relevant aspects of ratee performance; (4) mitigating cognitive biases; (5) training raters; (6) setting expectations in evaluations through transparency in all aspects of the process; and (7) incorporating any situational constraints on performance. Situational constraints on performance include inadequate resources, inadequate staffing, unexpected events (such as electricity outages or major weather events), and coworker pressure to lower productivity. As an example of the latter, suppose a new employee started producing one hundred widgets per hour, while the average productivity for other employees was only fifty. Those coworkers may pressure the new employee to reduce her performance so they aren't viewed negatively by superiors.

Performance Assessments

Are people realistic about their own performance? Poor performers are generally less realistic about their performance than good performers.[149] In 4 studies, researchers found that people who scored in the bottom quartile in tests of grammar, logic and humor grossly overestimated their own performance.[150]

Performance Improvement Programs

In an ideal workplace, everyone would be highly engaged and productive, yet in the real world, workplaces are plagued by some employees who are less engaged and productive than ideal. In these cases, managers often intervene to try to increase productivity of these employees rather than immediately terminating them. Oftentimes, human resource managers may put the less productive employee on a **performance improvement**

plan for a specific time period (often 90 days) to try to improve his performance. Managers set goals and communicate them with the employee who strives to reach the goals to increase performance. Managers also monitor the employee's performance over the specified time period and provide feedback on progress. They may choose various means of monitoring employees, whether electronically though company computers, in person, or based on output figures.

Recent Trends in Performance Management

Appraising employee performance annually and formally is sometimes considered a pain to managers who feel that their time could be used better in other ways. Some also feel that performance appraisals fail to motivate and engage employees. For these reasons and other related reasons, some organizations have moved away from formal annual evaluations to more frequent coaching sessions in which managers meet with their employees every few months to let them know how they're doing and to offer ways they could improve.

Balanced Scorecard

Perspective	Indicators
Financial or Stewardship	Financial performance
	Resource deployment
Internal Processes	Efficiency and Quality
Customer and Stakeholder	Customer value
	Satisfaction
	Retention
Learning and Growth	Human capital
	Culture
	Infrastructure and Technology

Balanced Scorecard

The Balanced Scorecard aligns the big picture strategy elements such as an organization's vision, mission, and strategic goals with its operational elements, such as objectives (continuous improvement activities), measures (key performance indicators) and initiatives (projects to help achieve targets). Balanced Scorecards are used extensively in business and industry, nonprofit organizations, and the government. The **balanced scorecard** is a strategy performance management tool that can be used by managers to monitor the alignment of business strategies with operational strategies and can make adjustments for continuous improvement.

Change Management

Change management refers to the management of change and development in organizations. Oftentimes, the cultures are flawed in some way. They may be toxic, as the culture of Enron was toxic. They may be complacent, ignoring significant environmental changes that could impact their long-term sustainability, as with Kodak, Sears, and Smith Corona. There may be an abundance of entitled, unproductive, and disengaged workers. In these cases, and other similar cases, organizational leaders need to step in with a vision for change.

HR managers need to manage change too. In a study of over 12,000 peer and supervisory assessments of about 2,000 HR managers, the ability to change was considered the most important competency, followed by HR knowledge and delivery and knowledge of the business.[151]

Harvard Business School professor John Kotter authored a book entitled "Leading Change" in 1995 that many organizational leaders have used to initiate and implement change management programs. He has identified the following eight steps that leaders should take to manage change.

Step One: Create Urgency

According to Kotter, 75 percent of the management in an organization need to "buy into" the change. They need to share a sense of urgency to be sure the change is effectively embraced and expediently implemented.

Step Two: Form a Powerful Coalition

Leaders should identify highly engaged, influential "change agents" within their firms to help them lead change.

Step Three: Create a Vision for Change

Leaders also need to establish a clear, relevant, and forward-thinking vision that people can easily appreciate and understand.

Step Four: Communicate the Vision

Leaders also need to communicate their new vision frequently, consistently and powerfully. They need to "talk the talk" and "walk the walk" by leading by example.

Step Five: Remove Obstacles

In any organization, there will be people who resist change. These people may be entrenched and entitled, disengaged employees whose motives could be dubious. Leaders should identify detractors and skeptics and should work with them to diminish their influence and obtain some level of buy-in.

Step Six: Create Short-term Wins

Success breeds success, so highlighting and praising those involved with early "wins" and achievements is important to keeping morale high and overcoming resistance. Short-term wins also help to build trust in organizations, as organization members can witness and imitate the successes of others to create future successes.

Step Seven: Build on the Change

Change management is an ongoing process, so leaders should be sure not to declare victory prematurely. A long-term, careful, and dedicated approach is best to create real and lasting change that penetrates all aspects of the organization. Continuous improvement should be embedded in the company's culture.

Step Eight: Anchor the Changes in Corporate Culture

The final step is to ensure the changes are anchored in the corporate culture. For example, if an organization created a vision to serve customers and deliver happiness, all functions of human resource management, from hiring to training to compensating to structuring the organization, should correspond to the vision. Extraverted, enthusiastic people who exude happiness should be targeted in the hiring process. People should be trained on ways to deliver happiness and good customer service. Incentives and compensation packages should reward customer service. The organization should be structured to best respond to customers to meet their needs. By focusing on all functions of human resource management, leaders can best anchor the changes into the company's culture.

Conclusion

An important component of the employer – employee relationship is performance management and within this large umbrella are performance appraisals. Organization managers can employ a variety of methods to evaluate performance, whether absolute or relative. Each offers advantages and disadvantages. So long as the tool used to assess performance is considered reliable and valid, the tool should be legally defensible.

QUESTIONS FOR REVIEW

1. What is a behaviorally anchored rating scale?

2. What are Kotter's 8 steps to change management?

3. Define the elements of a legally defensible performance appraisal.

4. What is a forced distribution rating system? What are its advantages and drawbacks?

5. What is the ranking method of performance evaluation?

6. What is representative bias?

7. Define leniency and severity biases. How do those biases differ from halo and horns biases?

8. Which is preferable – behaviorally anchored rating scales or scales with low, medium, and high anchors?

9. Which bias do forced distribution rating systems mitigate?

10. How else can organizational leaders mitigate rating biases in evaluation systems?

11. What are the current trends with respect to performance evaluation systems?

APPLICATIONS

1. An Ethical Dilemma for a New CFO

You are the new chief financial officer of a Fortune 500 organization. The organization was once thriving, but over the past few years times have been difficult. The competition in your industry has intensified, and shareholders have been complaining that stock prices have decreased. The pressure is intense.

One of your direct reports is a 59-year old woman who is the sole provider for her three college-age children and two children in high school. Her husband passed away years ago. After a few weeks, it becomes obvious to you that the woman lacks the skills needed for her position. The reports that she has generated are of poor quality and it seems she has little potential for improvement.

After some consultation with the HR department, you discover that she has been with the organization for twenty years and has never received less than a 4 on a 5-point evaluation scale. You suspect that your predecessors gave her relatively high evaluations out of leniency. Perhaps they felt sorry for her family situation and the way that she is the sole provider of five children. You're not sure.

You wonder about your other direct reports and whether the leniency bias is prevalent in the department you oversee. An investigation suggests that this is the case, as no employees received lower than a 4 on a 5-point scale in your department over the past five years.

1. What is the ethical dilemma that you're facing?

2. Given the leniency bias prevalent in the organization and other issues presented, identify measures that you would take to resolve the situation.

3. Should you terminate the employment of the 59-year old woman? What are the legal implications involved?

2. Discipline Role-Play

Form teams of three. Assign the roles of manager, subordinate, and observer. The manager will counsel the employee on each of the following scenarios. The employee should accept the disciplinary action and play along as the manager provides disciplinary feedback. The observer will offer constructive criticism to the manager at the conclusion of each feedback session. Feel free to improvise. For each successive scenario, teams should rotate roles.

1. The employee frequently is late to work. In the last 90 days, the employee has been late 18 times. In some cases, the employee is more than an hour past the time he is supposed to arrive at work.

2. The employee works in a warehouse and operates machinery unsafely. The equipment has a safety guard, but the employee has altered the mechanism so that it does not engage. According to the employee, the safety device slows down production.

3. The employee is a customer service representative who answers calls all day long from customers who are either placing orders or requesting to return their orders. The manager is receiving complaints from customers regarding the employee's rude behavior.

4. The company stipulates that employees take two breaks each day: one from 10 – 10:15 a.m. and another from 3 – 3:15 p.m. each day. Employees are also permitted a one-hour lunch hour at noon. These breaks and lunch periods can be used to smoke. Smoking is not permitted at other times. The employee can often be found on the outside of the building smoking during non-break periods. Other employees have complained that he/she is not has his/her workstation when he/she is supposed to be.

3. A Valid Performance Evaluation?

All of the 150 employees at Aardvark Corporation are evaluated using the same performance evaluation form, which is pasted below. Identify whether the form seems valid.

Aardvark Corporation Performance Evaluation

Name of employee:
Title of employee:
Name of supervisor rater:

1 = Does not meet expectations
2 = Sometimes meets expectations
3 = Meets expectations
4 = Sometimes exceeds expectations
6 = Exceeds expectations

Job Knowledge_____

Job skills_____

Attitude_____

Physical appearance_____

Mathematical skills_____

Verbal skills_____

Efficiency_____

Effectiveness_____

Overall likeability_____

Overall job performance_____

Recommend for promotion_____

Recommend for demotion_____

Recommend for termination_____

CASE STUDIES

1. The Younger, More Diverse Workforce

John Sanchez is 58 years old and has been working at ABC Company for 15 years. John's performance has always "exceeded expectations" but on his most recent performance appraisal he failed to meet expectations. Recently, the CEO of ABC told a large crowd at the ABC Annual Meeting that he desired a "younger, more energetic, more diverse" workforce. The CEO further implemented a new forced distribution performance appraisal system this past year, which limited A ratings to 20 percent, B ratings to 70 percent, C ratings to 10 percent. This program was similar to that advocated by Jack Welch who recommended that companies relieve those who receive C ratings of their duties.

When John asked his supervisor to explain his C rating, his supervisor could offer no explanation and no examples. John talked to several colleagues who had also been with ABC for a long time and who also received low ratings. Within a few weeks, ABC Company decided to fire John and replace him with a younger worker, leading him to wonder whether he has a legitimate ADEA case. Does he? What do you need to know in this case?

2. Built-In Bias?

Sociologists Frank Dobbin, Daniel Schrage, and Alexandra Kalev analyzed data from the Equal Employment Opportunity Commission (EEOC) for 816 establishments over a period of thirty years, from 1971 to 2002. They found that as firms became more likely to implement performance evaluation systems, women and minority men became less likely to hold management positions.

"According to the results of the study, the only group impacted at a statistically significant level (with a likelihood greater than 5 percent) were white women. Silicon Valley influencer Kieran Snyder also found that women get the short end of the stick when it comes to reviews. She looked at 248 reviews across 28 companies, and found that while 58.9 percent of the reviews received by men contained critical feedback, 87.9

percent of reviews received by women did. Many of these reviews were critical of women's personalities, with feedback on presentation and tone surprisingly common."[152]

Another study found that appearing self-confident at work is enough to gain influence for men, but not enough to gain influence for women.[153] Women are additionally "required" to be pro-socially oriented. Further, through the appearance of self-confidence, job performance enables men to exert influence in their organizations, yet that again is not enough for women. High performing women need both self-confidence and a pro-social orientation.

What would you do if you found the same biases in performance evaluations or gender perceptions in your organization?

3. Gaming a Forced Distribution Rating System

For ten years, profits at U.S.-based Beauty Bath and Bodyworks (BBB) were impressive. Each year the new cosmetics manufacturing company grew in sales, customers, and employees. By 2006, profits at BBB were just over $12,000,000 and owner Kallie Lopez threw a huge party for BBB's 75 employees at the end of the year in celebration.

Three years later, the great recession had hit and BBB found itself in a much less comfortable position. Sales had steadily declined over the past two years and it seemed BBB was going to be reporting its first loss in December of 2009. Lopez decided to forego the company party at that point, instead focusing on strategic ways to turn BBB around.

Kallie Lopez asked Jillian Jackson to gauge the satisfaction, engagement, and commitment of employees. She had heard through the grapevine that some employees were unhappy and a few departments had "motivational issues." Jackson was the human resource manager at BBB.

Within a few days, she had completed and collected the results a survey, which found that employees were unhappy about their performance evaluation system. Many were uncommitted to BBB and too many were disengaged. BBB was using a standards-based performance evaluation system. Employees were ranked between 1 and 5 with 1 representing a ranking that did not meet expectations and 5 representing a ranking that far exceeded expectations.

Most managers in BBB over the past five years had been giving everyone rankings of 3. They neither wanted to elevate the rankings of any employees by giving them a 4 or 5, nor downgrade them to a 1 or 2. Several high performers had left. A few anonymous surveys indicated that several high performers who stayed had reduced their output to the same levels of their peers since all were making the same scores (and hence, all were earning the same percentage of merit pay increases) anyway.

One wrote, "My boss must be a communist. He thinks we should all be paid equally, despite our very uneven contributions."

Another wrote, "I stopped coming in early and leaving late. Why should I do anything extra? The slackers have won. Now we're all slackers."

A third wrote, "Why even have performance evaluations? Why bother? Everyone gets the same score and the same pay increases."

Jillian Jackson knew a change needed to be made, so she worked with Lopez to implement a new forced distribution performance evaluation system. Managers were told they needed to use a 10/70/20 plan, where 10 percent would earn A scores and "significant" merit pay increases of 10 percent of their salaries; 70 percent would earn B scores and would earn "solid" merit pay increases; and 20 percent would receive "unacceptable" ratings. Employees who received 2 consecutive years of C grades would be terminated.

Over the next two years, the plan seemed to work beautifully. Surveys indicated that most employees were satisfied, engaged, and committed and revenues for BBB started to increase. By 2015, profits topped $14.5 million, so the company threw another huge party for employees at the end of the year to celebrate. No one knew whether the new performance evaluation system was driving productivity and sales increases or the end of the recession had spurred growth. Jackson figured both had contributed positively.

During the party, however, nine employees separately approached Jackson to air their grievances. Their managers had started playing games with the forced distribution rating system. They didn't want to give anyone C scores, so they started rotating employees into A, B, and C categories each year to avoid doing so. What can BBB do now?

Chapter 7: Training and Development

Introduction

Always a pioneer in innovation, St. Paul, Minnesota-based 3M is a leader in leadership development.[154] According to Marlene McGrath, 3M senior vice president of human resources, "Our global business plans require aggressive people plans. Our new program is developing leaders who can develop other leaders, empower teams that can create and innovate, and inspire all people to be their best. By preparing our leaders to thrive in a changing world and focus on customer needs and market opportunities, we'll achieve sustainable and successful business results." Global 3M Leadership Way and supervisor development leader Yaprak Gorur notes that the "Catalyst program moves leadership development from a limited, time-based event to a continuous journey over 12 months. It incorporates multiple face-to-face learning opportunities with executive leaders, customers and peers, all blended with online and mobile-enabled experiences." Training and development programs can enhance employee satisfaction, resulting in stronger organizational commitment and retention. For this reason and more, training and development are key components in high performance work systems.

Kim Roneree, the chief HR officer at College Hunks Hauling Junk, says, "One of the development concepts I have had success with in the past is having lunch and learns. If a member of management attends a conference or off-site training class, when they return, they must give a 30 minute to 1-hour lunch presentation on the conference or class attended. They share what they learned from it and what the key take-aways were."[155] Lunch and learns are informal and less structured that some other traditional training options, yet they provide a convenient way to engage employees and to offer learning opportunities.

Objectives:

After reading this chapter, you should be able to:

- Recognize various approaches organizations use to train and develop employees.
- Understand the steps used to develop and evaluate training programs.
- Discuss ways to equip organizations for present and future talent needs.
- Discuss the benefits of coaching in the workplace.
- Articulate the benefits of trust in the workplace.

According to the Association for Talent Development's 2017 State of the Industry Report,[156] organizations spend an average of $1,273 per employee on training and development. The average number of hours per employee spent on formal learning was 34.1 hours. According to the Organization for Economic Cooperation and Development, the United States ranks near the top for training as 66 percent of employees in the U.S. received training in 2017. **Training** refers to any approach an organization uses to improve the performance and learning of employees, while **development** refers to a longer-term approach that may incorporate various types of training to guide an employee's career path.

Many employers teach "tightly specified, highly standardized tasks" that will soon be taken over by computers, according to John Hagel, the co-chairman of the Center for the Edge, which is a unit of Deloitte LLP devoted to researching business and technology. Hagel says that employers should instead be investing in drawing out employees' "curiosity, imagination, creativity, emotional intelligence [and] social intelligence," which are harder for machines to replicate.[157]

Share of Workers Who Received Employer-provided Training in 2017 (OECD, 2018)

Country	Percent of workers who received employer-provided training
Finland	71
Sweden	69
United States	66
United Kingdom	62
Canada	62
Germany	57
South Korea	56
Israel	53
Chile	51
Japan	48
France	42
Turkey	31
Italy	30
Russia	24

"Because worker training benefits the society as a whole, not just the individual employer, there's an economic case that government should provide it directly or at least subsidize it. Yet in the U.S., public spending on labor markets (which includes unemployment benefits) has fallen from .8 percent in 1985 to .3 percent in 2016, according to OECD data...To upgrade the world's workforce for the skills of the future, the ideal environment is what economists call a high-trust equilibrium: Each employer invests in training because it's confident others will do likewise. We're not quite there yet."[158]

Training and development are integral components of **succession planning.** Succession planning is the process for identifying and developing new leaders who can replace current leaders when the latter leave their organizations, retire, or pass away. Identifying pools of talent for key positions in organizations is an effective means of ensuring smooth transitions during times of change.

Steps in the Training Process

The following steps should be taken in the training process: (1) assess organizational training and development *needs;* (2) define objectives, purpose and proposed deliverables; (3) design the training program to meet objectives; (4) implement the training program; and (5) evaluate its success and make any necessary revisions.

When conducting the training and development needs assessment, consider any deficiencies or areas in need of improvement at the organizational, department, team, individual, or task levels. For example, if the customer surveys have indicated bank tellers in a particular location are acting rudely, consider offering them training on ways to better handle customers. Set objectives for the training program. In this case, managers would consider the objective of "excellent customer service." This objective should be woven into the company culture so everyone is aware of the value company leaders place on customer service. Trainers should then design the method of training that would most effectively convey the message, whether delivered by a lecture, on-line, or by other means. After implementing the training, evaluate its success by collecting feedback from the bank tellers, feedback from customers, and the return on the training investment. How much money did the training cost? How much better is customer service? Customers who have positive interactions with the bank tellers may be more loyal, resulting in better business over time.

Evaluations of training can be based on the *reactions* of people who were involved, whether *behaviors* changed, whether l*earning* occurred, whether *results* were achieved and whether the return surpassed the investment. Reaction, learning, behaviors, and results are the four components of Kirkpatrick's four-level training evaluation.

Learning Theories

People learn in different ways and researchers have identified theories to try to explain variations. **Behaviorism** proposes that people are essentially passive, responding to external stimuli. They start off with blank slates and behavior is shaped through positive or negative reinforcement. People who endorse behaviorism often point to animal experiments to prove them, such as the famous experiment on Pavlov's dogs who began to respond in predictable ways each time bells were rung to let them know food was available. The dogs started to salivate when they heard the bells.

Some researchers have rejected behaviorism and replaced it with **cognitivism,** which states that mental processes are influenced by both intrinsic and extrinsic factors. Knowledge is seen in this theory as schema or symbolic mental processes and people build upon their existing knowledge (or schema) when they make new observations.

Others such as David Kolb[159] have argued that knowledge is created through the transformation of **experience**. According to Kolb, people (1) have a concrete *experience*; (2) they make observations and *reflect* on that experience; (3) they *conceptualize* and learn from the experience; and (4) they *test* what they learned. Learning is facilitated when people go through all four steps.

Trainee Characteristics

The following trainee characteristics are correlated with greater training success: high cognitive ability, high basic reading and math skills, strong orientation toward learning, less anxious, high levels of conscientiousness, high achievement motivation, high self-efficacy (confidence in oneself), high motivation to learn, perceptions that training is useful and relevant to the trainee's career, and the trainee values the learning outcomes. In a nutshell, intelligent trainees who are interested in the training and value the learning outcomes are the most likely to succeed. Less intelligent, less motivated, and apathetic trainees are least likely to be successfully trained. Younger trainees may learn more from training than older adults. Age is negatively correlated with learning outcomes and with learning in organizational settings.[160]

Conditions of the Learning Environment

Whole vs. Part Learning

When complex tasks are to be learned, breaking them up into their components is helpful. For example, if one were going to learn to play the game of golf, it is better to spend a day practicing chipping, another day putting, and a third day driving golf balls than to start playing a full game of golf all at once.

Massed vs. Spaced Practice

Spacing training over a longer period of time is more effective than using massed training.[161] If given the choice to take a class over five eight-hour days in a week or to learn two hours twice weekly over ten weeks, better retention of the material will result from the latter approach. Learning requires reflection of the material and spaced practice allots time for reflection.

Overlearning

Would you rather your doctor learned to remove your appendix "just in time" or had overlearned the procedure such that it was routine? Overlearning is beneficial in complex, highly stressful jobs. Consider why professional football players practice "drills" over and over prior to game time. When it's game time, players who have overlearned the coordinated skills they need to move the ball across the field can focus on other aspects of the game as their motions have become routine.

Goal-Setting

Goals should be SMART: specific, measurable, attainable, relevant and timely. SMART goals are superior to "do your best" types of goals because they are more motivating. Research in industrial and organizational psychology has consistently found that once employees have mastered a task, they perform better when given specific, difficult performance goals than "do your best."[162]

Edwin Locke recently pointed to the benefits of writing down goals.[163] He posits that writing objectifies and clarifies goals and values, making them more likely to be acted upon. Writing goals down may make one more consciously aware of his goals, which may increase commitment to action and self-efficacy.

Knowledge of Results

Trainees also need to have knowledge of their results. If salespersons were given sales training, they should have knowledge of the results of that training: did sales improve? Trainers should provide trainees with feedback on the training and any outcomes that were improved.

Attention and Retention

Trainees who are better able to translate training into learning objectives will be more attentive during training than their counterparts. Retention is enhanced when trainees are required to periodically recall what they have learned through tests.

Types of Training

Orientation is the most common form of training. **Orientation** (also called induction) is an *event* in which new hires or transferred workers are introduced to the organization, coworkers, and supervisors. Oftentimes orientations will include setting expectations, sharing the employee handbook, communicating the company's vision, mission, and goals, and sharing any other relevant, job-related information.

Orientation is often confused with onboarding, yet the two are distinct. **Onboarding** is also known as organizational socialization. Onboarding is the *process* of integrating a new employee into the company's *culture*. Managers may use a variety of ways to engage their new employees, such as hosting periodic social events, icebreakers and team-building events. The most effective onboarding practices teach new employees not only *what* they will be doing on the job but also *how* they are expected to work with others and for what *greater purpose*.[164]

Organizations offer numerous types of training. One form of training is **technical skills training,** which is offered to improve the abilities and knowledge of employees to perform certain tasks. These often include information technology, scientific tasks, quantitative tasks, or mechanical tasks. **Soft skills training** is offered to improve non-technical skills. These include training on interpersonal skills, communication skills, leadership, problem-solving, time management, emotional intelligence, diversity awareness, sensitivity, flexibility/adaptability, work ethic, and the ability to interact well within teams. **Products and services training** are offered to enhance the knowledge, skills, or abilities of employees on the products and services offered by their organizations. Finally, **mandatory training** is offered by organizations to comply with legal obligations. For example, employees may be required to take **sexual harassment training** by companies seeking to have an affirmative defense against sexual harassment claims.

Common Training Methods

Lectures give instructors the maximum opportunity to control the learning experience, which is one reason why they are so widely used. They can be delivered to large or small audiences, in person or via electronic modes, so they are considered convenient and effective. Yet depending on the quality and content of the lecture and the instructor, their effectiveness may vary quite a bit. Instructors who engage their audience with exercises, experiential applications, stories, and jokes may have more appeal than their counterparts who don't. Those who apply Aristotle's *ethos* (establish credibility), *pathos* (appeal to emotions with a story) and *logos* (appeal to rationality and logic) tend to be the most effective.

Other training approaches and exercises are also popular. Other approaches include **computer-based training, E-learning (podcasts and web-based learning)** and blended learning. **Blended learning** combines on-line methods with traditional classroom approaches. These approaches can be relatively inexpensive and convenient to learners, especially when access to the training can be scheduled when the trainee desires. Some of the exercises that can enhance the training experience include **role playing exercises, adventure learning, simulations, case studies**, and **team-building exercises.** These interactive approaches may appeal to trainees by facilitating engagement, problem-solving, and learning.

Some organizations use **behavior-modeling, job shadowing,** or **on-the-job training** approaches. In these approaches, trainers identify workers whose work behavior is highly valued and new employees are instructed to model those behaviors by shadowing (or closely following) the person. These are types of on-the-job training, which can be efficient and relatively inexpensive.

Companies may also offer **apprenticeships** and **internships** to people interested in enhancing their knowledge, abilities, and skills on particular jobs. They may also use **job rotation**, in which employees are rotated from one job to another to learn more about other jobs in their organizations.

A growing trend in many organizations is to provide coaches for workers. A recent meta-analytic study found that workplace **coaching** enhances employee learning and development, whether offered in person or virtually.[165] Companies may hire internal or external coaches and these individuals work with employees to help them solve problems, achieve their goals, and live life in desirable ways. Coaches often say that everyone needs a coach, whether at the top, middle, or bottom of an organization.

Can coaching change people for the better? In a study of employees from a high technology company based in Greece, a researcher found that person-centered coaching significantly increased the emotional and social intelligence of those being coached. More specifically, the research indicated that the emotional intelligence competencies of an achievement orientation, adaptability, emotional self-control, and a positive outlook increased after monthly sessions of coaching over a year of time.[166] The research also indicated that the social intelligence competencies of empathy, organizational awareness, conflict management, coach and mentor relationships, influence, inspirational leadership and teamwork improved.

Trust is another important factor in retaining top talent. One recent study from *Human Resource Management* found that trust in a leader is critical in reducing the turnover intentions of high performers, while trust in coworkers is more important in retaining low performers.[167] Trust is defined as the willingness of an individual to be vulnerable to the actions of someone else. Trust has been identified as a key variable in building relationships between employees and their leaders. Researchers have found that trust is related to a variety of beneficial workplace outcomes, such as organization citizenship behavior, effort, negotiation behaviors, communication, conflict reduction, group performance and individual performance.[168]

Conclusion

Organizations that invest in their employees by offering training and development opportunities are able to increase employee satisfaction, commitment, and retention. Establishing a learning organization in which people are motivated to enhance their knowledge, abilities, and skillsets further benefits organizations in adding meaning and purpose to employees' lives.

QUESTIONS FOR REVIEW

1. Which types of training are the most widely used?

2. When would "overlearning" training material be the most useful?

3. Which is superior: massed or spaced practice?

4. What are the benefits of coaching in the workplace?

5. How do organizations determine whether they should offer training to employees?

6. Which employee characteristics are most suited for training?

7. Identify characteristics of a training environment well-suited for training.

8. How can organizations determine whether the training programs offered are successful?

9. Which sorts of training should organizations offer to mitigate legal actions?

10. Which is more beneficial – part or whole training?

APPLICATIONS

Team-building Exercises

1. Organizations are increasingly using team-building exercises to develop and promote collegiality, respect, and an appreciation for diversity. Get into groups of five or six people and identify a team leader to be the spokesperson of the group.

Each person is asked to complete the following statements for a session on general work attitudes and statements for a session on developing and improving people's potential. Each person needs to complete the following sentences:

I most enjoy school when…

I least enjoy school when…

Working in teams at school is…

Working in teams at school could be improved by…

The biggest opportunity for me in life is…

My underused potential…

If I could instead…

To be more effective, I…

2. Training Exercise

Get into groups of two or three people and answer the following questions. Scenario: You are about to enroll in a GMAT Preparation Course because you feel that taking such a course will benefit the score you can earn on the exam, which will better position you for a strong AACSB-accredited graduate program. You have a number of choices. Choose the answers that you believe will enhance your learning.

1. You can either take a one-week cram course in which you will attend a class from 8 a.m. to 4:30 p.m. on Monday through Thursday (with ½ hour lunch breaks) (36 hours in total) OR you can take a course on Mondays, Wednesdays, and Thursday nights from 6 – 9 p.m. for four weeks (36 hours in total). Which choice will best enhance your learning? Why?

2. What type of environment (classroom; outdoors; etc.) do you feel would best enhance your learning? Explain seating, room, lighting, etc.

3. What are the characteristics of the instructor who is best likely to enhance your learning?

4. What are the characteristics of instruction that will most likely enhance your learning? In other words, do you prefer on-line learning, lectures, practice exercises, group-based learning, cases, simulations, something else or a mix of these options? Please explain.

5. Would you prefer that the instructor focus on one area (e.g., verbal) first before moving to another area (e.g., math) or do you prefer to learn the material at once, more holistically?

ONE AREA:

ALL AT ONCE:

6. What are the characteristics of the person in the course who is most likely to retain the least amount of information? What are the characteristics of the person who is most likely to retain the most amount of information?

LEAST:

MOST:

3. Giving feedback to an unmotivated employee

Get into groups of two or three people.

Two people: One person should assume the role of the manager and one person should assume the role of the subordinate (Anderson).

Three people: Two people should assume the role of dual managers and a third person should assume the role of Anderson.

Information about the performance of the incumbent, J. Anderson (from the perspective of the manager):

You and Anderson work together in a large automobile dealership that offers a wide selection of new and "pre-owned" vehicles, from small hatchback economy cars to large SUVs. Prices range from around $8,000 to $60,000 per vehicle. Anderson was hired three years ago to work as a sales representative on a commission-only basis (no salary, no benefits), earning 3 percent of the selling price of each vehicle.

Anderson's duties include: (1) meeting and greeting customers, 2) taking customers around the parking lot to educate them on the vehicles in the lot, (3) convincing the customers to purchase the vehicles, and (4) closing the deals.

Anderson works six days a week (Tuesday through Sunday) for approximately 9 hours per day. When (s)he came to the dealership three years ago, Anderson was a star, consistently selling more vehicles than his/her peers. Lately Anderson's sales are rotten (only one car sold in the past month!) and many of his/her peers have left the dealership. Only four salespeople remain, just enough to cover the reduced stream of customers visiting the dealership.

The dealership is located in a region that was dominated by two major employers for over two decades, yet one recently relocated and the other closed down. Thousands who lost their jobs have been scrambling to find new ones and many in the region feel insecure about a ripple effect. They worry that other employers may also leave for better opportunities elsewhere. Buying a new car isn't in the minds of too many people in the area at this point.

Anderson was once a "diamond in the rough," but now s/he just seems rough. S(he) is: (1) consistently late to work; (2) dresses too casually, often in wrinkly shirts with stains on the collars and underarms; (3)

appears generally unmotivated; (4) spends downtime surfing the net; (5) drinks too much coffee; (6) takes too many "vape" breaks, (7) complains about the economy, and (8) seems pretty grouchy.

Your boss has noticed Anderson's demeanor and instructed you to meet with Anderson to discuss his/her performance and to motivate/inspire Anderson to do a better job. Your boss attributes Anderson's poor sales of late to a combination of the economic downturn and Anderson's flaws. On the bright side, your boss thinks that Anderson has the potential to raise his/her sales volume by "focusing." You're not so sure.

To the manager(s) evaluating Anderson:

What will you say? What external factors must you consider in your conversations? What internal factors must you consider? How will you motivate and inspire Anderson to stay and do a good job? Your boss told you that you have some freedom in modifying Anderson's schedule and incentives. What will you offer?

To Anderson:

You're a little angry at your employer and at the economy in general. You've worked the past four weeks for around 50 hours per week and only made $1,720. That's nothing compared with the money you used to make. You were easily bringing in $3,000 per month. Sometimes you'd make $5,000.

A few years ago, you used your inheritance from your grandma and your savings to buy a decent little condo, but its maintenance fees of $500 per month are killing you now. You really need at least $3,000 to pay your mortgage, car loan, and other expenses.

You're starting to think that being laid off wouldn't be so bad. At least you could collect unemployment pay while looking for a different job. Several of your peers who have been laid off now spend their time at home playing video games and collecting unemployment, which doesn't sound too bad to you.

If your boss could offer you some incentives, you might consider modifying your behavior and working a bit harder to close sales. Everyone loves your winning smile. Plus, it would be hard finding a job right now, given thousands in your area just lost theirs.

4. Ethos, Pathos, and Logos

The most persuasive job interviewees are those who incorporate what Aristotle labeled as ethos, pathos, and logos. Ethos refers to establishing credibility. Credibility is often established in a resume, yet credibility also needs to be established during the interview. Interviewers look for job knowledge that only "insiders" could have in higher level positions. Pathos refers to generating emotion through a story. Interviewees should have a group of life stories and work examples they can use to relate to their interviewer. Logos refers to logic. After the interviewee has demonstrated credibility and related emotionally with his or her interviewer through examples and stories, the logical next step is for the interviewer to hire the person being interviewed. But the interviewee sometimes must explain to the interviewer why the logical step is to hire him or her. What does he or she bring to the table that no one else brings?

In groups of two people, identify your own ethos, pathos, and logos. Consider these within the context of a job interview. Then share your ethos, pathos, and logos with the class.

CASE STUDY

1. Coach's Management in Foreign Subsidiaries

For decades, Coach has been recognized in the handbag industry as a leader in the production of premium ladies' handbags. In 2015, Coach's products were assembled in eighteen countries, including the U.S., Vietnam, China, India, Thailand, and Italy.[169] The company uses a global outsourcing model that maintains strong control over the sources and quality of raw material used in production.

To maintain this quality, Coach has established a management presence in the foreign firms with which it has contracted to produce its products.[170] Having managers who are familiar with Coach's image, reputation, employment expectations, health and safety regulations, corporate and business strategies, and company culture overseeing operations benefits Coach. Such managers ensure that the strategic decisions made in the headquarters transfer to the local offices. They can also be used to train local managers for the sustainability of long-term operations and interests. Finally, their local presence helps to mitigate the possibility of sweatshop conditions.

1. Organizations such as Coach that send expatriate managers from one country to another face a variety of challenges. One challenge is that they need to ensure that the expatriate managers have been prepared well for their roles as global managers. Consider the countries in which Coach has management contracts. What types of training should be provided to global expatriate managers in those countries prior to their departures from the home office?

2. What types of training would managers in the global contract manufacturing facilities need to offer their employees to ensure health, safety, and employment expectations have been met?

Chapter 8: Compensation

Introduction

In the fall of 2018, on-line retailer Amazon made an unusual move: they increased the minimum wage of all U.S. workers to $15 per hour. This move impacted over 250,000 employees, including those in its Whole Foods Markets, along with around 100,000 seasonal workers. Feeling pinched by a tight labor market and political pressures, CEO Jeffrey Bezos stated, "We listened to our critics, thought hard about what we want to do, and decided we want to lead."[171] Employers like Amazon who pay their employees higher than market rates are able to position themselves competitively in the marketplace, attracting more qualified job applicants than their peers who pay their employees less competitively.

Business leaders use pay to achieve a variety of goals. An article in Bloomberg Businessweek tells the story of McDonald's turn-around.[172] Around 2016, Steve Easterbrook, CEO of McDonalds, had to concede that McDonalds' arch enemy, Burger King, had taken away some of its market share by offering at-home-delivery services for its products. He had to come up with an innovative way to fight back. He decided to pair up with Uber and join the online delivery business. He commanded each of his managers to nominate their best executives to roll out an on-line delivery business in only two weeks' time. He tied management's compensation to the speed and breadth of the rollout. It worked. Only a few other companies have outperformed McDonald's returns since 2015.

Easterbrook wants McDonalds to be recognized as a "beacon of innovation," which some say McDonalds hasn't enjoyed since the Truman administration. And compensation is a tool he has used and probably will continue to use to make that happen.

Objectives:

After reading this chapter, you should be able to:

- Recognize external competitiveness and internal alignment strategies in compensation.
- Recognize various approaches to compensating special groups.
- Explain ways to determine pay increases, develop a base pay system and establish pay levels.
- Understand motivation theories in compensation.
- Explain compensation-related laws in the United States.

Compensation refers to the total cash and non-cash payments employees receive in exchange for their contributions to an organization.

Human resource managers (or other managers who are overseeing employee compensation) must ensure their compensation strategies and structures are internally and externally equitable. In other words, the pay plans should be perceived as fair to employees when they compare their pay to other employees within their organizations and to employees in similar positions in other organizations.

Human resource managers must also work with other organizational managers to ensure that the plans they establish align with the business strategy, goals, objectives, and company culture. Companies with business strategies focused on premium products and innovation are more likely to compensate their employees more generously than those with business strategies focused on keeping costs low.

Patagonia, which is headquartered in Ventura, California, is an organization focused on innovation, premium products, and a strong interest in contributing to the triple bottom line (people, profits, planet). According to "Great Place to Work," 96 percent of its employees say they're proud to tell others they work there, 95 percent say they feel good about the ways Patagonia contributes to the community, and 92 percent say people celebrate special events at Patagonia.[173] Patagonia offers a competitive pay package to its employees. According to Payscale, the average pay for Patagonia employees is $77,000 per year, which is well above the average pay of employees in the United States.

Patagonia was one of the first organizations in the United States to offer its employees on-site daycare. In 2016, CEO Rose Marcario indicated that she believes that providing employees high-quality daycare isn't just good for families, it's good for employee engagement and ultimately, the bottom line. "It's true, there are financial costs to offering on-site childcare, and they can be expensive if you offer high-quality programs or subsidize your employees' tuition when on-site care is not available. But the benefits, financial and otherwise, pay for themselves every year."[174] Other benefits at Patagonia, whose founder Yvon Chouinard has a philosophy of "let my people surf," include field trips to Yosemite National Park for rock climbing, fly-fishing lessons, yoga, free scooters, and an organic café.[175]

Some might presume that such benefits would be detrimental to the bottom line, but the opposite is true. The family-owned company doubled in size between 2008 and 2013 and tripled its profits during that period, earning a whopping $600 million in 2013, partially due to its fiercely loyal employees and strong company culture and values.[176] Earnings in 2017 were projected to reach $750 million.[177]

Patagonia is not alone in including benefits and incentives in its compensation package. According to one study, more than ninety percent of either non-profit or for-profit organizations use short-term incentives (e.g., spot awards, team incentives) and more than fifty percent use long-term incentives (e.g., profit-sharing and gain-sharing plans) to motivate their employees.[178]

Over the past ten years, salaries have grown in the United States, according to the Economic Research Institute's Salary Indicator.[179]

Occupational Category	Mean Salary $	Growth 2007 – 2018
Top management	165,715	26 percent
Middle management	102,837	27.8 percent
Supervisory	79,271	23.1 percent
Healthcare	116,431	25.1 percent
Information technology	89,560	28.7 percent
Professional	85,092	29.2 percent
Sales	60,159	21.6 percent
Technicians and skilled craft	60,994	27.8 percent
Field, shop, and services	44,129	26.2 percent
Clerical	42,132	28.2 percent

Motivating Workers with Compensation

Can compensation packages motivate workers? According to several motivation theories, compensation plays a role in employee motivation.

Equity theory[180] is based on the proposition that people are motivated by fairness, so when people perceive an inequality in the input to outcome ratio of their referent party, they will adjust their inputs to achieve equality. For example, if an individual is working as a human resource clerk in an organization for $25,000 and she finds out that another clerk (her referent party) in either her or another organization is earning $30,000 for the same job, she will reduce her performance accordingly. She may be absent more, less productive, less willing to work extra hours, or more likely to steal from her organization to make up the perceived $5,000 inequity.

Reinforcement theory posits that an individual's behavior is a function of its consequences. The theory is a form of operant conditioning that suggests that environmental factors correspond to behaviors. **Positive reinforcement** occurs when people provide a positive response when an employee behaves in an appropriate manner. Positive responses could include gift cards, bonuses, or other rewards. **Negative reinforcement** occurs when people remove a negative consequence when certain objectives, goals, or deadlines are met. For example, if an employee was required to report daily on sales goals and all reporting and goals are successfully achieved over a certain period of time, the supervisor may decide to eliminate the daily progress report requirement.

Agency theory is an economic theory that helps to explain the problems that arise when principals (owners) and agents (workers) have divergent interests. If agents prefer to act in their own self-interests, the outcomes may be detrimental to their principals. For example, picture a situation in which a principal offers an incentive of $100 to software developers for every computer virus they identify and remove. If one of the software developers decides to insert *his own viruses* into the software so that he can "remove" the virus to earn the extra income, he is acting in his own self-interests, to the detriment of his principal (organization). His goal (of maximizing his income) and his principal's goals (of keeping the software virus-free) are at odds.

Expectancy theory proposes that an individual will perform at higher levels when he expects that increased *effort* will lead to increased *performance* and that the performance will lead to outcomes he *values.* If he values the outcomes, *valence* is positive. If he does not value the outcomes, valence is negative. *Instrumentality* is his belief that his performance will *result* in the outcomes. As an example, if a human resource manager decides to set up an ***employee of the month*** recognition and reward program in which he plans to recognize and reward one employee each month for achieving $150,000 in sales, expectancy theory helps to explain his employees' reactions. If an employee believes that his efforts will result in $150,000 in sales and that this accomplishment will lead to the recognition, instrumentality will be achieved. If he considers the employee of the month recognition and reward to be of value (positive valence), he is likely to exert the effort. If he does not value the reward (negative valence), he is unlikely to exert the effort.

Internal Alignment and External Competitiveness

Internal alignment, also known as *internal equity,* refers to the relationship between the jobs, skills, and competencies in a single organization. Managers should be sure the pay structures and compensation systems are equitable, support the organization's strategies, support the workflow, and motivate behavior. Equity issues include whether **procedural justice** perceptions suggest the procedures used to derive the pay systems are considered fair. Issues also include whether **distributive justice** perceptions suggest the outcomes or results of the process are considered fair.

When pay must be reduced or frozen, managers can mitigate perceptions of procedural injustice by candidly explaining company situations in empathetic ways. Imagine a scenario where a company leader gets up in front of his staff and announces a 10 percent pay cut, which he labels "a fact of life." In a second scenario, another company leader gets up in front of his staff and announces the 10 percent pay cut. Then she details sales forecasts and troubles in the economy and in their industry. She says she's going to take a pay cut herself and will work with everyone to develop new strategies to increase sales. She refers to her staff as "family" and tells them that she doesn't want to have to lay anyone off, so this is the only alternative. Which company is much more likely to experience lower productivity, absenteeism, and theft? The first company is more likely to suffer dysfunctional outcomes.[181]

External competitiveness, also known as *external equity,* refers to the relationships between the jobs, skills, and competencies across organizations both within the industry, the geographic location, and outside of the industry. Employees have a variety of ways to assess whether their own pay package is fair, from surveying salary providers on the internet to asking friends. In a **tight labor market**, when there are more jobs than workers, workers who perceive low pay relative to their peers may be more likely to exit their organizations. In a **loose** or **slack labor market**, where there are more workers than jobs, workers who perceive low pay may be less likely to leave. Labor market conditions also impact whether company managers will need to make adjustments to pay to attract top talent. In tight labor markets, they may need to increase pay packages for new hires to attract top talent, while the opposite is true in loose or slack markets.

According to Linda Cox of the Economic Research Institute,[182] "Attracting employees purely through above-market compensation programs may lead to an employee-employer relationship with little emotional connections to the job and the company. Companies without a diligent process of environmental scanning (e.g., external market conditions and internal employee feedback) may be forced to raise salaries to prevent turnover in a reactionary manner. This is usually a short-term solution as there is generally some other driver triggering the employee to look outside of the company (e.g., the number one reason for turnover is dissatisfaction with a supervisor). The hard costs of total rewards programs include the compensation and benefits offered, retirement plan matching, profit sharing, paid time off, and vesting over time. The softer costs relate to internal equity, career development opportunities, recognition, job autonomy, effective leadership, collaborative peers, and overall culture."

"Like any other business function that requires on-going assessment and alignment, high performing organizations with engaged workforces have transparent compensation communications that reflect the realities of balancing compensation. These employers are proactive and guide the employees through information and communications on a decision framework, explaining the complexities of compensation decisions in a user-friendly, intuitive manner. The explanations focus on how the programs align the employee needs based on their demographic preferences and the business imperative to have standardization of scale that enables effective talent management."

Compensating Special Groups

Compensation ranges widely depending on the value of the job to the organization. Less complex *entry-level* jobs that are filled by unskilled workers pay less than more complex jobs that are filled by workers with greater skills, know-how, decision-making, and accountability. Entry level jobs such as order entry or customer service jobs tend to pay by the hour and the pay may be as little as minimum wage. The U.S. minimum wage is $7.25, so at minimum (and unless the state or municipality in which the worker lives pays higher), workers in the United States are paid $7.25 per hour.

Minimum hourly wages vary significantly around the world. The 2019 table below[183] offers a sample of some of the current wage rates, adjusted to U.S. dollars at purchasing power parity.

Country	Wage	Purchasing power parity	Country	Wage	Purchasing power parity
Australia	14.14	10.77	Japan	7.61	7.13
Luxembourg	13.14	10.67	U.S.	7.31	6.63
New Zealand	11.28	8.91	S. Korea	6.71	6.62
France	11.24	10.45	Slovenia	5.55	6.78
Netherlands	11.01	10.01	Spain	5.07	5.57
Ireland	10.87	8.75	Malta	4.09	6.01
Germany	10.06	9.75	Turkey	2.87	5.89
United Kingdom	9.74	8.67	Brazil	1.43	1.91
Canada	9.06	7.86	Russia	.94	1.87

In *sales* jobs, incentives in the form of commissions are often part of the compensation package. Salespeople are paid according to the sales they achieve and may be paid at an hourly plus commission, salary plus commission, or commission only plan. For example, realtors in Florida are paid when they close on a home a pre-negotiated commission. In Florida, the commission is typically three percent of the sale of the home for each side of a transaction (either the buyer's realtor or the seller's realtor). So, the buyer's realtor could expect to earn $6,000 (less any broker's fees) on the sale of a $200,000 home.

Some jobs are considered *contingent* positions. These positions are either part-time or temporary or both. Examples of contingent positions include free-lance work, work as independent contractors, consultants and temporary employees. Pay for contingent workers varies by the contracted rates between the contingent workers and the contracting organization. When a contingent worker's output is highly valued, the pay is higher than when the work is less valued. A temporary staff person filling in as a cashier during the holiday season may only earn minimum wage, for example, while a strategic consultant may earn several hundred thousand dollars or more upon completion of the project.

Higher level *executives* are often paid a salary (specific annual dollar amount) with benefits and / or bonuses. The higher level the employee, the greater the bonus will be expected.[184] Some of the most highly paid people in the United States are *private equity managers.* Private equity is a source of investment capital. It comes from high net worth individuals and firms that purchase shares of private companies or they take public companies private. In the process, much money is to be made. "There are more private equity managers who make at least $100 million annually than investment bankers, top financial executives, and professional athletes combined."[185] Private equity contributes to inequality between the rich and the poor, which is why presidential candidates such as Elizabeth Warren complained about them in 2019, likening them to vampires.

At the *chief executive officer* level, the pay package may be quite high. CEOs of the 225 Fortune 500 organizations with more than 14 million workers and $6.3 trillion in revenue in the United States earned $11.5 million annually on average in 2016, which was an 8.5 percent increase over the previous year.[186] According to another survey, CEOs of 350 of the largest U.S. firms averaged $15.6 million per year and between 1978 and 2016, inflation-adjusted pay for CEOs increased by 937 percent! CEOs earn anywhere from about two times to around 5,000 times their workers.[187] In 2016, average workers in the United States made around $58,000 per year, so CEOs of these large firms made around 268 times what average workers earned. The next highest country with a comparable ratio of CEO to average worker pay is India, with CEO pay at 229 times average workers.[188]

Founders Versus Hired CEOs

When determining whether these pay levels are equitable, people often consider first whether the CEO is a founder or one hired after the founder stepped down. Because founders are the entrepreneurs directly responsible for all aspects of the start of the business, people often give them more leeway when assessing the fairness of their pay packages. They may be more skeptical of hired CEOs.

CEO Pay: Is It Fair?

When judging whether the pay packages of CEOs are fair, employees may question whether they work 268 times as hard as average workers or whether their performance merits such high pay levels. They may take into account pay for CEOs in other companies, the CEO's qualifications, the stress levels and relatively low tenure in CEO positions, or their unique contributions to the visions, missions, and strategies of their organizations.

Not all CEOs earn such lavish salaries, which includes even those who founded their organizations. Billionaire Warren Buffett, founder of Berkshire Hathaway, makes $100,000 annually, which is about 1.87 times the average salary of $53,510 of his workers.[189]

Nonprofit CEO Pay

Median pay for CEOs of nonprofit organizations is much lower than CEO pay in for-profit industries in Fortune 500 companies, averaging around $100,000 per year for most industries.[190] Exceptions are in universities and hospitals. CEO pay for nonprofits tends to vary as a function of the organization's size as CEOs of larger organizations earn higher salaries.

CEO Pay in Nonprofit World[191]

Industry	Count	Mean $	Median $	S.D. $	25th percentile $	75th percentile $
Arts, Culture and Humanities	4,728	97,382	70,820	114,155	48,651	109,528
Education (excluding universities)	5,236	116,832	89,732	119,328	59,408	140,344
Universities	532	260,220	232,516	169,692	140,233	344,834
Environmental and animals	2,476	104,587	78,967	149,705	54,472	117,565
Health (excluding hospitals)	8,066	155,330	107,374	216,817	71,604	171,095
Hospitals	1,061	616,104	357,708	816,340	168,817	714,050
Human Services	22,197	107,877	84,660	112,989	58,017	127,336
International and Foreign Affairs	1,193	133,894	93,000	124,983	56,160	161,762
Public, Societal Benefit	16,496	163,426	105,770	254,817	65,962	179,696
Religion-related	2,375	82,133	63,203	92,383	43,217	94,100
Mutual/Membership Benefit	514	188,723	111,462	418,785	59,893	182,619

Golden Parachutes

Sometimes compensation seems unfair. Outsized lump sums paid to executives upon their departures, which are referred to as "**golden parachutes**," are often scrutinized when the executives exit their organizations amid accusations of misconduct or poor performance. When the former CEO of Fox News, Roger Ailes, was accused of multiple claims of sexual harassment, he allegedly departed with a golden parachute of $40 million.[192] The former CEOs of embattled companies like Wells Fargo and United Airlines also left with golden parachutes in the midst of allegations of inappropriate and unethical actions.[193]

The original intent of golden parachutes was not to serve as payoffs to remove CEOs who have failed their organizations. The original intent of creating golden parachute packages was to protect executives at risk of terminations in the wake of the corporate takeovers of the 1980s. They were also used to ensure that shareholders would not lose out on valuable merger and acquisition deals by serving as enticements for top management to agree to the merger or acquisition.[194]

Building a Pay Structure

A pay structure refers to the array of pay rates for different skills or work within a single organization. Included within the structure are the number of levels, differences between those levels, and criteria used to establish the differences between levels. According to the International HR Forum,[195] HR managers can build a pay structure in ten steps.

1. *Establish a compensation philosophy.* What is your desired market position? Does an organization want to lag, meet, or lead the market in compensation packages? At the outset, we noted that Amazon decided to lead the market when it established its $15 minimum wage.
2. *Gather market data.* Who are your competitors and how well are they compensating their employees? For example, if a company is in retail automobile sales, how are other retailers in the same industry paying their employees? Often companies choose to be "competitive" by adopting similar pay structures to their competitors. Information can be found on websites such as Indeed.com, Salary.com, Glassdoor.com, government websites, and the O*Netonline.org.
3. *Identify benchmark jobs.* Benchmark jobs are those found across many organizations, such as administrative assistant, manager, clerk, driver and accountant. Benchmark jobs are easy to identify and match, given multiple sources within and across industries for those common positions. Be sure to include geographic considerations, such as relatively high or low cost of living conditions. For example, employees working in companies in places with a very high cost of living, such as New York City, would expect higher wages than those in places with a relatively low cost of living, such as in a small rural city in Alabama.
4. *Measure your market position.* If you have multiple benchmark jobs, calculate the average pay for each of the positions across industries and within your industry. How much is the average accounting manager paid?
5. *Calculate the compa-ratio.* The compa-ratio is the ratio of your data to the market. If the ratio is 100, you're fully comparable, while a number

below 100 is *under market* and a number above 100 is *over market.* Managers often identify key positions in their organizations and pay over market for those, while remaining at or below the market for less valuable positions.

6. *Check your budget.* Calculate the average difference between your current scale and the market. Consider your internal budget constraints, your ability to pay, inflation and market rates, and the average market movement in your surveys. Certain "hot" jobs, such as jobs in cybersecurity, may be rising in value in the market, so factor these expectations in based on trends accordingly.
7. *Start allocating.* Build a model for your organization, ideally with the number of incumbents in each pay grade. Using your overall percentage of market (step 5) and your budget number (step 6), start increasing your scale. How close can you get to 100 percent of the market? Do you need to tweak the pay for certain positions or job families? A **job family** is a series of related job titles with progressively higher levels of impact, knowledge, abilities, skills, competencies, and related factors.
8. *Final adjustments.* Does your pay structure make sense? Is it equitable between jobs within job families, within departments, between departments, and in the overall organization relative to the external market?
9. *Management approval.* Review your compensation structure with management, presenting your rationale, budget, and overall market comparisons.
10. *Communicate.* Be transparent on your compensation structure, the effort you put into developing the structure, how and whom benchmarked, and how equitable the structure is both internally and externally in the marketplace.

Job Evaluation: Point Method

One method of evaluating the pay within jobs is called the point method. In the point method, managers consider the *skill, effort, responsibilities,* and *working conditions* and determine a point value for the levels of each for each position in your organization. Skill refers to items such as education, experience, and ability. Effort may be mental or physical. Responsibilities could be supervisory or fiscal. Working conditions include items such as location, hazards, or extremes in the environment. Jobs with a greater number of points would correspond to higher levels of pay.

See the table below for an example off the point factor method. As you will notice, the evaluator considers education and job knowledge to be the most important, while working conditions is the least important variable. The "factors" correspond to pre-determined criteria. For example, for the education factor, 1 could equal a high school degree and 5 could be a terminal (doctorate) degree. 2, 3, and 4 would be degrees between high school and the terminal degree. Once employees' positions are evaluated, points are assigned and those with the greatest number of points are paid the most highly.

	Point values				
Factor	1	2	3	4	5
Education	10	20	30	40	50
Experience	8	16	24	32	40
Skill	6	8	10	12	14
Effort	8	16	24	32	40
Responsibility	10	15	20	25	30
Working conditions	5	6	7	8	9
Job knowledge	10	20	30	40	50

Job Evaluation: Job Classification

Another method is the job classification method, which is typically used in larger organizations, civil service, nonprofit agencies, colleges or universities and the government. In the job classification system, managers define the duties, responsibilities, tasks, and authority levels of each job. They group similar jobs together and create a hierarchy of jobs by their comparable values within the organizations and then attach pay grades. For example, in the administrative staff (secretarial) family of positions, the job classification may contain level 1, level 2, and level 3 administrative staff positions. Level 1 is the entry level; level 2 is the middle-level; and level 3 is the top level in the administrative family. The pay for level 1 may range from $25,000 to $35,000, while the pay for level 2 may range from $32,000 to $42,000 and the pay for level 3 may range from $40,000 to $55,000. As you will notice, some overlap may exist between levels as a new hire in one level may be paid just under a person who's in a lesser level with many years of tenure in the organization. Some companies may have many levels within families, while others may prefer to use a **broadbanding** technique where the numbers of salary grades are consolidated into fewer, but broader pay ranges.

Legal Constraints on Direct Compensation

When establishing pay structures and compensation systems, managers should monitor protected groups based on Title VII, the Americans with Disabilities Act, and the Age Discrimination in Employment Act to be sure disparities are not adversely impacting the workforce.

Fair Labor Standards Act

One important law impacting compensation systems in the United States is the Fair Labor Standards Act (FLSA). The FLSA sets the minimum wage, child labor laws, overtime, and governs internships.

Minimum Wage

The minimum wage in the United States is $7.25 per hour, yet if the state minimum wage is greater than the federal level, employees must be paid at the higher level. For example, in California, the minimum wage as of 2020 is $12 per hour. Employees in California can therefore expect to receive at least $12 per hour for their contributions to their organizations. In San Francisco, the 2020 minimum wage is $15.59 per hour, which is relatively high when compared to other U.S. cities due to its relatively high cost of living.

Child Labor

Younger individuals must be at least eighteen years of age or more for hazardous positions, sixteen years or more for manufacturing, mining or transportation positions, and fourteen years or more for most other jobs. Children who are fourteen or fifteen years of age cannot work during the hours in which the local school system is in session. They are expected to be in school at that time, even if they are home-schooled, married, or excused from school.

Overtime

As of January 1, 2020, workers who earn less than $35,568 per year, or $684 per week, are guaranteed overtime protection. Employers have the option of using nondiscretionary bonuses and incentive payments (including commissions) to satisfy up to 10 percent of the standard salary level so long as these are paid at least annually.

The FLSA provides an exemption from both minimum wage and overtime pay if employees are considered executive, administrative, professional or outside sales employees. Certain computer employees are also considered exempt from the law. To qualify for exemption, employees must meet certain tests regarding their job duties and be paid on a salary basis at not less than $684 per week.

Highly compensated employees are those making a total annual compensation of $107,432 or more. A highly compensated employee is deemed exempt if: (1) The employee earns total annual compensation of $107,432 or more, which includes at least $684 per week paid on a salary or fee basis; (2) The employee's primary duty includes performing office or non-manual work; and (3) The employee customarily and regularly performs at least one of the exempt duties or responsibilities of an exempt executive, administrative or professional employee. As an example, an employee may qualify as an exempt highly compensated executive if the employee customarily and regularly directs the work of two or more other employees, even though the employee does not meet all of the other requirements in the standard test for exemption as an executive.

Non-exempt employees who work more than forty hours in a work week are entitled to time and a half for the time after the first forty hours. For example, a non-exempt employee who earns $10 per hour who works 60 hours will be entitled to ($10 x 40 hours) + ($15 x 20 hours) = $700 that week. There is no limit to the number of hours an employee who is sixteen years of age or older may work. Averaging the hours over two or more weeks is not permitted. In other words, if an employee worked 65 hours in one week and 35 the next, the employer is barred from averaging the two weeks' total of 100 hours to 50 hours each and paying only 20 hours of overtime instead of 25 hours for week one. Employees in executive, administrative, and professional positions are exempt from overtime rules. Doctors, lawyers, and teachers are examples in the professional category.

To be exempt, they must meet the following conditions: (1) the employee must be compensated on a salary basis at a rate at or above $684 per week; (2) the employee's *primary duty* must be managing the enterprise, or managing a department of the enterprise; (3) the employee must regularly direct the work of two or more other full-time employees; and (4) the employee must have authority to hire or fire. Many class-action lawsuits have centered on the "primary duty," as employers often attempt to avoid paying overtime, while employees are interested in maximizing their paychecks.

Internships

According to the U.S. Government Department of Labor, courts have used the primary beneficiary test to determine whether an intern or student is an employee under the FLSA. The primary beneficiary test allows courts to examine the economic reality of the intern-employer relationship to determine which party is the "primary beneficiary" of the relationship. Courts have identified the following seven factors as part of the test:[196]

1. The extent to which the intern and the employer clearly understand that there is no expectation of compensation. Any promise of compensation, express or implied, suggests that the intern is an employee—and vice versa.
2. The extent to which the internship provides training that would be similar to that which would be given in an educational environment, including the clinical and other hands-on training provided by educational institutions.
3. The extent to which the internship is tied to the intern's formal education program by integrated coursework or the receipt of academic credit.
4. The extent to which the internship accommodates the intern's academic commitments by corresponding to the academic calendar.
5. The extent to which the internship's duration is limited to the period in which the internship provides the intern with beneficial learning.
6. The extent to which the intern's work complements, rather than displaces, the work of paid employees while providing significant educational benefits to the intern.
7. The extent to which the intern and the employer understand that the internship is conducted without entitlement to a paid job at the conclusion of the internship.

Courts consider the primary beneficiary test to be flexible, so whether a student or intern should be considered an employee under the FLSA depends on the unique circumstances of the case. Students or interns who are deemed employees are entitled to both minimum wage and overtime under FLSA. If they are not deemed employees, they are not entitled to minimum wage or overtime.

Volunteering

What happens when an employer wants to demonstrate its corporate social responsibility by rewarding employees who engage in charitable work with bonuses or other incentives? Are the hours an employee contributes to the community doing charitable work subject to the provisions of the Fair Labor Standards Act?

On March 14, 2019, the United States Department of Labor and Wage Hour Division (DOL) responded to an inquiry by an employer who wanted to know whether the hours employees contributed under its volunteer program were subject to the FLSA. Under the program, employees could volunteer for charitable programs of their choice during non-working hours and the employer would award a bonus to certain participating employees at the end of the year.

The DOL determined that because the program was completely *voluntary* and the employees had volunteered at *non-profit charitable, civic, humanitarian or public-interest organization,* the employer was not subject to minimum wage and overtime payments of the FLSA. If employees were compelled to contribute or the conditions of their employment would be negatively impacted if they did not contribute volunteer hours, then the FLSA would apply. Also, if employees contributed volunteer hours to for-profit organizations, the FLSA would apply.

Furthermore, the DOL noted that employers may consider an employee's participation in a volunteer program as a factor in determining bonuses or raises. Financial incentives are acceptable so long as the (1) volunteering is optional; (2) declining to volunteer will not adversely affect one's employment conditions; and (3) the financial incentive is not guaranteed.

The Equal Pay Act

A second important law impacting U.S. compensation is the Equal Pay Act. This act states that men and women in "substantially equal" jobs in terms of skill, effort, responsibilities, or working conditions must be paid the same. Job content, not job titles, determine whether jobs are considered "substantially equal." Exceptions are legal when pay differentials are based on seniority, merit (better performance), quantity and quality of work, or another factor other than sex. The latter includes education, experience, and credentials.

The Lilly Ledbetter Pay Act modified the Equal Pay Act in 2009 as follows: when pay disparities occur, employees have the right to file suit within 180 days of the last pay violation.

Gender Pay Gap

Women are paid less than men in all countries of the world. These pay differences may be based on their personal choices, as some women may choose jobs that typically pay lower, such as administrative positions or K-12 teaching positions. They may work fewer hours, due to traditional gender roles associated with childcare duties. They may leave the workplace to watch their children for a few years. Or they may not lean in for promotions when opportunities arise. According to Warren Farrell,[197] author of "Why Men Earn More: The Startling Truth behind the Pay Gap," women often put a premium on flexibility (25 – 35 hour work weeks and proximity to home), autonomy, fulfillment and safety. Farrell also noted that men average more hours and they are more likely to take dirtier, more dangerous, and outdoor jobs (such as garbage collecting, trucking and construction). They are also more likely to travel for their jobs, to relocate, and to train for technical jobs with fewer people.

Do these findings mean that discrimination does not persist? No. We still have evidence of some more insidious reasons behind pay gaps between males and females, including the glass ceiling to female advancement or the "old boys' network." An old boys' network refers to an informal system of support and friendship through which men use their positions of influence and prior school or work connections to help their male peers advance in the workplace.

According to the Organization for Economic Cooperation and Development (2018), variations persist globally. See the table below.

Women's Pay Gap as a Percentage of Men's Pay

Country	Wage gap percent	Country	Wage gap percent	Country	Wage gap percent
Austria	15.67*	S Korea	34.62	Sweden	13.42
Belgium	4.67	Mexico	16.49	Switzerland	14.76
Canada	18.22	New Zealand	7.15	Turkey	6.88
Denmark	5.73	Norway	7.12	United Kingdom	16.84
Germany	15.51	Poland	9.42	United States	18.17
Greece	4.49	Romania	1.55		
Ireland	10.61	Slovak Republic	15.04		
Israel	19.28	Slovenia	5		
Japan	24.52	Spain	11.54	*OECD Avg	13.89

*For every $100 a man earns, females in Austria average $84.33

Legal Constraints on Indirect Compensation

Social Security Act of 1935: Requires that companies cover employees under a comprehensive program of retirement, survivor, disability, and health benefits. Employees contribute 6.2 percent of their pay (up to a cap of $132,900 in 2019) to social security, which is equally matched by their employers. Employees pay 1.45 percent of their pay to Medicare (with no cap), which is also matched by their employer. Individuals whose pay exceeds $200,000 pay 1.9 percent to Medicare for the amount they earn over $200,000, while married contributors pay 1.9 percent to Medicare for earnings over $250,000. This amount is also matched by their employers.

Workers' Compensation Laws: Requires that employers finance a variety of benefits (i.e., lost wages, medical benefits, survivor benefits, and rehabilitation services) for employees with work-related illnesses or injuries on "no-fault" basis.

Federal Unemployment Tax: Requires that employers pay taxes to cover laid-off employees for up to 39 weeks (additional Act -FUTA- extensions possible in times of high unemployment).

Consolidated Omnibus Budget Reconciliation Act (COBRA): Requires employers to provide access to health care coverage in particular instances when COBRA coverage would otherwise be terminated. Cost of coverage may be completely passed on to worker. Administrative record-keeping fees also may be charged.

Family and Medical Leave Act (FMLA): Requires employers with 50 or more employees to continue providing health care coverage to employees who are on the FMLA Act of 1993 (FMLA) unpaid leave (up to 12 weeks per year).

Health Insurance Portability and Accountability Act (HIPAA): Provides benefits for working Americans and their families with pre-existing medical conditions.

Employee Retirement Income Security Act (ERISA): Sets minimum standards for most voluntarily established pension and health plans.

Conclusion

Managers may use pay as a means of attracting employees, yet pay is not the only means. Other factors important to employees include whether the job gives employees a sense of mastery, autonomy and purpose, according to Daniel Pink. To establish effective compensation systems, managers need to be sure such systems attract employees, motivate them to work hard, and comply with local, national, and any applicable international laws. Managers should structure pay systems to ensure they are both internally equitable and externally competitive.

QUESTIONS FOR REVIEW

1. What is the Fair Labor Standards Act?

2. What is the difference between a defined benefit and a defined contribution pension plan?

3. Go to the internet to the website of the OECD. List other countries in which Fortune 500 CEOs are paid as much as U.S. CEOs relative to average workers.

4. If two people work for the same company doing the exact same thing and have the same background and experience - but they are located in different offices (one is in Florida and the other is in Maryland), must they be paid the same under the Equal Pay Act?

5. What are the advantages and disadvantages of increasing the minimum wage to $15 per hour?

6. What are the advantages and disadvantages of keeping the minimum wage in the U.S. "as is?"

7. What are some reasons behind the male/female pay gap?

8. What percentage of an employees' pay do employers pay into social security?

9. Is there a cap on social security? Medicare?

10. What are several ways to address the social security deficit?

APPLICATIONS

1. Will Social Security Survive?

As recently reported in *Forbes*,[198] social security has a $2.8 trillion trust fund, which was built up by baby boomers over generations of working. With tax revenues, earnings, and principal from the trust fund, social security should be solvent until 2034. Without additional revenue, the social security fund will only be able to pay out 77 percent of what it has promised to recipients. Currently, anyone born in 1961 or later can receive their full social security benefits at the age of 67. The federal administration has four choices: (1) increase the cap of $128,400; (2) increase the percentage paid of 6.2 percent; (3) increase the retirement age; or (4) ignore all three options and let what happens happen. What should they do? Who will be impacted with each of the four decisions?

2. CEO Pay

Conduct a web search to identify the average pay for the current year for chief executive officers of Fortune 500 organizations. Now identify the average pay for workers in the United States. What percentage of CEO pay is average worker pay?

CASE STUDIES

1. Pay Equity Survey

Since the passing of the Lily Ledbetter Fair Pay Act in 2009, organizations are becoming increasingly aware of the need to conduct internal pay equity studies. A pay equity study can be conducted in a variety of ways, but all such studies involve an assessment of the current salaries of employees in various job classifications. Those who conduct pay equity studies may use a series of regression analyses to analyze relationships between predictors of salary predictors and the salary outcomes. Such regressions include predictors such as the tenure in the organization, the job level and category, the highest degree attained, and years of work experience overall. Regressions are initially conducted by isolating the predictors and outcomes of the reference group (always white males). Next, regressions are generated for the comparison groups (women and minorities). Based on such analyses, many organizations have found that the salaries of women and minorities are lower than those of white men in comparable positions.

As an example, the American Associate of University Professors conducted a pay equity study in a large U.S. public university, finding that many women and minorities were being paid "below the regression line," which basically means that they were being paid less than the rate they could have expected if they were white males. The results of the study were used to increase the salaries of women and minorities to achieve equity.

The authors of the study noted that "a particularly unhappy white-male associate professor of physics explained that he and a woman faculty member had been hired at the same time six years earlier with what he admitted were equal credentials. They had both been promoted the same year, four years after hire. He had been paid $1,300 more annually than she until the gender equity adjustment. Under the remedy, she would be making $300 more than he was making. In the six years since their hire, he had made $7,800 more than she. At $300 more a year, it would take her twenty-six years to merely catch up. He was not bothered when the inequity was in his favor, but when the tables turned in a non-stereotypical direction, he felt the injustice keenly."[199]

1. Go to the Internet for information on the Lily Ledbetter Fair Pay Act in 2009. How did the Lily Ledbetter Fair Pay Act change the Equal Pay Act?

2. What are the benefits of conducting a pay equity study? What are the drawbacks from an organization's perspective?

2. Is CEO Pay in the U.S. Too High?

CEOs of Fortune 500 organizations in the United States make more money relative to their average workers than CEOs in any other country of the world. But is their pay justified? In 2016, the board of directors at Coca-Cola increased the salary of its CEO Muhtar Kent by 20 percent, to $17.6 million, despite the fact that in the same year earnings plunged by 11 percent. That same year, Humana's pretax income dropped by 36 percent, while CEO Bruce Broussard's salary tripled, increasing $4.8 million to $17 million. Yet the salaries of CEOs Kent and Broussard are dwarfed by railroad powerhouse CSX's CEO Hunter Harrison. When he agreed to take over CSX, 72-year-old Harrison demanded a four-year, stock and cash pay package that would cost $230 million. Such an astounding pay package no doubt stunned his predecessor, who only made $39.8 million in total at CSX over the prior four years.

What impressive feat did Harrison pull off at his previous stint as the CEO of the Canadian Pacific Railroad? He engineered a massive cost-cutting program by reducing the size of his workforce by 34 percent while increasing the number of cars per train by 25 percent.

1. What factors should be considered in the evaluation of CEO pay?

2. How does CEO pay compare with the pay of star athletes or celebrity movie stars?

3. Following the financial collapse in the United States around 2008, the federal government stepped in and reduced the compensation in banks that borrowed from the government to $500,000 per year. Needless to say, the banks prioritized paying off their loans. Should such a limitation be put in place for all U.S. CEOs?

3. Should the Minimum Wage Be Increased?

During the Great Depression in 1938, President Franklin Delano Roosevelt initiated a federal minimum wage in the United States of 25 cents per hour. Since then, the wage has been increased 22 times and currently stands at $7.25 per hour.[200] Some states have higher minimum wages, so employers must pay higher minimum wages in those states. Living on $7.25 per hour and working forty hours per week would result in a pre-tax income of $15,080 per year. Is it possible in any part of the United States for a single person or a family to live on such low annual wages? Some people say no – and many are part of an effort to raise the minimum wage to $15 per hour. They argue that by raising the minimum wage, the federal government will stimulate the economy, putting more money in the pockets of the people will increase spending. Opponents argue that businesses cannot afford to increase wages. They believe that if the minimum wage is increased, business will be forced to close, reduce their workforces, or automate their services. In the long run, opponents believe that raising the minimum wage will have a detrimental effect on the overall health of the economy.

1. Should the federal government raise the minimum wage to $15? Why or why not?

2. What other options does the federal government have to address this issue?

4. Should College Athletes be Compensated?

California recently passed the "Fair Pay to Play Act," which will go into effect in 2023. Rather than playing for free, university athletes will be compensated. Other states may soon follow suit. One justification for paying university athletes is that *everyone else* who is involved in university athletics is making money. Why shouldn't the athletes also make money? Nick Saban, Alabama's head football coach is the highest paid – at $8.3 million.[201] Others make at least a million.

1. Should university athletes be compensated?

2. Discuss and debate.

Chapter 9: Benefits and Incentives

Introduction

In 2016, the Consumer Financial Protection Bureau, the Office of the Comptroller of the Currency, and the city and county of Los Angeles fined Wells Fargo $150 million for more than 5,000 of the bank's former employees who opened around 2 million fake accounts.[202] What would propel so many employees to open fake accounts? Sales bonuses. "For every clever person who goes to the trouble of creating an incentive scheme, there is an army of people, clever and otherwise, who will inevitably spend even more time trying to beat it," says Charlie Munger, vice chairman of Berkshire Hathaway.

As portended through agency theory, in the principal agent relationship, oftentimes agents (employees) engage in deceptive practices to maximize their own self-interests at the expense of their principals (employers). Accordingly, when employers create incentive systems, they should place themselves into the shoes of their employees and consider, "how could I beat this system?" Wells Fargo employees saw the opportunity to maximize their self-interests by opening fake bank accounts (apparently under-the-radar), earning undeserved sales bonuses.

Objectives:

After reading this chapter, you should be able to:

- Explain several types of individual incentive, commission, and bonus plans.
- Identify and differentiate between gainsharing plans.
- Articulate the reasons for pay-for-performance (PFP) failures.
- Understand ways to enhance PFP successes.
- Explain a variety of types of employee benefits.

As the old saying goes, "you get what you pay for." For centuries, the employer employee relationship has been based on the understanding of a contractual relationship between the employer who needs a job done and the employee who is willing to do that job. The two parties agree upon a wage and the work commences. Once complete, the exchange occurs as the employer pays the employee. Sometimes, the employer may feel that extra motivation is needed to add to sales, increase satisfaction, or generate greater customer satisfaction. In these cases, the employer may offer an incentive to the employee to further enhance his efforts.

Employers have had many successes with "**pay-for-performance**" (PFP) plans. Rather than paying a straight salary or hourly wages, some employers have turned to pay-for-performance plans where they incentivize workers at the individual, group, or company levels. These plans have been successful when strategically and carefully planned and implemented. New companies that placed a higher value on their employees and that included high levels of organizational-performance-based rewards had a significantly higher survival rate (of 92 percent) than organizations that were low on both dimensions.[203] The latter had a survival rate of only 34 percent.

At times, however, PFP plans are not successful in achieving goals. The following are six reasons why this problem occurs:

1. Poor perceived connection between performance and pay.
2. The level of performance-based pay is too low relative to base pay. The cost of more highly motivating programs may be prohibitive.
3. Lack of objective, countable results for most jobs, requiring the use of performance ratings.
4. Faulty performance appraisal systems, with poor cooperation from managers, leniency bias in the appraisals, and resistance to change.
5. Union resistance to such systems and to change in general. Unions tend to favor seniority systems, so oftentimes they challenge pay-for-performance incentive-based systems.
6. Poor (or negative) relationship between rewarded outcomes and corporate performance measures.

Individual Pay-for-Performance Plans

Pay-for-performance plans appeal to some employees more than others. Extraverts and high performers tend to like them, as many PFP plans are based on bonuses, incentives, and commissions that reward diligence, persistence, and sales. Americans often appreciate PFP plans, which is likely due to a tradition built from pride in a strong work ethic and value for achievement and recognition, along with high levels of individualism.

Most employees prefer straight salaries (63 percent), followed by individual incentives (22 percent) and organization-level incentives (12 percent).[204] This finding is likely attributed to a general desire to mitigate risk and maximize security.

Dramatic changes in performance can occur when pay is contingent on it, particularly in sales positions, as switching from salary-based or hourly pay to commission-only systems inspires salespeople to work harder to be sure they can pay their bills. Consider a situation in a furniture store where the salespeople are each paid a $40,000 annual salary. Customers come into the store, peruse the various floor models, and consider whether to buy. The salespeople may or may not approach them. They may or may not close the sale. Whether salaried employees approach and greet customers to show them around and eventually close the sale or not, they know that their paycheck will be coming. The dollar amount of the check will not vary as a function of whether they greeted and worked with customers. So, on days when they're not supervised, the following question arises: will they be **intrinsically motivated** to help? **Extrinsic motivators** in extra incentives are non-existent if the employee feels that she will retain her job regardless of whether she waits on customers. In these types of situations, switching to either a salary-plus-commission, commission-only, or hourly wage-plus-commission plan is highly effective. By switching to a **commission** plan, employers can add an extrinsic motivation for salespeople to work harder. A sample commission-only plan in a furniture business would be to pay employees 5 percent of all sales. So if an employee sells $2,000 one day, she makes $100.

Individual PFP plans should have three characteristics. They should be: (1) tailored to the particular work situation; (2) perceived as attainable; and (3) equitable with expected outcomes. As pointed out in Chapter 8, expectancy theory applies.

Expectancy/Instrumentality Theory

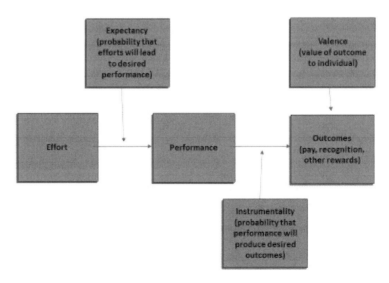

Merit pay plans are commonly used plans where increases in pay are based on appraisals of an individual's performance. The pay increase is usually in the form of a percentage, which is folded into an individual's pay along with any relevant **cost-of-living allowances** (COLAs). Cost-of-living increases are increases given to employees to keep up with inflation. For example, if inflation in the economy increases by 3 percent, the price of goods and services have increased, so employers will often increase their employees' base pay levels to keep up.

When merit pay is tied into base pay as a **percentage**, the increase will benefit the employee year after year, so long as he remains with his company. For example, if an employee who is making $100,000 per year as a base salary performs well, his company may decide to give him a 5 percent raise, increasing his pay to $105,000. Every year after that, he still retains his 5 percent raise and new salary level of $105,000. If the employee instead receives a $5,000 **lump sum bonus**, in year one he would receive $105,000 and in year two, if he receives no bonus, he would receive his original $100,000 salary. His base pay would remain the same in the lump sum bonus type of an incentive system. For this reason and for the purpose of keeping payroll expenses low, consultants often advise companies to offer lump sum bonus systems instead of percentage increases. Why? They're cheaper in the long-run.

The most challenging problem in individual merit pay systems is ensuring that performance appraisals are accurate. As you will recall from Chapter 6, accurate performance appraisals are valid, reliable, objective, unbiased, based on 360-degree evaluations, and legally defensible in court. Systems that are subjective and based on top-down evaluations are fraught with problems, particularly when **leniency** is an issue. The most lenient raters have high levels of agreeableness, low levels of conscientiousness, low levels of assertiveness, and high levels of discomfort in assessing their subordinates. Managers with high levels of discomfort tend to be those with less experience in conducting performance evaluations. When performance appraisals are compromised, the relationship between merit pay plans and important organizational outcomes, such as increased profits or sales, is minimal.

Employers have a variety of **individual incentive plan** options. These include straight piece-rate plans, differential rates, standard hourly rates, commission plans and draw-plus commission plans. Each of these plans should be tailored to the particular work situation, which in these situations should be at the individual level. In other words, in each of these plans, managers should be able to distinguish the work of a single worker from within his department or group.

In a **piece-rate system**, employees are paid by the piece. If an employee worked in a flower shop producing floral arrangements and is held individually accountable and responsible for each of the floral arrangements she produces, a piece-rate plan could work well. Her employer could pay her a certain dollar amount or percentage per arrangement. For example, if she makes floral arrangements that retail for $25 each, her employer may pay her a $5 incentive per arrangement or 20 percent.

The **differential rate** is another incentive system in which an employer agrees to pay a certain amount below a standard level and another amount above that level in a specified period of time. For example, the employer in the flower shop may agree to pay $5 per arrangement for the first 100 arrangements produced in a single month and $7 per arrangement for any produced beyond the first 100. This incentive motivates workers to work more quickly and productively.

The **standard hourly rate**, which is often called the "Halsey 50/50" plan is a third option. In the standard hourly rate, the standard time for completion of a job is fixed and the rate per hour is determined. If the employee takes more than the set amount of time, then she is paid according to the time rate, which is the time taken multiplied by the rate per hour. If she takes less than the set amount of time, she is paid for the actual time plus she earns a bonus for the amount she saved her company. In the Halsey 50/50 plan, she and her employer would split the bonus amount. In this case, she would be paid for the time rate plus the bonus calculated at a specified percentage (50 percent) of the saved time.

For example, if the standard hourly rate a worker earns is $20 and the standard time to complete a job is 10 hours, then the worker would expect to earn $200 for completion of the job on time. If she completed the job in 11 hours, she would earn $20 x 11 hours, or $220. If she completes the job in 9 hours, she would earn $20 x 9 hours, or $180 plus $20(.5), or $190. Because she has multiple jobs to complete in a week, she would earn more when completing the jobs in less time than that which was budgeted. For example, if she completed 5 jobs in her workweek of 45 hours (9 hours each), she would earn $950. If she completed 4 jobs in 44 hours and started a new job for the last hour, she would earn $880 plus $20 for the last hour, or $900. She earns more by being efficient.

Commission plans are typically used in sales positions. People who work in jobs selling real estate, automobile dealerships, insurance, pharmaceuticals, and retail oftentimes work on a commission basis. A commission is a percentage of the sale. For example, when a salesperson working in an automobile dealership sells a car, he may earn a certain percentage of the sale. For a $20,000 car, he might earn 5 percent, or $1,000. **Draw-plus commission** plans are those that are offered to people who need an early draw from a future commission. For example, in real estate, salespeople may not make any money for the first couple of months as they work with customers and set dates for future closings on residential or commercial properties. They may draw a set amount of money against their future earnings to pay their bills in the present timeframe.

Group Pay-for-Performance Plans

Oftentimes, organizations structure functions and tasks that need to be completed around teams. **Self-managed work teams** are used in technology companies, for example, as a means of producing dynamic and creative innovations in a fast-paced environment. Oftentimes, these teams work very well together, with everyone contributing equally and at high levels of productivity. Companies may reward these highly cohesive teams by giving them **team rewards**, recognizing the contributions and successes of all members of the teams at once. Team rewards work well when teams are cohesive and each member contributes equally to the overall effort.

Gainsharing plans are another group-based option, which reward workers for increased productivity, cost reductions, improved quality and other achievements through regular cash bonuses, usually monthly or quarterly. These plans establish a direct relationship with a company's performance and what it pays its employees and are therefore highly motivating. Effective gainsharing plans can increase employee productivity.[205]

The **Scanlon Plan** is the most common type of gainsharing plan. The Scanlon plan measures the relationship between the sales value of production and labor costs. Managers add sales plus inventory to establish a *sales value of production baseline* and a percentage of *expected labor costs.* When the *actual labor costs* bill comes in, if the actual labor costs are less than the expected labor costs, the savings is split between employees and management and distributed. For example, if the sales value of production baseline is $100,000 and expected labor costs are 40 percent, the expected labor bill will be $40,000. If the actual labor cost bill is $30,000, the $10,000 savings is divided between employees and management.

The **Rucker Plan** is similar to the Scanlon Plan in that it includes the focus on sales value of production and labor costs. The Rucker Plan adds in costs for materials and supplies. Managers add sales and inventory, and then subtract the costs for materials and supplies to establish a *value added baseline.* They then calculate their *expected labor costs,* which is a percentage of the value added. If the *actual labor costs* are less than the expected labor costs, the savings is split between employees and management.

Examples of Scanlon and Rucker

Scanlon Plan	
Sales	90,000
+ Inventory	10,000
Sales Value of Production Baseline	100,000
Expected Labor Costs	40,000 (40%)
Actual Labor costs	30,000 (30%)
Bonus to be distributed	10,000 (10% x 100,000)

Rucker Plan	
Sales	90,000
+ Inventory	10,000
- Purchases (Materials, Supplies, etc.)	20,000
Value Added	80,000
Expected Labor Costs	40,000 (50%)
Actual Labor Costs	20,000 (25%)
Bonus to be distributed	20,000 (25% x 80,000)

Some companies may be hesitant to share specific costs with their employees. Some employees may also find this information difficult to understand. In such cases, some managers have considered offering the **IMPROSHARE** plan. IMPROSHARE, which is short for "improved productivity through sharing" is a plan that is easier to understand than gainsharing plans because they do not require knowledge of cost accounting. IMPROSHARE plans are like Scanlon Plans, with the exception that the *labor costs* in Scanlon Plans are replaced by *standard* *labor hours*. Workers who complete their work in less time than was expected and allocated split the savings with management.

Company-level Pay-for-Performance Plans: Profit-sharing Plans

Another way to boost employee satisfaction and productivity is to offer profit-sharing plans. One such approach is to offer employee stock option plans (ESOPs). Employers offer employees the option to purchase shares of stock in the company, usually at a discount, within a certain period of time. ESOPs are extremely popular in mid-size and larger organizations.

Multiple studies have indicated that workers who belong to employee stock option plans and group-based incentive plans identify more strongly with their organizations than workers who are not affiliated with such plans.[206] "Shared capitalism," which is what researchers have labeled these group and profit-sharing programs, results in "lower turnover, greater loyalty and willingness to work hard, particularly when combined with high-performance policies, low levels of supervision and fixed pay at or above market levels."[207] The strongest benefits resulted from profit-sharing and gainsharing programs. Most workers indicated that ESOP plans, cash incentives, stock, and employee stock pension plans motivated them to work harder.[208] One study found that companies that offer stock options to 80 percent of managers have 25 percent higher returns on assets than those that offer stock options to only 20 percent of managers.[209]

Employee Benefits

Consider the fact that around fifty years ago in the United States, the typical worker was a white male who traveled to work from 9 to 5 and then returned home, unencumbered by emails or keeping up with work occurrences in his off hours. Not only have the demographics changed in the workplace, with a greater representation in higher level roles from women and minorities, but the way work is scheduled and organized varies between organizations, companies, and people. According to the Society for Human Resource Management, **telecommuting** has tripled over the past two decades.[210] People are on-call during the office hours, managing emails, text messages, virtual meetings and other electronic forms of communication. "In short order, we need to be creative and flexible in the way we approach every aspect of human resource management, including by crafting benefits that reflect the changing needs and wants of today's worker."[211]

Employers have competing goals of creating benefits packages that attract top talent while ensuring the costs of the packages do not exceed budgeted allocations. In short, they must consider the most effective and efficient means of appealing to today's diverse workforce. An employee benefits package is an expected component of an overall compensation package. But the costs could spiral out of control if not planned, budgeted, and monitored.

Federally Mandated vs. Voluntary Benefits

One critical function of benefits administration is to identify and budget for the federally-mandated (or "statutory") benefits first, followed by an identification of those voluntary benefits that employees may expect given the benefits offered in other competing organizations. Federally-mandated benefits for employees in the United States discussed in chapter 8 include **social security**, **Medicare**, **COBRA**, and **FMLA**. Additionally, employers must provide **unemployment insurance** and **workers' compensation insurance** to their employees. Unemployment insurance requires that employers pay taxes to cover laid-off employees (for reasons other than performance deficiencies) for up to 39 weeks. Additional extensions are possible during times of high unemployment. Workers' compensation insurance requires that employers finance a variety of benefits (e.g., lost wages, medical benefits, survivor benefits, and rehabilitation services) for employees with work-related illnesses and injuries on a "no-fault" basis. Employers with over fifty employees are also required to provide **healthcare** coverage to their employees under the **Affordable Care Act**.

After budgeting for mandatory benefits, managers can consider benefits that may distinguish their organizations from other organizations. As noted at the outset, Patagonia distinguished itself by offering on-site daycare. Such a benefit is expensive, yet Patagonia leaders felt the return was worth the investment. Benefits managers should conduct a cost-benefit analysis on any non-mandated benefits to determine whether they should be included in the budget and offerings for employees.

Components of a Strategic Benefits Plan

Employees of small "Ma and Pa" type of organizations typically do not receive the benefits packages that are offered in larger organizations, partially attributable to a lack of resources. Yet once companies begin to grow, expectations of competitive benefits packages increase. Competitive benefits packages often include the following components: healthcare plans (including medical, dental, and vision coverage), life insurance and survivor benefits, paid time off, vacation and holidays, paid family and medical leave, and paid sick days. Some organizations go beyond that, offering on-site childcare, on-site medical or dental facilities, sabbaticals, free meals, tuition reimbursement, travel reimbursement, early retirement plans, employee wellness programs, relocation expenses, and housing reimbursements. Sabbaticals are extended periods of leave typically offered to university instructors or other workers to allot time for research or travel. They often last between six months and a year and are usually offered after every seven years worked.

Flexible benefits are becoming popular with organizations as they compete for top talent.[212] At Proctor and Gamble, each employee (of 95,000 global employees) gets between 1 and 2 percent of his or her salary set aside for the benefits of choice. Options range from extra vacation time to financial planning to disability insurance. Hershey's "SmartFlex" offer a variety of leave options for new parents and expanded opportunities to work flexible hours or work from home.

Healthcare

In the United States and due to the fact we do not have universal healthcare (as other developed societies have), employees who work for companies with over fifty full-time employees (or a combination of full-time and part-time employees that equals fifty employees) are subject to the Employer Shared Responsible Provisions of the **Affordable Care Act.** Under these provisions, they must provide healthcare to employees and they must report coverage to the Internal Revenue Service annually. Employers with fifty or fewer employees may be eligible to buy coverage through the Small Business Health Options Program (SHOP).

Benefits managers have a variety of choices in their healthcare offerings. In countries in which healthcare is universally free and accessible, offering supplemental prescription coverage or other supplemental coverage may help them to differentiate themselves from their competitors. In countries in which healthcare is not universally free and available, offering coverage can be attractive to employees. Next, we will examine healthcare in two countries where healthcare is universally available.

Comparisons of Healthcare in Canada, Germany and the United States[213]

Canada has a universal national health insurance program called Medicare. This program is run by the Canadian government and covers its entire population for a well-defined medical benefits package. The program is financed through general taxes on the Canadian population and consumers' co-payments for services are negligible. Healthcare is provided by private organizations and physicians receive payments for their services from the government (single payer) based on a negotiated fee. Hospitals receive global budget payments. This method establishes total expenditure limits for medical services over specified periods of time. The key elements in Canadian healthcare are to (1) keep costs low by keeping payments to physicians and hospitals relatively low; (2) regionalize and restrict access to high tech services, such as services for open heart surgery and organ transplant; and (3) delay treatments.

In Germany, all individuals are required by law to have healthcare insurance. Healthcare premiums are calculated on the basis of income and not the age or number of dependents of the insured. Coverage in Germany is provided through a relatively large number of third-party small and independent plans. Around 500 localized independently-operated sickness funds pay providers directly for services provided to members at negotiated rates. Doctors, dentists, and hospitals negotiate rates and payments from these funds represents around 70 percent of healthcare spending. The central government is responsible for policy and jurisdiction, while the state governments are responsible for hospital planning, supervising the sickness funds, managing state hospitals, and supervising physicians' associations. The key elements in the German system is (1) an assumption that incomes will steadily increase, since medical expenses are expected to increase and incomes fund expenses; and (2) costs will be contained. Because German consumers do not pay directly for their medical expenses, their motivation to contain expenses is not significant.

The United States has no single nationwide system of health insurance. Instead, consumers have the option to purchase health insurance in the private marketplace if health insurance is not provided to them by their employing organizations or the government (for certain groups such as the military). Doctors and physicians are not as restricted to keep costs down, so services can be expensive. Wait times are lower in the United States when compared with Germany and Canada and access to high technology services is more easily attainable (though relatively expensive).

In the United States, consumers may purchase a conventional plan where they are unrestricted in their choice of a healthcare provider. This type of plan reimburses consumers a portion of the costs of the service rendered.

They may instead be part of an HMO (health maintenance organization) or PPO (preferred provider plan). HMOs are pre-paid and in return, they provide comprehensive services for consumers. PPOs require that consumers receive services from a designated list of providers, with whom they have contracted and incentivized to provide lower cost services. Some consumers do not buy insurance, preferring to pay a fee for each service as needed. This choice is risky as healthcare costs can be significant for unexpected health conditions.

Employers often provide health savings accounts (HSA). An HSA is a tax-advantaged savings (and flexible spending) account for current and/or future medical expenses. Consumers can use these accounts to save for eligible out-of-pocket medical, dental, and vision expenses.

Types of Retirement Plans

Another attractive voluntary program that employers may provide are retirement plans. Retirement plans help employees to plan for their future retirement from the workplace. Several types of retirement plans are popular: the defined benefit plan, the defined contribution plan, and hybrid plans. The **defined benefit** plan is a plan where an employee's pension payments are calculated according to his length of service and salary earned at the time of retirement. Federal and state government workers most often receive these plans, which offer tremendous security in retirement. For example, a firefighter may work for a set period of 30 years. Over the last five years of his employment, his pay averaged $75,000 per year. His pension plan may have stipulated that he would receive 90 percent of this average income for the rest of his life, whether he lives for another year or another thirty years. These plans typically include benefits for surviving widows or widowers as well. This type of plan was popular in private industries and universities in the 50s, 60s, and 70s, but with longer life expectancies, most (if not all) private companies and universities have dropped this offering.

Instead, many private organizations offer **defined contribution** (401k type of) retirement plans. In these plans, a portion (or percentage) of an employee's pre-tax paycheck is deposited into an investment fund. Oftentimes, employers "match" the deposit and may even add additional funding. Upon retirement, employees may start withdrawing from their pension plans at their current (usually very low) tax rates (since they are no longer working). Employees cannot collect the amount of their employer's contributions into the fund until they are **vested.** If an employee is 100 percent vested, it means that she owns 100 percent of her employer's contributions into her pension fund. Employers may grant full vesting after a certain agreed upon period of years. A **hybrid** pension fund offers a combination of the defined benefit and defined contribution pension plan.

Conclusion

Employers have a variety of tools that they can use to make themselves attractive to top talent in the marketplace. Pay-for performance incentive plans tend to be popular, yet employers should take care to be sure the systems are carefully developed. Poorly developed PFP plans can hurt organizations' bottom lines and reputations, as we witnessed from several examples in the chapter. Employers further are mandated by the federal government to pay social security and Medicare taxes and to fund workers' compensation and unemployment insurance plans. They further must fund COBRA and FMLA plans. Employers in the United States with over fifty employees must also provide healthcare to their employees. To be attractive to top talent, many employers offer additional voluntary benefits, such as paid time off, vacation time, tuition reimbursement, and more. Such benefits may help employers to attract and retain strong human capital.

QUESTIONS FOR REVIEW

1. What are some of the problems associated with pay for performance plans?

2. Unions prefer seniority systems over pay for performance systems. Why?

3. In merit pay systems, what is the advantage to employers associated with paying employees a lump sum bonus instead of awarding a percentage increase?

4. Define the Scanlon plan. How is it different from the Rucker plan?

5. What is the advantage of IMPROSHARE over the Scanlon and Rucker plans?

6. In what positions are commission systems most likely to be used?

7. When would piece-rate plans be most appropriate?

8. What are the characteristics of individuals who prefer pay-for-performance systems?

9. What is an employee stock option plan?

10. Do profit sharing programs benefit organizations financially?

APPLICATIONS

1. The Scanlon Plan

Calculate the Scanlon Plan

Sales Value of Production (SVOP) = $10,000,000

Total wage bill = $4,000,000

Total wage bill/SVOP = 4,000,000 / $10,000,000 = 40 percent

Operating Month, January	
SVOP	= $950,000
Allowable wage bill	= .40 ($950,000) = $380,000
Actual wage bill	= $330,000
Savings	= $50,000 (available for distribution as a bonus)

If the SVOP in February is $890,000 and the actual wage bill is $316,000, what would be the Scanlon savings?

2. The Empathetic Boss

Jody Kaplan was the operations manager for an educational publishing company. As the manager, she oversaw fifty-two employees and was well-liked by most of them. She considered herself fair, kind, and service-oriented and prided herself on going the extra mile to help her employees whenever she could. She would even dig into her own pockets when her employees ran into money troubles and she rarely even asked for the money back. When people needed time off to help out family members or work on personal troubles, Jody gave them the time off with no questions asked.

Everything seemed to be going well. At the end of the year, Jody began preparing her annual performance evaluations for each of her employees. She ranked them all on a five-point scale based on the tasks they performed. Those who received 5 on the 5-point scales were considered excellent and they received the highest raises. Those who received 4 scores received solid raises, while those who received 3 scores only received cost-of-living adjustments.

When she began to complete Terrence Hayden's appraisal, she paused. Terrence had been a solid performer for the first ten years in his tenure at the company, but over the past year, his family problems had gotten the best of him. His performance was at best considered mediocre. He had serious financial issues due to his son's medical bills and Terrence had to take out two mortgages on his house to try to make ends meet.

Jody decided that she would give Terrence a score of 5, just to help him out. After all, she thought, he would do the same thing in return if they were in each other's shoes. Other employees would certainly appreciate her kindness and empathy for her employees.

She wasn't surprised when Terrence arrived a few days later in her office with a huge smile on his face. "I really don't deserve a 5, Jody. You know I really deserve a 3…if that."

"That's OK Terrence. We support our own here. You're family. Just consider it a gift," Jody replied.

"Thanks. I really can't thank you enough. I appreciate it. The raise will really help me out. I can't wait to share this news with the guys in production."

1. From the company's standpoint, what difficulties might Jody's performance appraisal practices create?

2. Might a forced distribution performance appraisal system overcome the problem that Jody has created? Discuss.

CASE STUDIES

1. Ethical Issues with Pay-for-Performance Incentive Plans

Consider the following cases:

A variety of factors led to the housing bubble in the United States in the early 2000s and the subsequent financial collapse of 2007.[214] One reason related to the incentive plans given to bank employees for mortgages underwritten. Since the banks often bundled mortgages (i.e., securitization) and sold the bundled packages to other organizations (which subsequently purchased insurance on the bundled packages from organizations such as AIG), the incentives to ensure that the mortgages could be repaid by homeowners were not in place. Instead, the incentives to lend money to anyone who requested were great. Subprime mortgages ballooned with the popularity of "no income verification" loans. Following the financial collapse of 2007, several large banks were sued for housing foreclosure fraud. The lawsuits allege common law fraud. Part of the problem is likely attributable to the incentive system that awarded bank employees for expediting foreclosure paperwork, so employees rushed to complete the paperwork often signing off on papers they didn't verify.

Green Giant had to abandon a bonus plan that was intended to reward employees for thoroughly cleaning the peas harvested for its vegetable packages.[215] Employees starting bringing in their own insects, dropping them into the vegetables, and removing them for the incentive pay.

By late 1996, ailing Sunbeam's well-paid new CEO Al Dunlap had fulfilled his mission to turn the company around by laying off 12,000 employees and closing plants.[216] Sunbeam's stock price soared. Then in 1998, the stock price fell from $53 per share to less than $4 and the SEC began to investigate Sunbeam's accounting practices. Dunlap had improved Sunbeam's short-term performance, but he couldn't find a company to purchase Sunbeam, leading the board of directors to terminate him, giving him a golden parachute.

What do all of these cases have in common? What can be done to ensure that incentive plans are in alignment with company strategies?

2. Zombie Companies?

According to the Bank for International Settlements, 12 percent of all companies globally are "zombie" firms with profits lower than the interest payments on their debts. This number has substantially increased over the past twenty years. In the early 1990s, the rate was only 2 percent. Consider that you are working for a zombie organization, so you are severely limited in what you can offer your employees in benefits and incentives. How will you motivate them?

Chapter 10: Unions

Introduction

Imagine a business model in which your organization was notorious for its low service quality, yet still received funding from state subsidies of 14 billion euros each year to remain in operation. Despite such provisions, your organization runs a 3-billion-euro deficit annually and has a rising debt of 45 billion euros. Clearly you must think that your organization is hemorrhaging and will need to close its doors soon. Think again.

You're in France and you oversee France's rail networks and your workers are unionized. They enjoy lifetime employment, free railway passes for their families, automatic pay increases, and a retirement age of 52. As the editors of Bloomberg BusinessWeek disclosed, France's president Emmanuel Macron is not happy about this arrangement.[217] He intends to reduce workers' exorbitant privileges as part of a plan to loosen restrictions on hiring and firing, overhaul education, cut business taxes, and to make changes to pensions, training, and other previously forbidden areas.

Unionized workers have been striking against his proposals. To go on strike is to suspend all work. Garbage collectors, teachers, nurses, and employees in state-owned Air France-KLM have all been striking to protest his plans for austerity. Striking is one of the ways unions flex their muscles against employers when negotiations for better wages and other working conditions fail.

Objectives:

After reading this chapter, you should be able to:

- Recognize and distinguish trends associated with domestic and international unionization.
- Articulate major components of U.S. laws that impact labor unions.
- Understand the conditions that make it likely for workers to want to form or join unions.
- Discuss the means that workers can use to exert power against their organizations when in unions.
- Discuss the options available to employers to exert their power against unions.

Workers globally have a long history of organizing in groups to present a stronger voice to those leading, managing, or overseeing them. People realized long ago that there is power in numbers and the voice of many is more powerful than the voice of one. The freedom to join unions to negotiate with employers and receive better working conditions is a fundamental right that is recognized in many countries around the globe. In the United States, this right is protected by the U.S. Constitution and by U.S. labor laws. **Labor unions** are defined as organized associations of workers, often in trades or professions, which have been formed to protect workers' interests and rights.

A Brief History of Labor Unions and the U.S. Economy

Around the turn of the last century, working conditions in the United States were dismal. Employees worked long hours in unsafe and unhealthy environments for low pay. Only around 7 percent in the nonagricultural private sector were seeking worker protections collectively in unions, however.[218] Labor unions had been representing workers for hundreds of years, yet the workers were not legally protected from discrimination for being in unions by their employers. Discrimination against union members occurred frequently, especially during times of volatile wage negotiations or strikes. Yet that ended in 1935 with the **National Labor Relations Act (NLRA)**, which is also known as the Wagner Act. Under the NLRA, unions were prohibited from discrimination against employees who were interested in forming unions, trying to start unions, or were already unionized.

A powerful union at that time was the **American Federation of Labor (AFL).** The AFL was formed in 1886 by Samuel Gompers as an alliance of *craft unions,* which are unions of people organized based on a specialized craft or trade. The AFL was reluctant to organize unskilled workers, so in 1935, John L. Lewis formed the **Congress of Industrial Organizations (CIO)** to represent unskilled industrialized workers. The AFL clashed with the CIO as both grew in power over the Great Depression and the types of workers each represented began to blur. In 1955, the two organizations merged into the AFL-CIO.

Unions and the Economy

According to the National Bureau of Economic Research,[219] union membership displayed a ∩-shaped pattern over the twentieth century, while the distribution of income displayed a U-shaped pattern. At the beginning of the last century, the top 10 percent of workers earned 41 percent of the pre-tax income. Income inequality declined, and around mid-century, the top 10 percent of workers earned 31 percent of the pre-tax income. That number steadily increased to around 41 percent in 2000.

Unions benefit the least skilled workers the most, so union membership tends to vary as a function of the total productivity levels of unskilled workers. High productivity corresponds to many *unionized* unskilled workers, while low productivity corresponds to fewer. Economists have determined that when the productivity of unskilled workers is high, unions benefit by organizing and demanding generous wages.

Over the past century, as workers shifted from an artisan economy to an assembly line economy, the demand for unskilled workers increased with the need for more workers on the assembly lines. Generous wages for assembly line workers followed. Yet when the assembly line economy started to decline with the information age, the need for unskilled workers declined. Hence, we witnessed the inverse ∩ pattern in membership, which corresponded to a U-shaped pattern in income inequality. In other words, in the height of productivity of the assembly line economy when unionized unskilled workers were demanding generous wages, the income gap between the rich and the poor was smaller.

Union Demographics in the United States

Though the percentage of U.S. workers represented by unions reached as high as 25 percent in the 1970s, in recent times, union membership has declined. According to the Bureau of Labor Statistics,[220] union membership in 2019 was at 10.3 percent of the U.S. population. 14.6 million workers were unionized. In 1983, which is the first year comparable union data were available, 20.1 percent of workers were unionized, or 17.7 million workers. 33.6 percent of *public-sector workers* were unionized, which is more than five times higher than private sector workers. Only 6.2 percent of private sector workers were unionized. The most heavily unionized occupations were in education, libraries, and training. More males were unionized than females and black workers are more likely to be unionized than their white, Asian, or Hispanic counterparts. Of the U.S. states, New York had the highest union membership (23.5 percent), while South Carolina (2.2 percent) and North Carolina (2.3 percent) had the lowest.

Unions tend to win gains when more Democrats are in political office, while they tend to lose when more Republicans are in office. In general, Democrats represent labor, workers' rights, job security, and economic equality while Republicans represent big businesses, the desire for lower corporate taxes, less unionization, and programs that tend to fuel economic inequality.

Why Do Workers Join Unions?

Workers join unions due to perceptions of improvements in their working conditions. When they believe that unions can help them garner bigger paychecks, better hours, longer vacation times, and more security, unions seem attractive.

Workers' perceptions about greater pay levels are accurate. According to the Bureau of Labor Statistics,[221] salaries of nonunionized workers in 2019 were around 80 percent of those of their unionized counterparts: $892 versus $1,095 per week. Furthermore, during negotiations (also known as collective bargaining), unions have had a long history of improving the working conditions of those they represent.

Arguments against Unions

Some argue against unions. A lower level of unionization is a **high performance work systems characteristic**, yet not for political reasons. Greater unionization means less control over operations and decisions for management. Unions tend to prefer that pay raises and promotions are based on seniority systems rather than on employee performance and incentives, which can have a detrimental impact on motivation and productivity.

Consider the hypothetical example of XYZ Company. XYZ employs 100 employees and has successfully been operating its business since 1950. In 2007, XYZ employees began a drive for unionization and eventually certified and formed a union. XYZ's employees once were motivated through a variety of incentive plans, but in recent years, the union has successfully eliminated those. Once the union stepped in, XYZ managers were given constraints on hiring and firing. The union preferred that XYZ base promotions on the people who have been at XYZ the longest rather than those who performed the best. The new hires, freshly charged to make an impact on XYZ, have been quickly becoming demotivated. To them, it seems advancement would be a long, dreadful haul into the far too distant future. In fact, the only recognition programs still in place since the union formed are those that celebrate the greatest years of service with XYZ. Today, anyone would label XYZ's culture as one of mediocrity.

Another reason some have argued that unions are no longer needed is due to a greater prevalence in offerings of generous pay and benefits packages and innovative employee enrichment, engagement and empowerment programs. The less innovative, less flexible programs of the past have been replaced, so employees are more engaged and no longer need union help to achieve such benefits.

Arguments in Support of Unions

Some have lamented the declines of unions in the United States. Researchers found that union families had a median wealth of $80,993 in 2016, compared with non-union family median wealth of $45,025 – a difference of 80 percent![222] The same study indicated that between 2010 and 2016, 52.8 percent of union families had a defined benefit pension plan, while only 19.8 percent of non-union families had the same retirement security.

According to Christian Weller of *Forbes,* "Unions help families save more in three ways. First, union members enjoy a wage premium thanks to collective bargaining. These higher wages make it generally easier to save. Higher wages also mean that families receive more tax incentives to save, for instance, in a 401(k) plan. Because the tax code is progressive, higher income earners receive a greater boost in their after-tax income from deducting their contributions than is the case for lower-income earners. For example, if a unionized laborer earns $80,000 and his non-unionized counterpart earns $45,000 and both contribute 6 percent into their defined contribution pension plan each month, the unionized laborer would be contributing $4,800 of pre-tax income annually (often matched by his employer), while his counterpart would be contributing $2,700. Over many years, these differences become substantial.

Second, union members are more likely than non-union members to have a wide range of benefits from their employer. These include health insurance, pensions and life insurance. Such benefits can free money up for union members for the purchase of homes, cars, or other big-ticket items. From 2010 to 2016, for example, union members had a homeownership rate of 74.3 percent, while non-union members had a rate of 63.6 percent.

Third, union members have more job stability. Collective bargaining agreements make it easier to engage with employers on job related concerns, which gives employees fewer reasons to leave when things are not working out. They also establish processes for promotion, which further incentivizes the workers to stay on a job longer. As a result, union members are more likely to stay with one employer for longer periods of time than is the case for non-union members. Greater job stability makes it easier for people to plan for the future. And more job stability makes it more likely that people qualify for key benefits such as 401(k) pension plans."[223]

In summary, numerous arguments can be made either in support of or against unions. Where people stand could be a function of many factors, which is why unionization is considered a hot button political issue. Those who take sides in this debate are well advised to investigate the interests on all sides thoroughly before forming a strong opinion.

Which Laws Apply to Unions?

The following laws apply to unions: National Labor Relations Act, the Railway Labor Act of 1926 (RLA), the Civil Service Reform Act, the Landrum Griffin Act, and the Taft Hartley Act.

National Labor Relations Act (NLRA; aka, the Wagner Act) of 1935

Under the **National Labor Relations Act**, employees have the right to form a union if a union currently does not exist within their organizations. They also have the right to decertify a union if the union has lost the support of its employees.

The following are examples of employee rights under the NLRA:[224]

- Form, attempt to form, or work with a union to start a union;
- Join or participate in a union whether it is recognized by one's company or not;
- Refuse to form, attempt to form, work with unions to start a union, or join a union.
- Engage in a lawful strike.

Employees have the right to go on strike when negotiations come to a halt, so long as the strike is an economic strike or one based on unfair labor practices. Economic strikers are those who strike for higher wages, better hours, better working conditions or other similar economic factors.

In a recent NLRB ruling, employers are free to bar non-employees from soliciting union membership on company property that is open to the public. This reverses a long-time precedent in which employers could not bar this solicitation.

Strikes are considered unlawful when their purpose is unlawful, such as compelling one employer to stop doing business with another. Strikes are also considered unlawful when their timing violates no-strike provisions in a labor agreement or contract. They are also considered unlawful when strikers engage in unlawful activities, such as being violent.

According to the National Labor Relations Board, which oversees and enforces the NLRA, "the U.S. Supreme Court has ruled that a "sit down" strike, when employees simply stay in the plant and refuse to work, thus depriving the owner of property, is not protected by the law. Examples of serious misconduct that could cause the employees involved to lose their right to reinstatement (or getting their job back) are:

- Strikers physically blocking persons from entering or leaving a struck plant.
- Strikers threatening violence against non-striking employees.
- Strikers attacking management representatives."[225]

Companies can hire temporary replacement workers to replace workers who are on strike, yet they are limited in whether they can permanently hire replacement workers. If managers' intentions to hire permanent replacement workers are to punish or discriminate against union workers, the courts have ruled that their intentions are unlawful.[226] In such cases, managers cannot hire permanent replacement workers.

Employees who are not represented by a union also receive protections from the NLRA. This protection has recently been applied to **social media**, which is often a means used for employees to engage in protected concerted activities. A **protected concerted activity** is when two or more employees take action for their mutual protection or aid in regards to the terms of their employment. A single employee may also engage in a protected concerted activity if he or she is acting on behalf of other employees by bringing forward the views, opinions, or consensus of a group to the employer's attention. The single employee may also try to induce group action or try to prepare for group action.

When do employees engage in protected concerted activities? Oftentimes, employees have grievances that go unresolved. Perhaps a grievance process is not in place or their grievances have been ignored. They may choose to air their grievances publicly via the internet (e.g., social media). Some examples of terms of employment include pay concerns, safety concerns, workplace conditions, or co-worker concerns.

Most employees in the private sector are covered by the NLRA. The Act specifically excludes government workers (federal, state, or local), agricultural laborers, domestic workers, independent contractors, and employees employed by a parent or spouse. Further, the level of employment matters in the NLRA. Supervisors are not covered. Neither are employees subject to different union-related laws, such as those covered by the Railway Labor Act.

Mandatory arbitration agreements are a form of alternative dispute resolution in which two or more parties in a dispute submit their dispute to a third-party arbitrator. The arbitrator resolves the dispute rather than taking it to litigation in the courts. It is a means of avoiding litigation.

If employers choose to create mandatory arbitration agreements to respond to employees who opt into collective action (such as a strike), they are not in violation of the National Labor Relations Act. In the 2018 Supreme Court ruling on *Epic Systems Corp. v. Lewis,* the Court ruled that arbitration agreements that contain class and collective action waivers and require that disputes be resolved in arbitration are permissible. By using a class or collective action waiver, the employer asks employees to pursue their actions as individuals rather than as part of a larger class, group, or collective. A NLRB decision in *Cordua Restaurants, Inc.* extended this Supreme Court Decision by holding that employers may enforce such arbitration agreements and waivers and may discipline employees if they refuse the terms of the agreements. Yet note that the NLRB still holds that employers cannot terminate or punish employees for participating in collective action.

Railway Labor Act[227]

In 1926, nine years before the NLRA was passed in 1935, railway and transportation employees were protected against union discrimination under the **Railway Labor Act** (RLA). One of the main purposes of the RLA is to *take measures to avoid the strike*, which could cripple the transportation industry and ultimately the U.S. economy. The RLA avoids the strike by delaying its possibility. Two means are used: (1) the RLA prolongs the process of collective bargaining by requiring the National Mediation Board to release union and management for self-help thirty days before a strike can occur and (2) the RLA also requires mandatory arbitration of disputes about the interpretations of the labor agreement between the union and the organization. In other words, the RLA seeks to substitute bargaining, arbitration and mediation for strikes to solve labor disputes.

Who is covered under the Railway Labor Act? The RLA defines the term "carrier" as "any express company, sleeping-car company, carrier by railroad, subject to subtitle IV of title 49, and any company which is directly or indirectly owned or controlled by or under common control with any carrier by railroad which operates any equipment or facilities or performs any service (other than trucking service) in connection with the transportation, receipt, delivery, elevation, transfer in transit, refrigeration or icing, storage and handling of property transported by railroad." Under the RLA, Federal Express is considered a carrier, whereas the United Parcel Service (UPS) is not.

Taft Hartley Act

The Labor Relations Management Act of 1947, also known as the **Taft Hartley Act**, made changes to the NLRA to *further protect employees' rights from unfair labor practices by unions*. Under this Act, employees have the right to refrain from participating in union or mutual aid activities, except that they could be required to become union members as a condition of employment. The Act prohibited the secondary boycott, which is when a union calls on non-members (such as the greater American public) to boycott a company's products or services. The Act also prohibited the unions from charging excessive dues or fees or from "featherbedding," which is causing an employer to pay for services not rendered by an employee.[228]

Landrum Griffin Act

The Labor Management Reporting and Disclosure Act of 1959, also known as the **Landrum Griffin Act**, protects the interests of union members by granting them certain rights and promoting democratic procedures within labor organizations. The Act establishes a Bill of Rights for union members by specifying reporting requirements for labor organizations and those affiliated with such organizations. The Act also includes safeguards for protecting labor organization funds and assets.[229]

Civil Service Reform Act

The Civil Service Reform Act was modified in 1978[230] to guarantee certain rights to members of unions who are Federal government workers. The Act establishes a Bill of Rights for these workers, specifying their equal rights to participate in union activities, their freedom of speech and assembly, their voice in setting dues, fees, and assessments, and their protection of the right to sue. The Act also includes safeguards against improper discipline.

The Civil Service Reform Act also prohibits certain activities, such as secondary boycotts and strikes for Federal government workers. The Act also created the Federal Mediation and Conciliation Service, which assists in resolving labor disputes that carry the risk of turning into national emergencies.

How Do Workers Join Unions?

If at least 30 percent of workers in an organization sign cards or a petition stating that they want union representation, the NLRB conducts an election. If a majority of those who vote in a secret ballot choose the union, the NLRB certifies the union as the employees' representative in collective bargaining. Employers could also voluntarily recognize a union based on evidence that a majority of employees want to form a union. The evidence could be signed union-authorization cards. Once a union has been certified or recognized, the employer must bargain in good faith over the terms and conditions of employment.

If employees decide they no longer want union representation, they can vote to decertify the union. First, they must obtain signatures from 30 percent of employees in a petition to decertify the union. Then an election is held. If a majority of employees (over 50 percent) votes in a secret ballot to decertify the union, the union will no longer be their representative.

If employers plan to hold this vote, they must inform the unions no more than 90 days prior to the expiration of their Collective Bargaining Agreement with the union. The union then has 45 days to try to re-establish majority status by holding a new election. The party with the majority status in the secret ballot determines whether or not the organization remains unionized.

Why do workers vote for **decertification**? Some workers feel that unions have outlived their usefulness. They may believe their dues are too high relative to what they receive in return from the unions in collective bargaining. Union dues are typically around 2 percent of pay. According to the Labor Relations Institute, Inc., between 2004 and 2013, unions lost over 11 percent of total membership, which was 1,110,000 employees.[231]

What Rights Do Employees Have Under Unions?

Unless prohibited by law or a union contract, employees have the right to picket or go on **strike** to protest economic or working conditions. On September 15, 2019, 46,000 auto workers at General Motors (GM) went on strike. They had taken pay cuts and made concessions to get GM through bankruptcy, yet since GM had posted near-record profits over the prior three years of around $12 billion, they demanded their share.[232] **Picketing** is a form of protest in which workers gather outside of their workplaces with pickets, or signs, to explain to the public the reason behind their protest. Employees may also engage in **primary boycotts** by refusing to purchase the goods or services of their employer. Under the Taft Hartley Act and the Civil Service Reform Act (if federal workers), they may not engage in secondary boycotts.

What Rights Do Employers Have with Unions?

When workers voted to unionize in a Walmart store in California, Walmart responded by closing that store and others in Texas, Florida, and Oklahoma, claiming the need to fix plumbing and make other repairs.[233] The move negatively impacted about 2,200 employees. Walmart offered employees 60 days' pay and the opportunity to transfer to other stores, placing around 75 percent of those who applied for transfers. The Commercial Workers International Union responded to Walmart by filing a complaint with the NLRB, stating that Walmart closed the California location due to its unionization plans. Rather than deal with an expensive and lengthy court case, Walmart said, "We are moving forward with the process to reopen all five stores."

Companies cannot close their doors in retaliation and Walmart appears to have been retaliating against the union vote. In a separate case, a court in Quebec found Walmart's Quebec store closure following a vote to unionize to be illegal.[234]

What rights do companies have? They can certainly close their doors when unprofitable or when corporate strategies shift or for other non-retaliatory reasons. They may choose to close down the company, the plant, or certain operations within the plant, transfer operations to another location, subcontract out certain jobs, or lockout their employees. A lockout is a temporary work stoppage or denial of employment initiated by management during a labor dispute.

Right to Work States

In 27 U.S. states with **Right to Work** laws, the law guarantees that no person can be compelled to join or not join a union or to pay dues to a labor union as a condition of employment. Most of these states are in the South, West, or Midwest. Further, unionized employees in Right to Work states may decide to resign from a union. They cannot be fired for that reason.

No matter the state, no public employees, including teachers, can be forced to join a union, as per a Supreme Court decision: *Janus* vs. *AFSCME*.

What is "Collective Bargaining?"

Collective bargaining refers to the negotiation of wages or other conditions by an organized group of employees. When unions bargain in good faith with the employers of the employees they represent, the term used to describe the activity is collective bargaining.

Ideally, the results of collective bargaining between union representatives and management is an **integrative bargaining strategy.** With an integrative negotiating strategy, both sides win.

The Pumpkin Patch

Consider the following situation in a classroom just prior to Halloween. A school teacher of 30 third grade students has the desire to purchase a pumpkin for each of her students so they can carve pumpkins for Halloween. She travels to a pumpkin patch and encounters a seller who happens to have 30 pumpkins to sell. The teacher carries all thirty pumpkins to the cash register and pulls out her wallet only to discover that the seller refuses to sell all 30 pumpkins. The seller says that she needs to keep one pumpkin so she can plant the seeds from that pumpkin for the following year for Halloween. The school teacher becomes upset, knowing that one of her students will be upset because he or she does not have a pumpkin to carve. If she purchased 29 pumpkins and left one student without a pumpkin, the situation would be a **zero-sum** situation in which one person won (the seller) and the other lost (the school teacher). A zero-sum negotiation is also called a **distributive bargaining strategy.** How can the school teacher convince the seller to sell all 30 pumpkins? This is where a bit of thinking outside of the box is helpful. The school teacher offers to buy all 30 pumpkins and to return the seeds from all pumpkins to the seller after her students have carved the pumpkins. This results in a win-win situation, or an integrative agreement.

Sometimes during collective bargaining, union representatives must make concessions. In a **concessionary bargaining strategy,** the union representative agrees to give back or surrender previous gains in wages or other working conditions. For example, consider the impact of the Coronavirus on the airline industry. Prior to 2020, when the Coronavirus was labeled a pandemic, unions may have been able to negotiate high wages for the employees they represented. Suppose one negotiated a five-year raise plan in 2017 in which airline employees of a particular airline received a 5 percent raise each year for each year after 2017. The market then collapsed in 2020 and people reduced canceled flights in droves, impacting all airlines negatively. The management team of the airline would likely renegotiate employee raises, since the raises had become unaffordable. In such situations, the union representatives are very likely to make concessions and to reduce the raise percentages.

Conflict Management

In the United States, relationships between unions and company representatives are often adversarial. Each party comes into the negotiation agreement with the mindset that he is going to battle and it is "us against them." For this reason, it is in a company's best interest to identify the right type of people to enter negotiations.

You may know someone who has the uncanny ability to "turn lemons into lemonade." You may have identified people who are just a bit better at managing conflict than their peers. Identifying and placing these types at the forefront of collective bargaining is critical to ensuring integrative negotiation results.

Conflict management is the practice of recognizing and dealing with disputes in a rational, effective, and balanced way. People who manage conflict should have high levels of emotional intelligence and the emotional stability to be able to effectively navigate negotiations in difficult situations. They should further be able to limit the negative aspects of conflict while maximizing any positive aspects. These skills are important on either side of the negotiating table.

Consider the example of Joey Anderson. Anderson is the union representative preparing to go into negotiations at XYZ Company. XYZ Company desires to increase productivity of its workers, to minimize pay raises, and to maintain high levels of overall employee satisfaction. Anderson wants to focus on maximizing pay raises and employee satisfaction, yet he is less concerned with productivity. But he knows XYZ cares about productivity, so he prepares to make concessions if needed. When he comes to the negotiating table, he will focus most strongly on employee satisfaction. He knows that both parties agree on that point. He will bring research indicating that greater pay levels correspond to greater employee satisfaction. The approaches he uses will include efforts to minimize conflict between the parties and maximize agreement, while always keeping an eye on his end goal of maximizing pay raises.

Whenever a group works together, the potential for disputes arises. Organizations should be proactive in handling any disputes by establishing a **grievance policy.** A grievance policy is a constructive way for employees to voice their opinions or disputes before they become a distraction in the workplace. They may reduce the potential for gossip and other counterproductive work behaviors. If employees have a grievance (complaint), they should be instructed on the steps to take to communicate the grievance. Typically, the steps they complete take the following form:

1. The employee discusses the grievance with his supervisor.
2. He submits a written complaint to the second-level supervisor (i.e., the supervisor's supervisor).
3. The second-level supervisor holds a meeting with the employee.
4. The second-level supervisor investigates the complaint.
5. The second-level supervisor documents the decision or resolution.
6. The second-level supervisor shares her decision with the employee.

Establishing policies where employees can voice their concerns and grievances is a useful tool for keeping the communication lines open and mitigating the possibility for litigation. Along these lines, organizations may also adopt **alternative dispute resolutions (ADRs).** ADRs involve the use of mediation and arbitration instead of costly litigation when conflicts arise. Mediation and arbitration are synonyms for intervention in a dispute. In ADRs, the parties in disputes get together with a neutral third party, either a mediator or an arbitrator. The mediator has no power to impose a resolution, other than his power of persuasion. The arbitrator, in contrast, is given the power to decide on the resolution of the dispute. The benefits of ADRs over litigation are that they are less formal, less expensive, and less time-consuming than litigation.

Differences between U.S. Unions and International Unions

The United States differs from some European countries in its relationships with unions. In the United States, workers in an organization are only represented by one union. In Europe, they may have more than one. In the U.S., the government is passive in labor relations as they do not get involved in wage negotiations, labor disputes, or collective bargaining. In Europe and in most of the world, government is active in labor. Relations between unions and management in the United States is often adversarial, or "us" versus "them." In other countries, the relationship is more amicable. Economic issues are at the forefront in the U.S., whereas political issues are tops in other countries. For example, the retirement age of 52 years in France is a political issue that is the subject of much focus among the French people. Collective bargaining in the U.S. is decentralized. For example, automobile manufacturers Ford, Chrysler, and General Motors negotiate separately with the United Auto Workers. In other countries, similar companies in the same industry would negotiate together so none have a competitive advantage based on negotiation skills.

Unions in other parts of the world use some of the same approaches when negotiations fail. Strikes, picketing, and secondary boycotts are used all over the world. As one example in 2019, British Airways had to cancel almost all of its departures because its pilots went on strike. One estimate suggested that strike cost British Airways the equivalent of $49 million a day![235] This was the first strike for British Airways pilots since 1979.

Conclusion

Over the past fifty years, union membership has slowly been in decline in the United States, which is attributable to shifting labor markets, the information age and the declining need for unskilled workers, along with perceptions that unions are no longer needed. Employees have many legal protections in the workplace and in some workplaces, leaders value their human capital, keeping them highly satisfied, so union protections may be redundant. Yet some lament these trends, as unionized workers have more security and income than their non-unionized counterparts. To completely eliminate the need for unions, one would need to eliminate the reasons for workers' interest in them. Workers are typically interested in joining unions when they are dissatisfied with their working conditions and pay. Organizations that take measures to ensure satisfaction may be able to lessen their chances of union certification.

QUESTIONS FOR REVIEW

1. What is the "National Labor Relations Act" of 1935?

2. How are unions formed in U.S. firms?

3. If collective bargaining between unions and employers fails, what can unions do to exercise their power?

4. If a majority of workers in a plant vote to join a union, can plant managers fire the employees? What can they do if they don't want a unionized plant?

5. What is the Taft-Hartley Act?

6. What specific benefits do employees receive as union members?

7. Which types of employees benefit the most from unions?

8. Cite some examples of how international unions differ from unions in the United States.

9. What is the Civil Service Reform Act?

10. What is the Railway Labor Act?

APPLICATIONS

1. Bureau of Labor Statistics

Go to the Bureau of Labor Statistics website and look up the current rates of unionization in the United States. How does the pay of public workers vary from private workers? How does the rates of unionization vary around the world?

2. FedEx's Competitive Advantage

Consider the fact that Federal Express is categorized under the Railway Labor Act and United Parcel Service is categorized under the National Labor Relations Act. What benefits has Federal Express derived by this categorization?

CASE STUDIES

1. The Divergent Interests of Unions and Government in Europe

According to the Bureau of Labor Statistics, [236]union power and recruitment worldwide have been limited by globalization, the rise in service employment, a slow growth of government employment, higher unemployment rates (especially in Europe), an increased use of flexible employment contracts, and the control of inflation through tight monetary policies. However, these relationships are mitigated by politics and legal rules.

With over 60 million members from 39 countries, the European Trade Union Confederation (ETUC), which is an alliance of the European trade unions, is a strong force in the global union environment. The group "defends fundamental social values such as solidarity, equality, democracy, social justice, and cohesion."[237] ETUC fights for high quality jobs, high levels of social protection, gender equality and fair pay, health and safety, social inclusion and fundamental rights, action to combat climate change while protecting workers' jobs, and the promotion of these values worldwide. In 2015, ETUC crafted a Manifesto, which calls for social dialogue and collective bargaining to be strengthened across Europe.

Yet persistent underemployment in Europe, particularly in Croatia, Spain, and Greece, have resulted in calls for austerity, structural reforms, and deregulation. ETUC recommendations fail to change the growing share of short-term one-month employment contracts in France or job insecurity in Cyprus, where 95 percent of workers are in temporary positions.[238]

1. How do companies save money by hiring employees in temporary positions?

2. Why are unions interested in replacing temporary positions with permanent positions?

3. What market conditions would help ETUC to strengthen its global position?

2. Social Media: Was Walmart Justified?

The already complex employment environment has been further complicated in recent years by social media (e.g., Facebook, Twitter, Instagram, Tumblr, and blogs). Regardless of whether employees are on the job or not when they post material on social media, the material they post may be a mix of their opinions of their workplace and personal lives. The National Labor Relations Board protects workers who post information on their working conditions, wages, hours, and union organizing.

According to the NLRB, it is lawful to restrict employees' communication on the disclosure of trade secrets; commercially sensitive or confidential internal information that results in a competitive advantage; and discriminatory, obscene, threatening, bullying, harassing, or defamatory comments. But employers cannot restrict communication with respect to the aforementioned protected activities (e.g., working conditions).

Sometimes employees post material on social media that their companies find offensive, disrespectful, and hurtful to their public image. Such posts have led to the termination of some employees. When the NLRB steps in, company leaders are often advised to revise their social media policies and occasionally are required to reinstate fired employees. To determine the likelihood of an NLRB intervention, it's wise for company leaders to examine decisions made in past cases.

One such case is at Walmart. A Walmart employee was Facebook friends with about five of his Walmart coworkers. His privacy settings were set to "public" when he wrote this in 2011:[239]

> "The government needs to step in and set a limit on how many kids people are allowed to have based on their income. If you can't afford to feed them, you shouldn't be allowed to have them…Our population needs to be controlled! In my neck of the woods when the whitetail deer get to be too numerous, we thin them out! …Just go to your nearest big box store and start picking them off…We cater too much to the handicapped nowadays! Hell, if you can't walk, why don't you stay the f@*k home!!!!"

After reading these postings, one coworker wrote that she couldn't wait for her coworker to be punished. A Walmart customer referred to the comments as "beyond disturbing," especially given a fatal shooting that had occurred at that same Walmart just a year before.

When Walmart leaders contacted the employee to inquire about the post, the employee indicated that his comments were not angry comments, but just comments to "let off steam." He further acknowledged that the comments were in bad taste and that he showed poor judgment. He explained that his comments were part of his personal entertainment therapy. Walmart leaders then discharged the employee. Were they justified? The NLRB needed to determine whether the comments addressed working conditions or arose out of any concern or complaint about his working conditions.

3. Social Media: Was Chipotle Justified?

According to the National Labor Relations Board, "Federal law protects your right to engage in not only union activity, but also "protected concerted" activity, which is when two or more employees take action for their mutual aid or protection regarding their terms and conditions of employment. A single employee may also engage in a protected concerted activity so long as he or she is acting on the authority of other employees, trying to induce group action, bringing group complaints to an employer's attention, or seeking to prepare for group action.[240] You have the right to address work-related issues and share information about pay, benefits, and working conditions with co-workers and with a union. You have the right to take action with one or more co-workers to improve your working conditions by, among other means, raising work-related complaints directly with your employer or with a government agency, or seeking help to form a union. Using social media can be a form of protected concerted activity. You have the right to address work-related issues and share information about pay, benefits, and working conditions with coworkers on Facebook, YouTube, and other social media. But just individually griping about some aspect of work is not "concerted activity": what you say must have some relation to group action, or seek to initiate, induce, or prepare for group action, or bring a group complaint to the attention of management. Such activity is not protected if you say things about your employer that are egregiously offensive or knowingly and deliberately false, or if you publicly disparage your employer's products or services without relating your complaints to any labor controversy.

A Chipotle employee aired grievances about Chipotle with the following three tweets on Twitter:

1. In response to a news article concerning hourly workers having to work on snow days when certain other employees were off and public transportation was shut down, the employee addressed Chipotle's communications director and stated: "Snow day for 'top performers' Chris Arnold?"
2. In response to a customer who tweeted "Free chipotle is the best thanks", the employee tweeted "nothing is free, only cheap #labor. Crew members make $8.50hr how much is that steak bowl really?"
3. In response to a tweet posted by a customer about guacamole, the employee wrote "it's extra not like #Qdoba, enjoy the extra $2" – a reference to the fact that Chipotle charges extra for guacamole, whereas the restaurant chain Qdoba does not.

When Chipotle managers were informed of the tweets, they contacted the employee and asked him to delete the tweets, which he did. The NLRB would question whether he was airing an individual grievance or whether he was engaging in a protected concerted activity. Was this activity protected?

4. Social Media Role Play

Get into groups of 3 persons and select one of the following roles: employee, customer, and store manager. If there are uneven numbers of students, one group can have five students and two store managers. Read only the material relative to your role.

The place of employment is an upscale automobile dealership named for its founder: Chaumers Automotive. The mission of the dealership is to impress its customers with a high-touch approach. Chaumers has a social media policy, which stipulates certain rules to employees. Included in these rules are the following: "You may not make defamatory or disparaging remarks in any public forum (including social media and in on-line blogs) about Chaumers, its employers, officers, directors, vendors, customers, partners, affiliates, or our products and services unless you are specifically authorized to do so." Chaumers further states that "courtesy is the responsibility of every employee. Everyone is expected to be courteous and friendly to the aforementioned stakeholders. No one should be disrespectful and no one should use profanity."

Employee

You are a car salesperson who was required to attend an event in which Chaumers Automotive where they served free colas, hot dogs, potato chips, cookies and bottled waters to customers. Employees were permitted to partake in the food as well. You find the food to be extremely cheap, especially given Chaumers' upscale image. So, on Facebook, you posted the following comments: "I can't believe my employer. Chaumers should have champagne tastes, but it clearly only pays with a beer wallet. They were trying to ATTRACT business with cheap hot dogs – probably not even 100 percent beef – store brand potato chips and store-bought cookies. Such a joke. How am I ever going to make good money if they're going to be so cheap?"

The next day at work, you spotted the thirteen-year-old son of a customer who was about to test drive a vehicle in the driver's seat of the vehicle, which was parked next to a pond. The son must have stepped on the gas and the vehicle rolled into the pond. The son was able to climb out and walk away, but the car was damaged. "What an idiot!" You think as you take pictures with your mobile phone and post the event on Facebook.

Customer

You were about to test drive a high-end sports car at Chaumers' Automotive with your 13-year-old son. As you approached the car with the salesman and the keys, you see that your son is waiting for you in the driver's seat. To your horror, you watch as the vehicle rolled into the pond, which was just in front of it. Your son must have pushed the gas!

Fortunately, your son is able to free himself from the vehicle and walk away. You feel relieved. Then you spot another Chaumers' salesperson laughing and snapping photos with his mobile phone. "What kind of customer service is this? How rude!!!" You decide to inform the company's management.

Store manager

Your day began in a pleasant way, yet that quickly changed when an employee forwarded screenshots of Facebook posts by one of your salespersons. Some screenshots contained defamatory words about Chaumers. The employee apparently thought the hot dog event wasn't classy enough to attract high end customers. The employee was worried about his pay. Other screenshots from the employee's Facebook page contained photos of the customer and his son in front of one of your sports vehicles in a pond.

This frustrated you, so you decide to check the company's social media policy and its rules to see whether the employee is in specific violation. Are employees allowed to discuss their pay? Go to the NLRB's website to check whether your social media policy is consistent with the NLRB's rules. Was this a concerted effort? Your gut response is to fire the employee. Immediately. Clearly the employee is not a team player.

Role Play:

The first interaction will be between the customer and the store manager. The second interaction will be between the employee and the store manager. What actions were taken? Were the actions appropriate?

Chapter 11: Health and Safety

Introduction

In 2015, more than 11 million young adults ages 18 to 25 in the United States ingested marijuana.[241] In 2016, a survey of 45,000 students in 380 public and private secondary schools across the United States found that more than 24 percent of teens reported that they had used marijuana in the past year.[242] 28 percent of tenth graders had used an illicit drug and 27.7 percent had used alcohol, while 12.9 percent of eighth graders had used an illicit drug and 18.2 percent had used alcohol. The survey indicated that fewer teens considered marijuana (pot) to be dangerous. Such findings are consistent with the fact that states are increasingly loosening laws on the recreational use of marijuana and many more have legalized marijuana for its medical uses.

At issue are health and safety concerns. Over the past thirty years, the amount of THC (the active ingredient in marijuana that causes the "high" people feel) has increased significantly.[243] In the 1970s, THC levels were around one percent, while today levels range between 13 and 25 percent![244]

Higher THC levels correspond to a greater chance of adverse health impacts, such as the short-term impacts of impaired body movements, difficulty thinking and problem-solving, hallucinations, delusions, and psychosis. Long-term effects are further an issue, as one study[245] found that people who started smoking heavily in their teens had an ongoing marijuana disorder (addiction) and lost an average of 8 IQ points between the ages of 13 and 38. Those who started smoking later had fewer declines. In addition to physical effects, heavy marijuana users have reported less academic and career success, a greater chance of dropping out of school, and more job accidents, other accidents and injuries.[246]

Despite the potential for negative health and safety outcomes, proponents for the legalization of medical and recreational marijuana continue to advocate their positions on its benefits and more and more states are loosening their laws against marijuana. Some states prohibit employers from discriminating against workers on the basis of status as a registered medical marijuana patient. Laws in Delaware, Arizona, and Minnesota have indicated that a positive test alone does not indicate impairment. This may be attributable to the fact that impairment does not have a positive relationship with THC levels in the blood as the mode of ingestion and characteristics of the person ingesting vary the outcomes.[247] Furthermore, THC may remain in the blood for weeks or even months after usage.

State laws that have legalized marijuana do not require employers to compromise workplace safety and productivity. Impairment on the job, whether via marijuana, alcohol, or other drugs can still result in termination. Furthermore, federal laws, which prohibit marijuana ingestion, trump state laws.

The Drug-Free Workplace Act of 1988 requires that companies have a drug-free workplace policy that specifies what will happen in the event that an employee violates the policy by testing positively for drug use, whether termination or citation or counseling. Human resource managers need to pay attention to this rapidly changing environment and current state laws to determine appropriate policies and practices in the workplace.

Using marijuana is still considered illegal under federal law as the drug is still listed as a Schedule I drug under the Controlled Substance Act. Some have lobbied to change this classification, yet studies have yet to be produced that show the benefits of marijuana outweigh the risks. In some states, the courts have ruled that federal laws trump state laws, yet the courts haven't always made these determinations. The United States still lacks consistency across states with respect to medical or recreational marijuana use. Accordingly, testing and reprimanding or terminating employees who test positively for marijuana in states in which marijuana is legal for either recreational or medical use is a risky business.

In 2017, a Massachusetts high court ruled that a worker could sue her employer for disability discrimination for terminating her for a positive marijuana test.[248] She was a registered medicinal user (or cardholder), so she was given protections under the Americans with Disabilities Act.

Employers do not have to accommodate on-the-job use (or retain workers who show up to work "high" on marijuana), but they should review applicable state statutes before issuing blanket drug testing policies for those who test positively.

Objectives:

After reading this chapter, you should be able to:

- Discuss ways to create a healthy and well workplace environment.
- Recognize employee issues, such as job stress, burnout, and potential violence.
- Identify ways to achieve a work-life balance.
- Explain the purpose of OSHA.
- Recognize ways to enhance safety in the workplace.

Health and Wellness

According to the Society for Human Resource Management, many companies today have expanded the scope of their health and wellness programs, moving from a focus solely on physical health to a focus on physical, mental, and emotional health.[249] Companies such as Cisco Systems offer a wide variety of programs for employees, from financial education, flexible work policies, five paid days off per year for volunteer work, and a general paid parental leave program. They further offer on-site primary medical care, hiking and bike paths, outdoor sports courts, fitness centers, and a childcare center.[250] Keeping employees healthy is not only good for employee satisfaction, engagement, and commitment to the organization, it is good for business. Employees who are healthy and happy are more likely to be more productive and focused.

To establish a **wellness program**, human resource managers should take the following steps: (1) conduct assessments of needs and interests; (2) obtain support from management; (3) form a wellness committee; (4) develop goals and objectives; (5) establish a budget; (6) design wellness components; and (7) identify appropriate incentives and rewards.

Some companies may start small, with periodic healthcare screenings for high cholesterol, high blood pressure, dramatic weight gain or loss, vision testing, hearing testing, and other similar relatively low-cost programs. They may supplement payments for gym memberships or encourage employees to take time off for exercise and mental relaxation. Creating contests based on weight loss or walking distances could be enticing for employees and may motivate more sedentary ones to take measures to be healthier physically. Offering counseling programs, legal assistance, financial education, meditation and yoga programs, smoking cessation programs, faith-based and spirituality programs, and work-related educational or training opportunities could also pique the interest of employees. As organizations grow and funding for additional programs increases, managers may consider other more costly options, such as paid time off for volunteer activities or on-site childcare or on-site gyms and exercise facilities.

Research has found that wellness programs favorably relate to job satisfaction and the lowering of stress.[251] According to one study, workplace wellness is a $6 billion dollar industry in the United States offered by about 60 percent of U.S. companies, yet the benefits of wellness programs vary by their purpose.[252] 87 percent of employees participate in lifestyle management programs and 13 percent enroll in disease management programs, yet 87 percent of employers' healthcare cost savings come from disease management programs. For every dollar invested in wellness, companies get back $1.50, but the bulk of the return centers around *disease management programs* rather than lifestyle management programs. While lifestyle management programs can reduce absenteeism, smoking, obesity, and a lack of physical exercise, the best results come from targeting employees who already have chronic diseases to help them manage their diseases.[253]

Healthy Work Environments

Creating a healthy work environment is an additional concern, since not everyone is interested in engaging in employee wellness programs. WellSteps offers several options for companies of varying budgets:[254]

Low Cost Strategies

1. Create a company culture that discourages sedentary behavior, such as TV viewing on breaks and sitting for long periods of time.
2. Offer flexible work hours to allow for physical activity during the day.
3. Support physical activity breaks during the workday, such as stretching or walking.
4. Map out on-site trails or nearby walking routes.
5. Host walk-and-talk meetings.
6. Post motivational signs at elevators and escalators to encourage stair use.
7. Provide exercise/physical fitness messages and information to employees.
8. Have employees map their own biking or walking route to and from work.
9. Provide bicycle racks in safe, convenient, and accessible locations.

Medium Cost Strategies

10. Provide shower and/or changing facilities on-site.
11. Provide outdoor exercise areas such as fields and trails for employee use.
12. Provide or support recreation leagues and other physical activity events (on-site or in the community).
13. Start employee activity clubs (e.g., walking, bicycling).
14. Explore discounted or subsidized memberships at local health clubs, recreation centers, or YMCAs.
15. Implement incentive-based programs to encourage physical activity, such as activity tracker walking challenges.

High Cost Strategies

16. Offer on-site fitness opportunities, such as group classes or personal training.
17. Provide an on-site exercise facility.
18. Provide incentives for participation in physical activity and/or weight management/maintenance activities.
19. Allow for use of facilities outside of normal work hours.
20. Provide on-site child care facilities to facilitate physical activity.

Setting up healthy environments for employees may help them to manage their stress levels via healthy coping mechanisms. Some employees, however, deal with their stress and mental health issues with unhealthy coping mechanisms, such as drugs and alcohol. The National Council on Alcoholism and Drug Dependence (NCADD) states that drugs and alcohol in the workplace cause a variety of problems, such as injuries, high turnover, absenteeism, fatalities, theft, low employee morale, legal liabilities and lost productivity.[255] The NCADD points to the following industries where drugs and alcohol in the workplace are especially prevalent: food service, construction, mining and drilling, excavation, and installation, maintenance and repair.[256]

Job Stress and Burnout

Job stress and **burnout** are two problems faced in almost every organization. Too much chronic stress in the workplace leads to employee burnout. In a recent Gallup Study of 7,500 workers, 23 percent reported feeling burned out at work either often or always, while 44 percent reported feeling burned out sometimes. Healthcare spending for burnout costs an estimated $125 billion to $190 billion annually.[257] Diseases associated with burnout include type 2 diabetes, coronary heart disease, gastrointestinal issues, musculoskeletal pain, prolonged fatigue, severe injuries, high cholesterol and even death of people under the age of 45 years old.[258] The psychological effects include depressive symptoms, mental disorders, and the use of psychotropic and antidepressant medications.[259]

Why does burnout occur? When employees feel that they have unfair and unreasonable deadlines, or unmanageable workloads, or a lack of assistance, resources, or support from management, they become burned out. To alleviate burnout, companies should consider developing employee wellness programs, offering peer support, and giving their employees much job autonomy.[260]

Who gets stressed? People in all roles and levels may get stressed from time to time. Sometimes some of the firm's hardest workers are the most stressed. Conscientious workers are known for their dependability and strong work ethic. Many go beyond the minimum role requirements for their organizations, working extra hours and helping their colleagues achieve their goals. Yet this may come at the expense of their work-life balance and may cause conflict between their duties in the home versus their duties in the workplace.[261]

Work-Life Balance

Companies often take measures in the organization to ensure their employees achieve a **work-life balance.** Work-life balance refers to the time employees allocate to their work and other aspects of their lives, such as their social lives or families. Work-life balance has traditionally been viewed from the perspective of work as a full-time, permanent position and life as caring for children in the home, yet this view has changed with consideration of other types of either work or life. People without dependent children may desire a work-life balance too, as do those in part-time positions and those caring for others (such as elders or pets), pursuing an education, engaging in non-work-related training, engaging in hobbies or exercise, maintaining health, or participating in community activities or religious activities.[262]

Employees and managers can strive for healthy workplace environments. Employees can take steps to ensure they have maintained a healthy work-life balance, such as leaving their work at work, reducing their email access times, learning to say no, shortening commitments, and minimizing interruptions. Managers can also help their subordinates to achieve a healthy work life balance by not pressuring their employees to respond to work matters during their off hours. Managers who send emails or text messages in the middle of the night could be stressing out their subordinates who may feel compelled to respond quickly.

Stress can lead to insomnia and a lack of sleep. According to the National Sleep Foundation, nearly half of Americans say that sleep affects their daily activities. To alleviate this issue, some companies offer **nap rooms** or napping chairs, where employees can take time off during the middle of their workdays for power naps. Zappos, Google, Cisco, PWC, Capital One Labs, and Ben and Jerry's are examples.[263] According to Inc. Magazine, around 6 percent of employers have onsite nap rooms. The intentions are to recharge and reenergize the minds of drowsy employees, helping them to regain concentration, reduce anxiety and depression, and boost productivity.

Allocating time for reflection is another tool used in many organizations. Google famously tells its employees to devote 20 percent of their work weeks to tasks outside of their usual daily work activities. Employees use this time to be creative, thinking of new ways to do things at Google and new strategies to consider. 25 percent of Aetna's employees engage in meditations, or deep reflections. This measure has resulted in a 28 percent reduction in stress, 20 percent improvement in sleep quality, and 19 percent reduction in pain. After offering opportunities to meditate and reflection Aetna employees gained 62 minutes of productivity a week![264]

Violence in the Workplace

Workplace violence is usually in the form of physical threats or abuse, creates a risk to the health or safety of employees. Forms of violence also include verbal or written threats, harassment, physical attacks, and threatening behavior. These may occur in the workplace or in places associated with the workplace, such as in off-site meeting locations or conferences.

According to the Canadian Centre for Occupational Health and Safety, the following work-related factors increase the risk of workplace violence:

- Working with the public
- Handling money, valuables, or prescription drugs
- Working where alcohol is served
- Working alone or in small numbers (as in real estate) or in isolated or low traffic areas (washrooms, utility rooms)
- Providing services, health, care, or education
- Carrying out inspection or enforcement duties
- Working with unstable or volatile persons
- Having a mobile workplace (e.g., taxicab)
- Working in community-based settings (nursing homes)

As you will note, certain types of occupations lend themselves to a greater risk, such as occupations in banking, real estate, healthcare, pharmacies, retail stores, taxicabs, or nursing homes. Additionally, the risk of violence may be greater at certain times of the day (late hours of the night or early hours in the morning), on pay days, or during tax season.

What can human resource managers do to mitigate the potential for workplace violence? Managers can take measures to identify the right employees in the *hiring* process who are less inclined to violence. They should check job candidates' criminal background records, driving records, and references to help to identify those prone to violence. They can also administer questionnaires to identify job candidates' proclivity to violence. Managers should also train employees to understand what constitutes workplace violence and identify people who are likely to commit violence.

Employers may also adopt "if you see something, say something" campaigns to generate awareness and increase the likelihood that violence will be reported to the proper authorities and those prone to violence will be identified and treated appropriately. This campaign was initiated by the Department of Homeland Security in the United States as a means of countering terrorism, yet it can be applied in workplaces, schools, community facilities, and more.

Workplace Injuries and Illnesses

A **workplace injury** refers to a discrete occurrence in the course of work, leading to physical or mental occupational injury. For example, if an employee slips and falls down a stairwell at work and breaks his leg, he sustained a workplace injury. He can collect workers compensation to cover his related medical bills and a portion of lost wages. An **illness** is considered to be work-related if an event or exposure at work either caused or significantly contributed to the condition or significantly aggravated a pre-existing condition. Years of work in coal mines often result in lung disease, while exposure to asbestos can result in mesothelioma. Both conditions are considered work-related illnesses. If employers are found to be negligent in the conditions causing the workplace injuries or illnesses, they can be held criminally liable.

Workplace Accidents

Accidents also happen periodically in workplaces, especially in those of moderate size. The Bureau of Labor Statistics (BLS) reported that in 2018, 5,250 fatal accidents occurred in U.S. workplaces, which is a rate of 3.5 per 100,000 workers. In 2016, the BLS reported that 2.9 million nonfatal accidents were reported by U.S. private employers, which is the equivalent of 2.9 workers per 100 full-time equivalents (FTE) workers.[265] Private industry employers reported 48,500 fewer accidents in 2016 than in 2015. Most of the accidents reported were based on falls, slips, or trips. Other types of accidents reported included exposure to harmful substances or environments, fires and explosions, and violence and other injuries by persons or animals.

Workers Compensation

Employees who are injured in work-related accidents may be eligible to collect workers compensation. **Workers Compensation** is a no-fault insurance policy that covers injured employees and provides wage replacement and medical benefits in exchange for the employee to relinquish his or her rights to sue their employer for the tort of negligence. Workers compensation is a state-mandated program and its applications vary between states, so human resource managers are advised to check the particular applications and laws related to workers compensation in their own states. Most employers are required to carry workers compensation insurance, yet some exceptions are notable. Farm workers, seasonal employees, and domestic employees are usually excluded.

Workers compensation covers most work-related injuries, yet it does not cover injuries that occur because the employee was (1) drunk or using illegal drugs; (2) committing a serious crime; (3) violating company policies; (4) self-inflicting injuries; or (5) starting a fight with others. In these cases, employers can contest workers compensation claims. They can also contest non-work-related injuries.

Workers compensation may also cover injuries resulting from long-term overuse or misuse. For example, chronic back problems, chronic neck problems, and repetitive stress injuries, such as carpal tunnel syndrome, have been covered by workers compensation.

OSHA

"'A man is dead because this employer decided to break the law over and over again. Before this tragedy, OSHA cited this contractor twice for exposing workers to fall hazards, including at the same site just four months earlier,' said Dr. David Michaels, Assistant Secretary of Labor of Occupational Safety and Health."[266] The man fell 22 feet to his death because his employer didn't take the proper steps to ensure safety. Fines to employers in such cases can be over $300,000.[267]

The Occupational Safety and Health Act of 1970 (OSHA) was established as a means of reducing illnesses and injuries in United States' workplaces and ensuring safe and healthy conditions. OSHA establishes and enforces standards by providing training, outreach, education, and assistance. OSHA is an agency of the U.S. Department of Labor.

Workers' Rights

OSHA gives workers the following rights.[268]

"Under federal law, you are entitled to a safe workplace. Your employer must provide a workplace free of known health and safety hazards. If you have concerns, you have the right to speak up about them without fear of retaliation. You also have the right to:

- Be trained in a language you understand
- Work on machines that are safe
- Be provided required safety gear, such as gloves or a harness and lifeline for falls
- Be protected from toxic chemicals
- Request an OSHA inspection, and speak to the inspector
- Report an injury or illness, and get copies of your medical records
- See copies of the workplace injury and illness log
- Review records of work-related injuries and illnesses
- Get copies of test results done to find hazards in the workplace"

Employers' Responsibilities

Under OSHA, employers have a **general duty** to provide a workplace free from recognized hazards that are causing or likely to cause death or serious physical harm. Employers must also comply with standards, rules and regulations issued under the OSH Act. The following items are examples of employer responsibilities.[269]

- Examine workplace conditions to make sure they conform to applicable OSHA standards.
- Make sure employees have and use safe tools and equipment and properly maintain this equipment.
- Use color codes, posters, labels or signs to warn employees of potential hazards.
- Establish or update operating procedures and communicate them so that employees follow safety and health requirements.
- Employers must provide safety training in a language and vocabulary workers can understand.
- Employers with hazardous chemicals in the workplace must develop and implement a written hazard communication program and train employees on the hazards they are exposed to and proper precautions (and a copy of safety data sheets must be readily available).

- Provide medical examinations and training when required by OSHA standards.

Employers should also pay attention to workplace **ergonomics.** Ergonomics refers to the study of physiological and psychological principles to the design of products, processes and systems. Applied to the workplace, ergonomics refers to the study of how a workplace and the equipment used there can best be designed for efficiency, posture, comfort, safety, and productivity. Poorly designed workstations, cars, sofas, and chairs can contribute to aches and pains, suggesting poor ergonomics. Managers should design workstations that attend to ergonomics to ensure employees can work free from the aches and pains associated with poor designs. For example, chairs without lumbar supports, weak back rests, and computers without palm rests may result in either back injuries or carpal tunnel syndrome.

With the rise in the use of computers over the past few decades, **carpal tunnel syndrome** has become more commonplace. Carpal tunnel syndrome results in tingling, numbness, and weakness in the hand and it's caused by pressure on a nerve in the wrist. Tennis players have long experienced the condition, but prolonged computer use can also bring it about when one's palms flatly rest on the keyboard causing undue pressure on the wrists.

OSHA's Inspection Priorities

OSHA has jurisdiction over approximately 7 million worksites. The agency establishes priorities in its inspections by focusing in the most dangerous situations first. OSHA's priorities are ordered as follows:

1. Imminent danger situations, which are hazards that could cause death or serious physical harm. Compliance officers will ask employers to correct these hazards immediately or remove endangered employees.

2. Severe injuries and illnesses. All work-related fatalities must be reported within 8 hours of the occurrence. Within 24 hours, all work-related inpatient hospitalizations, amputations, or eye losses must be reported.

3. Worker complaints and allegations of hazards or violations. Employees may request anonymity when they file complaints.

4. Referrals of hazards from other federal, state or local agencies, individuals, organizations or the media receive consideration for inspection.

5. Targeted inspections, which are inspections aimed at specific high-hazard industries or individual workplaces that have experienced high rates of injuries and illnesses also receive priority.

6. Follow-up inspections to ensure that violations previously identified have been abated.

OSHA Violations[270]

For serious violations, other-than-serious violations, or failures to post signs, OSHA issues a penalty of $12,934 to employers. If employers fail to abate (or correct) a violation, OSHA issues $12,934 penalty per day beyond the abatement date. Employers who willfully or repeat violations receive a penalty of $129,336 per violation. In summary, OSHA violations can be extremely costly for employers, so attention to OSHA's citations and employer responsibilities is critical.

Proactive Safety Programs

Firefighters are in arguably one of the most dangerous professions. Proactively establishing and implementing safety programs in this profession could be the difference between life and death. In a recent study of firefighters, a successful risk management program was identified.[271]

This program began with a three-phase **risk management** process: (1) scoping; (2) risk assessment and (3) control evaluation. The **scoping** phase establishes the context of the operation or job task with special attention to potential hazards and unwanted events. The **risk assessment** phase formally details potential hazards and the likelihood or consequence of any potential hazard or injury. Hazards are labeled as unlikely, with < 10 percent chance of probability; likely with a 30 – 75 percent chance of probability; and almost certain with a > 75 percent chance of probability. Consequences of the hazard are then labeled as (1) minor effects, with first aid; (2) moderate, with lost time due to the injury; (3) major, with a loss in the quality of life; and (4) maximal, with single or multiple fatalities. Potential new or adaptive **control** strategies are then considered to mitigate the identified risks. Based on this structure, the aforementioned firefighter study developed the following list of recommendations.[272] This methodology is one approach that can reduce the potential for industries in a field in which the risk of injury is significant.

Recommendations	Considerations or suggestions
Planning and organizing the scoping sessions	Involve a diverse group of firefighters Incentivize participation Utilize best practices and a "bottom up" approach Choose a strong facilitator
Identify clear tasks for the RM process	Have clear steps to help identify specific control strategies
Use quality data	Use department-level or company-level data Present data clearly and by task
Understand culture	Consider elements of the firefighter culture Realize that not all will "buy in"
Recognize the importance of technical assistance	Provide technical assistance in compiling data and for other aspects of the RM process, such as the mapping and ranking of control strategies
Understand available resources	Highlight the cost savings of RM to garner support
Provide regular communication	Communicate expectations of the RM process up front Provide regular communication to all firefighters

Safety Culture

Creating a culture that focuses on safety is particularly important in industries in which safety could be compromised regularly in the nature of the tasks performed. Examples of such dangerous jobs include loggers, coal miners, fishers, firefighters, truck drivers, steel workers construction workers, and policemen. According to one recent study,[273] logging is by far the most dangerous job in the United States as it is considered 38 times more dangerous than the typical job. In 2016, there were 135.9 fatal injuries per 100,000 loggers. The most common accident in logging is for the logger to be struck by an object, such as a log or falling branch. They also deal with dangerous machines such as chainsaws and harvesters.

In such industries, it is essential that companies adopt **safety cultures,** which are cultures focused on the safety and health of their employees. Hiring employees who are more likely to embrace safety measures and rules is one way to build a safety culture. Very young and very old employees tend to be less safe than their middle-age counterparts, as evidenced by high automobile insurance rates for the two groups. The young may act less cautiously, while the old may be inhibited by slower reaction times and reflexes. Training employees regularly on ways to enhance safety in the workplace is also useful. Employees should be aware of the best practices in their industries to enhance safety and they should be able to use those practices in their jobs. Business leaders should also motivate their employees to follow instructions designed to keep them safe by holding them accountable for unsafe actions and recognizing and incentivizing them for safe actions. These approaches are among many that organizations can use to inspire safety cultures. Such cultures may help to save lives, especially in the most dangerous types of jobs.

Crisis Management

Unexpected weather events impact every society and culture in the world, yet given our particular locations we can establish probabilities of specific types of events. For example, in Florida, the probability of lightning strikes, hurricanes, and spin-off tornadoes during hurricanes is relatively high. Businesses operating in Florida should have a plan in place to deal with potential adverse weather events.

To prepare for disasters or crisis events, leaders should have a list of best-case and worst-case scenarios. Each scenario should be identified and appropriate responses delineated. Controls should be put into place to mitigate the damage in worst-case scenarios. In Florida, hurricanes are prevalent, so Floridians should consider (1) occupying buildings built of concrete block rather than frame construction; (2) accessing wood or metal shudders to cover all windows; (3) having back-ups for electrical power; (4) having back-ups for all data; and (5) having an evacuation plan. Leaders should also establish a plan for handling recovery after a worst-case scenario.

Conclusion

Health and safety are two of the most important functions of human resource management as engaging in healthful and safe workplace practices can enhance productivity, satisfaction, engagement, and ultimately, the bottom line. Companies can adopt a variety of human resource practices to ensure health and safety, from hiring the right workers to training and incentivizing them. These approaches can impact their long-term sustainability.

QUESTIONS FOR REVIEW

1. What situations are most likely to results in workplace violence?

2. Accidents occur most frequently in _____ size organizations. Why?

3. When can an employer contest a workers' compensation claim?

4. When must occupational injuries be recorded?

5. What is OSHA's top priority in workplace inspections?

6. Can OSHA require an employer purchase hard hats in construction sites under the "general duty clause?"

7. Identify some of the least expensive options in employee wellness programs.

8. How can organizations take actions to address high levels of employee stress?

9. What is the general duty clause of OSHA?

10. What is workers' compensation? When must workers' compensation be paid?

APPLICATIONS

1. Workers' Compensation Coverage for Injuries due to a Bank Robbery in Florida

Martha Landon was working as a branch manager at a bank in Florida when she was shot in the face during a robbery. After she recovered from her injuries, she sued the bank, alleging that it failed to protect her. The security guard who was hired to protect the bank was not present on the day of the robbery. The bank filed a motion to dismiss the case, stating that workers' compensation is the exclusive remedy for employees injured on the job. Conduct a search of Florida laws with respect to workers' compensation. Are the bank's claims accurate?[274]

2. Trends on Smoking Laws

What are the laws in your home state or country with respect to smoking in the workplace? Conduct a web search.

3. OSHA Safety Checklist for an Office Environment

Get into groups of between 4 and 5 students and visit at least three buildings on campus. Identify whether the buildings and campus are in compliance with OSHA. Circle the correct answer, whether "yes," "no," or "not applicable."

Basic life safety

1. Are hallways and exits free from obstruction?

Yes   No   N/A

2. Are exit signs visible and illuminated?

Yes   No   N/A

3. Are emergency instructions posted near telephones?

Yes   No   N/A

4. Is a fire emergency plan posted and visible?

Yes   No   N/A

General workplace safety

5. Are chairs in working condition or are they broken?

Yes   No   N/A

6. Are all equipment and supplies in working condition?

Yes   No   N/A

7. Are filing cabinets placed against a wall and bolted?

Yes   No   N/A

8. Are carts available for the transport of heavy materials?

Yes   No   N/A

Slips and falls

9. Are floor surfaces free of hazards?

Yes   No   N/A

10. Are wet floors marked with "wet floor" signs of warning?

Yes   No   N/A

11. Are inclines in floors covered in "no-skid" materials?

Yes   No   N/A

12. Are there stools/ ladders available to reach high objects?

Yes   No   N/A

Electrical

13. Are all electrical appliances properly grounded and insulated?

Yes   No   N/A

14. Is all electrical equipment in proper working order?

Yes   No   N/A

15. Are permanent use cords covered by runners in walk-ways?

Yes   No   N/A

16. Are extension cords taped to the floor?

Yes   No   N/A

CASE STUDIES

1. Alabama Incentivizes Healthier Behaviors for Employees by Punishing the Unhealthy

In 2009, The Alabama State Employees' Insurance Board approved a plan to incentivize the state's 37,527 employees to become healthier. Those who don't become healthier would be assessed $25 per month for health insurance that at the time was free.

In 2010, workers were required to undergo free health screenings. Those who failed to comply were charged a $25 fee. If the screening indicated serious problems with blood pressure, cholesterol, glucose or obesity, employees had a year to see a doctor at no cost, enroll in a wellness program, or take measures to improve their health. Those who showed progress weren't charged the $25 monthly fee (starting in 2011).[275]

What are the implications of such decisions? Which law is applicable to this situation? What other options could Alabama have taken to encourage its workers to be healthier?

2. The Compliance Officer at Coyote Corporation

Bill and Jim were having lunch when an OSHA Compliance Officer showed up and informed them that he wanted to conduct an inspection of the construction site where they were working. Bill is the president of Coyote Corporation, which is a 200-person private firm that oversees and manages construction of a variety of residential and commercial properties in Arizona. Bill said, "I suppose," as he grunted and watched the officer walk past him to inspect the site. About two hours later, the compliance officer returned to the trailer where Bill and Jim were working. He presented them with a list of violations and told them he would return in 30 days to see if they had abated them. Did the compliance officer follow the proper procedure?

Chapter 12: Servant Leadership and Ethics

Introduction

Earl Stewart is the dealer principal of Earl Stewart Toyota of North Palm Beach, Florida. For years, he engaged in what some consider to be "typical" dealer practices of high-pressure haggling, hidden fees, and deceptive tactics.

"Back in the day...I was a thief and I was surrounded by a bunch of thieves, so I wanted to be the smartest, best thief in the market. And I was."[276]

Then one day he had an epiphany. His sons abhorred his tactics. He had just become a grandfather. And he survived stage 2 colon cancer. Life was about more than being the best thief in the market. Life was about valuing people, not abusing them.

Stewart soon broke his bad habits and became determined to build a strong reputation with clients. The company code is "(1) Do whatever our customer asks if they believe they're right; (2) Your first loyalty is to our customers, not to Toyota; and (3) Always answer all calls, emails, texts, and messages of any kind from our customers ASAP."[277]

Five "red phones" are located throughout the dealership, which are landlines that directly connect customers to Stewart's personal cell phone. Stewart's son, Josh Stewart, considers the phones a value proposition. "Every one of them is one of our unique selling propositions. We want to set ourselves apart from the competition, and not with come-ons and gimmicks. You can't put a dollar amount on the red phone – how much value in there is that?"[278]

Helen Keller once said, "Character cannot be developed in ease and quiet. Only through the experience of trial and suffering can the soul be strengthened, vision cleared, ambition inspired, and success achieved." People who consider themselves servant leaders often embrace similar views and values.

One such leader is also in the auto industry: Richard Dimmitt. Richard Dimmitt is the owner of a highly successful automobile dealership with five locations and three hundred and fifty employees in Florida. To share his vision and mission with his company, Dimmitt wrote a book entitled "Servant Hearts" in which he has identified three core values that drive Dimmitt behavior on a daily basis: character, commitment and cooperation. Dimmitt sells high end, luxury vehicles and maintains a high touch, customer-focused business strategy that is consistent with the company's human resource management strategy. Employees at Dimmitt Automotive Group are imbued with the values of a servant leader whose purpose and mission are to serve others with personal integrity and to develop long-term relationships with customers, employees, and the community.

"At the Dimmitt Automotive Group, we believe that we can create trust in the work environment by expecting our managers to be servant leaders. We regularly ask our associates questions like, 'Is there anything that I can do to help you accomplish your tasks at work today?' or 'How can I better serve you as your manager and coach?' and we're confident that a 'servant leader coach' is the type of manager that can develop the talents of our people while at the same time fostering trusting relationships."[279]

We next turn to the topics of this chapter of servant leadership and ethics.

Objectives:

After reading this chapter, you should be able to:

- Define servant leadership and distinguish it from other types of leadership.
- Identify the nine dimensions and seven virtuous constructs of servant leadership.
- Discuss the benefits to organizations who have embraced servant leadership approaches.
- Identify the dimensions of the multidimensional ethics scale.
- Identify the universal moral principles that guide humanity.

Theories of Leadership

Over the past century, theories of leadership have taken several forms focused on leader traits, behaviors, or contingencies. **Trait** theories ask the question: what traits make a leader a "great man?" They focus on what leaders are. The **behavioral approach** focuses on what leaders do. Studies using this approach focus on task-oriented behaviors to initiate structure or relationship-oriented behaviors to show consideration. Both the task and behavioral approaches failed to incorporate important situational factors that may play a role in the traits and behaviors leaders exhibit. The **contingency approach** focuses on the fit between the leader's style and the situation. An example of a theory that fell under this umbrella is **path goal theory**. According to path goal theory, a leader's primary function is to motivate followers by increasing personal payoffs to subordinates for work achievements. Scholars also used this theory to better explain different leadership characteristics, such as transformational, transactional, and laissez faire leadership.[280] **Transactional leadership** motivates followers by providing task guidance, correcting performance flaws, and rewarding successful efforts. Transactional leadership involves an exchange or transaction process with followers. **Transformational leadership** motivates followers by inspiration, charisma, intellectual stimulation, and individualized consideration. **Laissez faire leadership** is a "hands off" non-directive approach in which the leaders let the followers work more autonomously.

According to the Society for Human Resource Management, leadership consultants Jack Zenger and Joseph Folkman surveyed over 300,000 business leaders to identify the top competencies from a list of key leadership skills.[281] The following are most important to leadership success:

- Inspires and motivates others.
- Displays high integrity and honesty.
- Solves problems and analyzes issues.
- Drives for results.
- Communicates powerfully and prolifically.
- Builds relationships.
- Displays technical or professional expertise.
- Displays a strategic perspective.
- Develops others.
- Innovates.

Innovation

It's also important that leaders be innovative. Professors Jeff Dyer of Brigham Young University and Nathan Furr of INSEAD worked with a consultant to develop a measure of innovativeness in leaders. They measure reputation for innovative by looking at leaders' media coverage, social connections and networks (on Twitter and LinkedIn), track record for value creation based on the market value growth for their organizations, and investor expectations of the future values of their organizations.[282] Jeff Bezos of Amazon tops the list of innovative leaders, followed by Elon Musk of Tesla, Mark Zuckerberg of Facebook, Marc Benioff of Salesforce.com, and Reed Hastings of Netflix.

"We need to have a beginner's mind to think about what is happening." – Marc Benioff

Servant Leadership

These competencies well align with those of servant leaders. What is servant leadership? Servant leadership is an approach that focuses on developing the potential of employees through community stewardship, self- motivation, task effectiveness, and future leadership capabilities.[283] Servant leadership expands upon transformational leadership as it focuses more on followers and encompasses altruism and humility. Transformational leadership is a broader term, which refers to leaders who inspire others to reach higher than they had anticipated to achieve organizational goals.

"Servant leadership is a holistic leadership approach that engages followers in multiple dimensions (e.g., relational, ethical, emotional, spiritual), such that they are empowered to grow into what they are capable of becoming. It seeks first and foremost to develop followers on the basis of leaders' altruistic and ethical orientations.[284] When followers' well-being and growth are prioritized, they in turn are more engaged and effective in their work. Servant leaders see themselves as stewards of the organizations,[285] who seek to grow the resources, financial and otherwise, that have been entrusted to them. As such, they do not ignore performance expectations even though they focus on the personal development of their followers. Unlike performance-oriented leadership approaches that often "sacrifice people on the altar of profit and growth,"[286] servant leaders focus on sustainable performance over the long run."[287]

Researchers in servant leadership have developed nine dimensions: [288]

Nine Dimensions of Servant Leadership

1. Emotional healing—showing sensitivity to others' personal concerns and issues

2. Creating value for the community—a conscious, genuine concern for helping the community

3. Conceptual skills—possessing the knowledge of the organization and tasks at hand so as to be in a position to effectively support and assist others, especially immediate followers

4. Empowering—encouraging and facilitating others, in identifying and solving problems, as well as determining when and how to complete work tasks

5. Helping subordinates grow and succeed—demonstrating genuine concern for others' career growth and development by providing support and mentoring

6. Putting subordinates first—using actions and words to make it clear to others (especially immediate followers) that satisfying their work needs is a priority (Supervisors who practice this principle will often break from their own work to assist subordinates with problems they are facing with their assigned duties.)

7. Behaving ethically—interacting openly, fairly, and honestly with others

8. Relationships—the act of making a genuine effort to know, understand, and support others in the organization, with an emphasis on building long-term relationships with immediate followers

9. Servanthood—a way of being marked by one's self-categorization and desire to be characterized by others as someone who serves others first, even when self-sacrifice is required

Servant Leadership is a Virtuous Theory

A virtue is a qualitative, spiritual characteristic that is comprised of three elements, according to Aristotle: (1) good habits; (2) the middle ground between the extremes of too much and too little; and (3) a habit that is a firm, settled disposition of choosing what is good and right.[289] Virtue theory refers to doing the right things with a focus on moral character. Virtue theory was originated by Aristotle in his book "Nicomachean Ethics."

Servant leadership includes seven virtuous constructs: (1) agapao love, which is the Greek term for moral love; (2) humility; (3) altruism; (4) vision; (5) trust; (6) empowerment; and (7) service.[290]

Are Servant Leadership-Focused Organizations Among the Best?

Each year, Fortune Magazine ranks one hundred top companies to work for. Seventeen companies on this list, including the #1 company SAS, are considered servant leadership organizations. In fact, five of the top ten practice servant leadership.[291] The seventeen are as follows:

- SAS (#1 on the list of Best Companies to Work For)
- Wegmans Food Market (3)
- Zappos.com (6)
- Nugget Market (8)

- Recreational Equipment (REI) (9)
- Container Store (21)
- Whole Foods Market (24)
- QuikTrip (34)
- Balfour Beatty Construction (40)
- TD Industries (45)
- Aflac (57)
- Marriott International (71)
- Nordstrom (74)
- Men's Wearhouse (87)
- CH2M Hill (90)
- Darden Restaurants (97)
- Starbucks (98)

Consider the example from the Container Store.[292]

"Our Foundation Principles were formalized in 1988, after we opened our Houston store. That store made us take a look at our business a little harder. From the day we opened the doors, the store did more business than we ever anticipated, which became quite overwhelming to our Houston store employees. We already had a 10-year-old company with strong values and culture; however, communicating this to an entire store of new employees, most whom never had been exposed to our stores or our way of doing business, was quite a challenge.

Our Chairman, Kip, struggled with how to clearly communicate our culture so that all the employees in the Houston store would act and make decisions using the same set of values and knowledge as the employees in the rest of the company.

In a moment of inspiration, he referred back to a file he had started many years ago called his "philosophy epistle file" where he'd saved various anecdotes, musings and philosophical phrases that he admired or thought of himself beginning in high school, through college and up to this time in the business. He invited the entire Houston store staff over to their Manager's home and chose many examples to communicate the message that no matter how big the company became, our guiding principles and values would stay the same. Kip was nervous to be sharing all of these ideas that were so near and dear to his heart – but to his surprise they were incredibly well-received by the team!

Over the years, the philosophies that Kip shared that night were condensed into what are now our Foundation Principles. By understanding and supporting these principles, we can all respond in unison to similar circumstances. In other words, we act as a unit, all working toward the same goal. Retail is far, far too situational to attempt to achieve anything through inflexible rules and policies. So, instead of using the typical phone-book-sized retail procedural manual to guide our decision making, we use these Foundation Principles to keep us on track, focused and fulfilled as employees. With this combination of values-driven business philosophies and a one-of-a-kind product selection, The Container Store's goal, with all due humility, is to become the best retail store in America!"

The following "foundation principles" guide Container Store employees: "(1) 1 great person = 3 good people in terms of business productivity; (2) communication IS leadership; (3) Fill the other guy's basket to the brim. Making money then becomes an easy proposition; (4) the best selection, service, and price; (5) intuition does not come to an unprepared mind. You need to train before it happens; (6) man in the desert selling, which corresponds to astonishing customers by anticipating their needs and exceeding their expectations; and (7) air of excitement!"

Do Organizations Practicing Servant Leadership Perform Well?

Marcel Schwantes of Inc. Magazine identified ten chief executive officers of organizations whom he considered high in servant leadership. #1 on this list is Cheryl Bachelder, the CEO of Popeye's Louisiana Kitchen. In her book "Dare to Serve: How to Drive Superior Results by Serving Others," Bachelder presents a compelling case for servant leadership and its ability to reinvent an organization.

According to Marcel Schwantes,[293] when Bachelder became the CEO of Popeye's in 2007, sales and profits were trending downward and the stock price had declined from $34 per share in 2002 to $13 per share in 2007. Relations between Popeye's owners and its franchise owners had become strained as the brand name had become stagnant. By 2014, sales were up twenty five percent and profits were up by forty percent and the stock price
By 2014, sales were up 25 percent, profits up 40 percent. Market share had grown from 14 percent to 21 percent, and the stock price was over $40. As of this writing (in April 2018), the stock price is at $55 per share.

What happened? Bachelder focused the workplace on treating employees with dignity and respect and challenged to perform at their highest levels. Egoistic managers were moved out and replaced by servant leaders. Thanks to her dedication and hard work, Bachelder was the recipient of 2015 Norman Award by the U.S. restaurant industry in recognition for her leadership and impact.

Another study found that when leaders and managers empowered their employees on a daily basis, workers are more proactive the next day and more willing to offer constructive suggestions for organizational improvement and take risks to benefit their performance.[294] These relationships work best when workers get a good night sleep.

Why Do Servant Leadership-Focused Companies Perform Well?

In Daniel Pink's Ted Talk entitled "The puzzle of motivation,"[295] Pink offered several motivators in the workplace: purpose, autonomy, and mastery. People desire to have a purpose to be a part of something bigger than themselves. They desire the autonomy and freedom to make their own decisions without feeling as if they're being micro-managed. They finally desire control over their destinies, performance, and circumstances, or what Pink terms as mastery. These concepts are similar to Abraham Maslow's motivation theory that suggests a hierarchy of needs in the form of a pyramid of motivation. Basic needs are at the bottom of the pyramid and one must satisfy these needs before advancing to higher needs. In order from the bottom to the top are the physiological, safety, love/belonging, esteem, and self-actualization. The highest need of self-actualization is consistent with Pink's purpose, mastery, and autonomy. People who are self-actualized believe that their lives have been fulfilled and they are doing everything of which they are capable. Self-actualization refers to personal growth and discovery.

The aforementioned virtues and dimensions of servant leadership correspond to developing employees' self-actualization. Employees working in organizations characterized by high levels of servant leadership are therefore likely to be motivated by purpose, autonomy, and mastery.

Recent research has further found that leaders may use servant leadership behaviors to set the vision for their organizations and to satisfy the needs of their followers. In a study of servant leaders and their employees, employees' needs for autonomy, competence, and relatedness were met through servant leadership.[296] Servant leadership has also been found to correspond to trust, perceptions of an ethical environment,[297] an empowerment climate and group creativity.[298]

"Today, new leadership strategies have emerged as new drivers of effectiveness in workplace relationships based on the leader-follower relationship. One of these leadership strategies is servant leadership, whose motto is 'put and promote followers' interests and needs first', which makes this leadership style strongly linked to exercising high ethics.

As agapao love and service to others are important distinctive features of these leaders' decisions and behaviors, the ethical influence relationship with their collaborators is thought to reach high levels. It is no surprise then that this ethical influence relationship leads to followers who serve others and inculcates followers with values such as acceptance, tolerance, empathy, love, or forgiveness. More importantly, these leaders might make followers who grow in maturity, intelligence, creativity, and self-management, among other aspects."[299]

Ethical Decision-Making Frameworks

Reidenbach and Robin's well-known Multidimensional Ethics Scale[300] contains ethical dimensions that people use to guide their ethical decisions. The dimensions are relativism, utilitarianism, deontology, justice, and egoism.

Relativism

Ethical **relativism** is the belief that what is right or wrong depends on the morals in the society in which it is practiced. For example, if love, justice, empathy and honesty are considered acceptable in a society, then ethical relativism suggests that people will act in accordance with those values. Conversely, if the practices of bribery, slavery, cannibalism, or rape are considered acceptable in a society, then ethical relativism *also* suggests those practices are right.

Utilitarianism

Ethical **utilitarianism** is the doctrine that actions are right if they benefit or are useful for a majority of the people. On the utilitarian view, one ought to maximize the good by considering the good of others as well as one's own good. The core idea in utilitarianism is that the consequences or effects on the greater portion of humanity of decisions inform whether actions or values are right or wrong. Like relativism, utilitarianism has flaws. Suppose four people in a hospital need organ transplants of a heart, liver, kidney and lungs. If a healthy person walks into the hospital, the utilitarian decision would be to kill one to save the four. Obviously, this is not an acceptable course of action and it is not morally right.

Deontology

Deontology is an ethical theory that states that the morality of an action is not based on its consequences but rather whether the action is right or wrong under a set of rules, or duties. Deontology is considered a "non-

265

consequentialist" view. For example, one could posit that all people have a moral obligation to follow the Golden Rule, treating others as we want to be treated.

Justice

Justice is an ethical theory that focuses on the fairness of decisions by considering equity and equality. Morals are considered right when they maximize fairness and wrong when they maximize mistreatment and inequality.

Egoism

Unlike the first four dimensions of the multidimensional ethics scale, which focus on ethics relative to others, egoism is focused on the self. **Egoism** is the ethical theory that people should maximize their own self-interests. Egoism has two variants: descriptive egoism states that people act in ways to maximize their own self-interests, while normative egoism states that people *should* act in ways to maximize their own self-interests. Egoism is not the same as egotism, which is the psychological overvaluation of one's own importance.

What Is and What Ought to Be

Cross-cultural scholars have distinguished what "is" from what "ought to be" in societies. In the United States, for example, Shalom Schwartz[301] found many people value self-enhancement, which is characterized by higher levels of hedonism, achievement and power. In eastern societies, more emphasize self-transcendence, which is characterized by benevolence and universalism. People in the United States may value self-enhancement while concurrently recognizing that they ought to place a greater emphasis on self-transcendence, or others' focused values.

Interestingly, Schwartz found that across the 82 countries in his cross-cultural surveys, there was a surprising consensus in the hierarchical order of the values. He examined the following values: **self-transcendence** (benevolence, universalism), **openness to change** (hedonism, stimulation, and self-direction), **conservation** (security, conformity, and tradition) and **self-enhancement** (achievement, power). Hedonism split evenly between the openness to change domain and the self-enhancement domain, so Schwartz grouped the value with the former, though noting its presence in the latter. Benevolence, universalism, and self-direction values were considered the most important, while power and stimulation were considered the least important across all cultures.

According to Shalom Schwartz,[302] "This implies that the aspects of human nature and of social functioning that shape individual value priorities are widely shared across cultures. I presented the initial, functionalist explanation that has been offered for this phenomenon. It deserves much more analysis in depth." "The high importance of benevolence values (ranked 1st) derives from the centrality of positive, cooperative social relations in the family, the main setting for initial and continuing value acquisition. Benevolence values provide the internalized motivational base for such relations. They are reinforced and modeled early and repeatedly. Universalism values (2nd) also contribute to positive social relations. They are functionally important primarily when group members must relate to those with whom they do not readily identify, in schools, work-places, etc. They may even threaten in-group solidarity during times of intergroup conflict. Therefore, universalism values are less important than benevolence values."

University professors and studies often focus on our differences, but numerous studies have found that we're more the same. The above cited studies suggest we all support values of goodness. They suggest we're hard-wired to seek meaning and purpose.

Schwartz's Ten Values:

Power: social status and prestige, control or dominance over people and resources (power, authority, wealth)

Achievement: personal success through demonstrating competence according to social standards (successful, capable, ambitious, influential, intelligent, self-respect)

Hedonism: pleasure and sensuous gratification for oneself (pleasure, enjoying life)

Stimulation: excitement, novelty, and change in life (daring, varied life, exciting life)

Self-direction: independent thought and action-choosing, creating, exploring (creativity, freedom, independent, curious, choosing own goals, self-respect)

Universalism: understanding, appreciation, and tolerance and protection for the welfare of all people and for nature (broadminded, wisdom, social justice, equality)

Benevolence: preservation and enhancement of the welfare of people with whom one is in frequent personal contact (helpful, honest, forgiving, loyal, responsible, true friendship, mature love)

Tradition: respect, commitment and acceptance of the customs and ideas that traditional culture or religion provide the self (humble, accepting my portion in life, respect for tradition, moderate, devout)

Conformity: restraint of actions, inclinations, and impulses likely to upset or harm others and violate social expectations or norms (politeness, obedient, self-discipline, honoring parents and elders)

Security: safety, harmony, and stability of society, of relationships, and of self (family, security, national security, social order, clean, reciprocation of favors, sense of belonging, healthy)

A Universal Set of Moral Values

People seeking to resolve value conflicts may call upon an innate and universal set of moral values. Previous research based on the seven most practiced religions in the world and several secular groups has identified a "short list of universal moral values."[303] These are as follows:

"1. Commitment to something greater than oneself
- To recognize the existence of and be committed to a Supreme Being, higher principle, transcendent purpose or meaning to one's existence
- To seek the Truth (or truths)
- To seek Justice

2. Self-respect, but with humility, self-discipline and acceptance of personal responsibility
- To respect and care for oneself.
- To not exalt oneself or overindulge – to show humility and avoid gluttony, greed, or other forms of selfishness or self-centeredness.
- To act in accordance with one's conscience and accept responsibility for one's behavior.

3. Respect and caring for others (i.e., the Golden Rule)
- To recognize the connectedness between all people.
- To serve humankind and to be helpful to individuals.
- To be caring, respectful, compassionate, tolerant, and forgiving of others.
- To not hurt others (e.g., do not murder, abuse, steal from, cheat or lie to others.

4. Caring for other living things and the environment."[304]

Other global studies have found similarly. One examined the ancient texts from eight religious traditions (Christianity, Judaism, Athenian philosophy, Taoism, Confucianism, Islam, and Hinduism).[305] The authors found six recurrent values: courage, temperance, justice, transcendence, humanity, and wisdom. In a survey using psychological, historical, juridical, theological, and ethnographical research, another study identified universals in the approval of honesty, charity, mutual aid, and generosity, along with the prohibition of theft and homicide.[306]

Psychologists have surveyed evolutionary theories about human and primate sociality, along with lists of virtues and taxonomies of morality from psychology and anthropology to moral concerns or virtues that were shared widely across cultures. They established five "foundations" of morality: care/harm, fairness/reciprocity, ingroup/loyalty, authority, and purity/sanctity.[307]

Researchers have also identified political variations in the attention to the five foundations. People considered more liberal (or "Democratic") on the political spectrum were primarily concerned with care/harm and fairness/reciprocity, while more conservative (or "Republican") individuals were more even in their attention to all five foundations.[308] These findings suggest that corporate events and volunteer activities that tap into people's patriotism and country loyalty may be more effective in "red" conservative states, while events about diversity appreciation and equity may be more effective in "blue" liberal states.

Why Do Ethics Matter to Human Capital Leadership?

When motivating employees to treat one another well, attend events, become engaged, and do the "right thing" in organizations, one can draw on the universal moral axioms that we all hold to be true. One way to do so is to establish a strong corporate code of ethics to help shape and guide employee decisions. A corporate code of ethics can be defined as a "written, distinct, and formal document which consists of moral standards which help guide employee or corporate behavior."[309] Research has identified universal moral values that should be included in these codes. These values are (1) trustworthiness; (2) respect; (3) responsibility; (4) fairness; (5) caring; and (6) citizenship.[310] These (unsurprisingly) correspond with the values and duties we all hold to be self-evident.

But when leaders "talk the talk," do they "walk the walk?" Once a corporate code of conduct is established and communicated, it's critical that human capital leaders lead by example. No one will follow the values that a leader establishes if he or she does not follow them himself or herself.

The University of Tampa's President Ron Vaughn stepped into the president's role in 1995 when the University was struggling with only around 2,000 students. Today, the University of Tampa has almost 10,000 students and its campus is more beautiful and vibrant than ever. President Vaughn's focus on marketing has certainly helped, along with his vision, mission, and the fact he leads by example.

When people see him walking around the campus, his attention to detail and care for UT become obvious. You're always "on camera" when you lead. Everyone watches the leaders. People want to know how their leaders treat their subordinates and peers. They want to know whether their leaders are "for real." They want to know whether their leaders truly embrace the values they tell them to follow.

When President Vaughn comes into contact with garbage on UT's campus (such as an empty water bottle on the ground), he bends down, picks it up and carries it to a garbage can. That example demonstrates that he values (1) a beautiful university campus, (2) the organization he's leading and (3) humility. President Vaughn is a servant leader.

Conclusion

The #MeToo movement has garnered much attention in social media, which has led to greater reporting of unethical (and even illegal) issues in workplaces. Sexual harassment, discrimination, and reports of unethical workplace behaviors abound in companies of all sizes. Human capital leaders can mitigate the possibilities that harassment, discrimination, and unethical behaviors are wreaking havoc in the organizations for which they work by identifying and hiring people with strong ethical foundations. Identifying and hiring ethical employees and leaders are beneficial to organizations seeking to maximize the Triple Bottom Line: people, profit and planet. Servant leaders empower human capital, ensuring talent development and personal growth. They promote pleasant work environments and highly engaged employees. They further contribute to a climate that endorses a strong corporate code of ethics, which emphasize the universal moral values and duties we all hold to be self-evident.

QUESTIONS FOR REVIEW

1. What are the ethical dimensions of the "multidimensional ethical scale?"

2. Why are servant leaders effective?

3. Which of Schwartz's ten values is considered the most important to people universally?

4. Why should companies establish a "corporate code of conduct?"

5. What are the universal moral values that should be included in corporate codes of ethics?

6. Do cultures vary in what "is" in values with what "ought to be?"

7. What are the risks of hiring unethical people?

8. Why do companies focused on servant leadership perform better than those that don't?

9. What are the ethical dimensions of utilitarianism and relativism? Are these two dimensions mutually exclusive?

10. Do moral values (or practices or "what is") vary cross-culturally? Do moral duties (or "what ought to be")?

APPLICATIONS

1. Crafting for Success

1. You are a marketing manager who oversees ninety employees. You have heard that seven of your employees have been coming to work late and leaving early – more frequently than not. Though the workers are salaried employees and not tied to specific office hours, they aren't present to handle phone calls and customer visits when they arrive late or leave early. You need to do something, because you don't want the problem to grow. Craft a message for your employees.

2. You are the CEO of an organization with 75 employees. You are working with a local charitable organization (the Children's Pediatric Cancer Association) on an upcoming weekend event in which you hope that many of your employees will choose to participate. Craft a message for your employees.

3. Your organization hosted an event for its suppliers in which you charged members of your marketing department to oversee. Though those employees came to the event, no one from other departments attended, so your employee presence at the event was notably small. Your organization will be hosting several more events in coming months and you hope to increase your employees' presence at these optional events. Craft a message.

4. For well over ten years, one of your subordinates has always said "yes" when you ask her to "go the extra mile." When asked to head up a new project, lead departments, work with multiple committees, and pick up the slack of the slackers in your organization, she has always agreed to do what you've wanted. Yet one day, she contacts you to say she made a mistake. She took on too much. Her plate is too full. She had agreed to a work schedule three months ago that is three months away. She says the schedule involved so much preparation on her part that she suddenly realized (late in the game) that she didn't think she could do a good job for your organization. Even though she agreed three months ago, she now determined that she couldn't fulfill her side of the bargain. She wanted out of the agreement. This will cause some work for you. You will need to juggle schedules you had already established. You will need to contact your higher-ups to make changes. You feel very inconvenienced. Do you

agree to change her schedule? Do you scold her – or do you try to accommodate her request?

2. Servant Leadership Short Scale[311]

Rank your answers to the following questions about a leader you know who has an influence on you on a five-point scale: 1 = strongly disagree; 2 = disagree; 3 = neutral; 4 = agree and 5 = strongly agree

1. My leader can tell if something work-related is going wrong.

2. My leader makes my career development a priority.

3. I would seek help from my leader if I had a personal problem.

4. My leader emphasizes the importance of giving back to the community

5. My leader puts my best interests ahead of his/her own.

6. My leader gives me the freedom to handle difficult situations in the way that I feel is best.

7. My leader would NOT compromise ethical principles in order to achieve success.

Add up your scores.

Scores between 25 and 35 indicate that your leader has the characteristics of a servant leader. Scores less than 25 indicate these characteristics are less pronounced.

CASE STUDIES

1. EDUPUB

You are a human resource manager who has just accepted a position working for an educational publisher in Miami, Florida, "EDUPUB." The company produces and sells articles that it has collected (and obtained the rights to) on a number of social issues (e.g., pollution, population, drugs, environment, sexuality, money, health, etc.). The company sells its products to thousands of school libraries all around the world. Currently, 102 people are employed at EDUPUB, yet it has never had an HR department or an HR person.

On your first day at EDUPUB, you survey employees, finding that they had received an extensive orientation on the company's vision, mission, products, and strategy - yet received little training on their specific jobs - or any other type of training for that matter. In fact, they don't have job descriptions.

Most of them found their positions at EDUPUB on CareerBuilder, the sole source of recruiting for EDUPUB. After submitting their resumes and interviewing with the manager of their particular department, they were hired. One employee noted that the interview was "weird" as the manager asked a number of questions unrelated to the position for which she was being hired. One question was whether she had a boyfriend. Another employee pointed out that the 65-year old CEO is a "flirt."

Departments in the company include (1) Accounting, (2) Sales, (3) Customer Service, (4) Marketing, (5) Graphic Design, (6) Publishing, and (7) Shipping. The company also employs an outside sales force. Employees in its Miami location are evenly distributed between first 6 departments. Within the first 6 departments, the demographics are as follows: 60 percent female; 75 percent White; 15 percent Hispanic; 5 percent African American; 5 percent other. 80 percent of the employees in all 7 departments are under 30 years of age. Within the shipping department, 100 percent of the employees are male; 80 percent of the employees are African American; 10 percent are Hispanic, and 10 percent are white. The CEO says that the company is an "Equal Opportunity Employer," yet no EEO practices are evident.

Employees are forbidden to discuss their hourly pay or salaries and a few relate to you that they believe that a few "golden" female employees are receiving much better pay than they are despite the similarity in their jobs and performance. Employees receive medical and dental insurance, defined contribution pension plans, 4 weeks paid vacation, and the hourly employees receive 1.5x overtime pay. The company offers no incentive plans. Despite the benefits, many employees feel that they are paid below the market and are unhappy with their pay. Turnover is high, at 50 percent per year. The CEO has confided to you that he is constrained financially and can't afford to raise everyone's pay much. Yet he resides in a mansion on the Intracoastal Waterway in Miami Beach and hosts numerous employee events at his home. People think he's a braggart who likes to showcase his mansion and yacht.

In an effort to reduce costs, the CEO recently eliminated most overtime pay by switching about 20 employees from hourly pay to salary pay. 10 of the 20 employees make between $22,000 - $25,000 per year. Another 5 make between $25,001 and $35,000 per year.

A few employees have started generating some discussion about joining a union. The CEO is very disturbed by this, and has formed a task force to identify union sympathizers and create an anti-union internal marketing campaign.

The shipping department is managed by a Haitian gentleman who confides to you that he feels uncomfortable with a few colleagues who have said derogatory things about his heritage. Also, four accidents were recently reported in the shipping department and two caused serious injuries. One employee had to be hospitalized due to an injury in a conveyor belt. A second employee fell off some scaffolding and broke his leg. These accidents occurred about a month ago, yet the employees have yet to report back to work.

The customer service department is comprised of a variety of happy-go-lucky employees in their early 20s. Rumors of dating within this department abound, perhaps due to its weekly happy hour events at the local Chili's.

Identify the issues that need to be addressed in this case. How would you remedy these problems?

2. Ethical Dilemmas

1. You are in charge of a nonprofit organization with one hundred employees that serves the community through outreach and rehabilitation programs. Your firm also provides full benefits to its employees, including health insurance. One of your employees has just approached you to let you know that his cancer, which had gone into remission, has recurred and that he will need to have multiple rounds of chemotherapy. He says that he would like to keep working to help him pay for his treatments and his other bills. He is his family's sole source of income. If you let him go, you will save your organization money, so it will be able to provide more services to others. If you retain him, you will generate good will among employees. How would a person who advocates utilitarian ethics respond? How would one who advocates egoism respond?

2. You have been out of work for 11 months and you've exhausted your savings account. You worry that it will be difficult to find a job, having been out of a job for so long. A friend offers to let you add his company to your resume and to list him as your boss. You ask your friend if he would truly be willing to hire you, but he says he has no open positions and really can't afford it at this time. Do you list him on your resume as your boss? How would a person who focuses on moral deontology respond? How would an egoist respond? How would a person who focuses on justice respond?

3. You are working in southern Italy when a member of the Italian mafia shows up to your workplace and demands that you pay him a monthly "protection" fee. You refuse, telling him that your organization does not tolerate threats from the mafia or anyone who is without legal justification. He leaves. When you discuss the situation with people from other businesses in the area, you discover that many are paying the mafia for "protection" and those who hadn't had been robbed. What do you do? How would an ethical relativist view this situation? How would this situation relate to Aristotle's virtue ethics?

Answers to "The Research-Practice Gap" from Chapter 1

Work in teams of two or three people to answer whether each of the following questions is true or false. This survey comes from a cross-cultural study of human resource practitioners.[312]

1. Leadership training is ineffective because good leaders are born, not made. FALSE
2. The most important requirement for an effective leader is to have an outgoing, enthusiastic personality. FALSE
3. Once employees have mastered a task, they perform better when they are told to "do their best" than when they are given specific, difficult performance goals. FALSE
4. Companies with vision statements perform better than those without them. TRUE
5. Companies with very low rates of professionals' turnover are less profitable than those with moderate turnover rates. FALSE
6. If a company feels it must downsize employees, the most profitable way to do it is through targeted cuts rather than attrition. TRUE
7. In order to be evaluated favorably by line managers, the most important competency for HR managers is the ability to manage change. TRUE
8. On average, encouraging employees to participate in decision making is more effective for improving organizational performance than setting performance goals. FALSE
9. Most managers give employees lower performance appraisals than they objectively deserve. FALSE
10. Poor performers are generally more realistic about their performance than good performers are. FALSE
11. Teams with members from different functional areas are likely to reach better solutions to complex problems than teams from single areas. TRUE
12. Despite the popularity of drug testing, there is no clear evidence that applicants who score positive on drug tests are any less reliable or productive employees. FALSE
13. Most people over-evaluate how well they perform on the job. TRUE
14. Most errors in performance appraisals can be eliminated by providing training that describes the kinds of errors managers tend to make and suggesting ways to avoid them. FALSE
15. Lecture-based training is generally superior to other forms of training delivery. FALSE
16. Older adults learn more from training than younger adults. FALSE

17. Training for simple skills will be more effective if it is presented in one concentrated session than if it is presented in several sessions over time. FALSE
18. The most valid employment interviews are designed around each candidate's unique background. FALSE
19. Although people use many different terms to describe personalities, there are really only four basic dimensions of personality, as captured by the Myers-Briggs Type Indicator (MBTI). FALSE
20. On average, applicants who answer job advertisements are likely to have higher turnover than those referred by other employees. TRUE
21. Being very intelligent is actually a disadvantage for performing well on a low-skilled job. FALSE
22. There is very little difference among personality inventories in terms of how well they predict an applicant's likely job performance. FALSE
23. Although there are "integrity tests" that try to predict whether someone will steal, be absent, or otherwise take advantage of an employer, they don't work well in practice because so many people lie on them. FALSE
24. On average, conscientiousness is a better predictor of job performance than is intelligence. FALSE
25. Companies that screen job applicants for values have higher performance than those that screen for intelligence. FALSE
26. When pay must be reduced or frozen, there is little a company can do or say to reduce employee dissatisfaction and dysfunctional behaviors. FALSE
27. Most employees prefer to be paid on the basis of individual performance rather than on team or organizational performance. TRUE
28. Merit pay systems cause so many problems that companies without them tend to have higher performance than companies with them. FALSE
29. There is a positive relationship between the proportion of managers receiving organizationally based pay incentives and company profitability. TRUE
30. New companies have a better chance of surviving if all employees receive incentives based on organization-wide performance. TRUE
31. Talking about salary issues during performance appraisal tends to hurt morale and future performance. FALSE

32. Most employees prefer variable pay systems (e.g., incentive schemes, gain sharing, stock options) to fixed pay systems. FALSE
33. Surveys that directly ask employees how important pay is to them underestimate pay's true importance to employees. In other words, pay is more important to employees than they let on in surveys. TRUE

REFERENCES

[1] Banjo, S. (2018). Over 30 need not apply. China's fast-moving tech industry runs on youth, not experience. *Bloomberg BusinessWeek.* May 7.

[2] Heathfield, S.M. (2017). Find out the ways Zappos reinforces its company culture. *The Balance.* September 9. Accessed March 7, 2018 at https://www.thebalance.com/zappos-company-culture-1918813.

[3] Ibid.

[4] Ibid.

[5] Stebbins, S., Comen, E., Sauter, M.B. & Stockdale, C. (2018). Bad reputation: America's top 20 most hated companies. *USA Today.* February 1. Accessed March 8, 2018 at https://www.usatoday.com/story/money/business/2018/02/01/bad-reputation-americas-top-20-most-hated-companies/1058718001/

[6] Ibid.

[7] Kim, N. & Kang, S. (2016). Older and more engaged. The mediating role of age-linked resources on work engagement. *Human Resource Management, 56*(5): 731-746.

[8] Anonymous. (2016). 7 trends for workforce 2020. How to make today's ever-changing workforce work for you. Instructure. Accessed October 6, 2019 at: https://www.instructure.com/bridge/pdf/2016_5_Workforce_Evolution_eBook_Collateral_Bridge_12.pdf?newhome=bridge

[9] McBride, J. & Sergie, M.A. (2018). NAFTA's economic impact. Council on Foreign Relations. Accessed October 27, 2018 at https://www.cfr.org/backgrounder/naftas-economic-impact

[10] Johnson, R. (2011). New sweatshop scandals for Disney, Mattel, and Apple. *Business Insider.* Accessed March 5, 2018 at http://www.businessinsider.com/mattel-disney-chinese-sweatshop-child-labor-2011-8

[11] Goetz, L. (2018). Why is Hong Kong considered a tax haven? *Investopedia.* https://www.investopedia.com/ask/answers/060916/why-hong-kong-considered-tax-haven.asp

[12] Kagan, J. (2019). Tax haven. *Investopedia.* Accessed October 13, 2019 at: https://www.investopedia.com/terms/t/taxhaven.asp

[13] Bosshart, S., Luedi, T. & Wang, E. (2010). Past lessons for China's new joint ventures. McKinsey. Accessed March 5, 2018 at https://www.mckinsey.com/business-functions/strategy-and-corporate-finance/our-insights/past-lessons-for-chinas-new-joint-ventures

[14] Associated Press. (2006). Walmart selling its 85 stores in Germany. NBC News Accessed March 5, 2018 at http://www.nbcnews.com/id/14073098/ns/business-world_business/t/wal-mart-selling-its-stores-germany/#.Wp3Rk03fNYc

[15] Society for Human Resource Management. (2017, March 7). Introduction to the global human resources discipline. *SHRMOnline.* Accessed October 12, 2019 at: https://www.shrm.org/resourcesandtools/tools-and-samples/toolkits/pages/introglobalhr.aspx

[16] Mulkeen, D. (2017, February 20). How to reduce the risk of international assignment failure. Communicaid. Accessed October 1, 2018 at: https://www.communicaid.com/cross-cultural-training/blog/reducing-risk-international-assignment-failure/

[17] Hall, E.T. & Hall, M. (1990). Understanding Cultural Differences. Yarmouth, ME: Intercultural Press. Hofstede, G. (2001). Culture's Consequences: Comparing Values, Behaviors, Institutions, and Organizations across Nations. Thousand Oaks, CA: Sage. House, R.J., Hanges, P.J., Javidan, M., Dorfman, P.W., & Gupta, V. (2004). Culture,

Leadership, and Organizations: The GLOBE Study of 62 Societies. Thousand Oaks, CA: Sage. Kluckhohn, C. & Strodtbeck, F. (1961) Variations in Value Orientations. Evanston, IL: Row, Peterson. Schwartz, S. (1992). Universals in content and structure of values: theoretical advances and empirical tests in 20 countries, in Mark Hanna (ed.) Advances in Experimental Social Psychology. Vol XXV. New York, NY: Academic Press, pp. 1-65. Trompenaars, F. (1998). Riding the Waves of Culture: Understanding Diversity in Global Business. New York, NY: McGraw Hill.

[18] Hubbard, B. (2017). Saudi Arabia agrees to let women drive. *The New York Times.* September 26. Accessed March 5, 2018 at https://www.nytimes.com/2017/09/26/world/middleeast/saudi-arabia-women-drive.html.

[19] Avakian, T. (2015). 16 odd things that are illegal in Singapore. *Business Insider.* August 4. Accessed March 5, 2018 at http://www.businessinsider.com/things-that-are-illegal-in-singapore-2015-7

[20] Anonymous. (2018). Employees' rights in Germany. Chuck Emerson Media Services. Accessed March 5, 2018 at https://www.howtogermany.com/pages/employee-rights.html

[21] Heymann, J. & Vogelstein, R. (2017). Commentary: When sexual harassment is legal. *Fortune.* November 17. Accessed March 6, 2018 at http://fortune.com/2017/11/17/sexual-harassment-legal-gaps/

[22] Transparency International. (2017). Corruption perceptions index. Accessed March 6, 2018 at file:///C:/Users/STHOMASON/Downloads/CPI percent202017 percent20global percent20map percent20and percent20country percent20results.pdf

[23] Anonymous. (2017). A report from De Beers' new diamond mine. *Economist.* February 25. Accessed March 6, 2018 at https://www.economist.com/news/international/21717369-production-worlds-most-valuable-gem-may-be-about-peak-report-de-beerss

[24] Tenhiala, A., Giluk, T., Svenkepes, C., Simon, I. & Kim, S. (2014). The research-practice gap in human resource management: A cross-cultural study. *Human Resource Management, 55*(2): 179-200.

[25] Embar, W. (2015) Sweatshops and child labor. Accessed July 18, 2016 at http://www.veganpeace.com/sweatshops/sweatshops_and_child_labor.htm

[26] Ibid.

[27] Carpet slaves – abusing children. Accessed July 18, 2016 at http://whitengreen.com/carpet-slaves--abusing-children-71-video

[28] Ibid.

[29] Ibid.

[30] Ibid.

[31] Goodweave. Accessed July 18, 2016 at http://www.goodweave.org/child_labor_campaign/child_labor_handmade_rugs_carpets

[32] Lawrence, D. & Abelson, M. (2018). Woman vs. Wall Street. *Bloomberg BusinessWeek.* May 7.

[33] Equal Employment Opportunity commission (2018). Title VII of the Civil Rights Act of 1964. Accessed May 15, 2018 at https://www.eeoc.gov/laws/statutes/titlevii.cfm

[34] Equal Employment Opportunity Commission. Civil Rights Act of 1991. Accessed May 15, 2018 at https://www.eeoc.gov/laws/statutes/titlevii.cfm

[35] Chang, E., Green, J. & Paskin, J. (2018). Can Amazon deliver diversity? *Bloomberg BusinessWeek.* May 14th.

[36] Ibid., pp. 15.

[37] Del Carmen, M., Jayasinghe, M., Pieper, J.R., Delgado, D.M., & Li, M. (2019). Perceived Workplace Gender Discrimination and Employee Consequences: A Meta-Analysis and Complementary Studies Considering Country Context. *Journal of Management, 25*(6): 2419-2447.

[38] Steele, E. & Schmidt, M.S. (2017). Bill O'Reilly settled new harassment claim, then Fox renews his contract. *The New York Times.* October 21.

[39] Nagele-Piazza, L. (2016). Pregnant Chipotle worker awarded $550k in discrimination lawsuit. *SHRM.* Accessed May 17, 2018 at https://www.shrm.org/resourcesandtools/legal-and-compliance/state-and-local-updates/pages/chipotle-pregnancy-verdict.aspx

[40] Townsend, M. & Deprez., E.E. (2018). Is the corporate bully the next workplace pariah? *Bloomberg BusinessWeek.* May 14th.

[41] Ibid., pp. 23.

[42] Ibid.

[43] Ibid.

[44] Ibid.

[45] Ibid.

[46] Howard, M.C., Cogswell, J.E. & Smith, M.B. (2019). The antecedents and outcomes of workplace ostracism: A meta-analysis. *Journal of Applied Psychology.* Advance online publication. http://dx.doi.org/10.1037/apl0000453

[47] Ozcelik, H. & Barsade, S.G. (2018).No employee an island. Workplace loneliness and job performance. *Academy of Management Journal, 61*(6): 2343-2366.

[48] United States Department of Justice Civil Rights Division. Americans with Disabilities Act. Accessed May 17, 2018 at: https://www.ada.gov/ada_title_I.htm

[49] Ibid.

[50] Sherbin, L. & Kennedy, J.T. (2017). The case for improving work for people with disabilities goes way beyond compliance. *Harvard Business Review.* December 27. Accessed May 17, 2018 at: https://hbr.org/2017/12/the-case-for-improving-work-for-people-with-disabilities-goes-way-beyond-compliance

[51] Kaye, H.S., Jans, L.H., & Jones, E.C. (2011). Why don't employers hire and retain workers with disabilities? *Journal of Occupational Rehabilitation, 21:* 526-536.

[52] Horn, L. (2019). NYC restaurant owner ordered to pay $64,000 for repeatedly discriminating against service dogs. VICE US.

[53] Stuart, D. & Nordstrom, T. (2016). Generational differences: Why they matter and when they don't. *Forbes.* August 16.

[54] Hinchliffe, E. (2019). GM's board will have more women than men. It's not the only one. *Fortune Magazine.* May 20th.

[55] Glass, C. & Cook, A. (2018). Do women leaders promote positive change? Analyzing the effect of gender on business practices and diversity initiatives. *Human Resource Management, 57*(4) 823-837.

[56] Anonymous. (2019). State social media privacy laws. NCSL. Accessed October 12, 2019 at: http://www.ncsl.org/research/telecommunications-and-information-technology/state-laws-prohibiting-access-to-social-media-usernames-and-passwords.aspx

[57] Equal Employment Opportunity Commission. (2017). EEOC Releases Fiscal Year 2016 Enforcement and Litigation Data. January 18. https://www.eeoc.gov/eeoc/newsroom/release/1-18-17a.cfm

[58] See Knowles versus Knight, Case 8-09-cv-01920-RAL-AEP. United States District Court, Middle District of Florida, Tampa Division.

[59] See SHRM's Business and Legal Reports for further discussion. Was machinist's request for accommodation reasonable? 1/31/06.

[60] Aguiluz, R.N. (2007). 11th Court: Strict adherence to punctuality policy may have violated ADA. SHRM. 8/10/2007.

[61] Bell, M. P. (2011). Diversity in Organizations. 2nd ed. USA: South-Western Cengage Learning.

[62] See Jones Versus Transportation Agency. (1987). 85-1129
[63] Myers, C. (2017). Why everyone at your company should have this simple job description. *Forbes.* February 4.
[64] Economic Research Institute (2018). How to conduct a job analysis. Part 1. Accessed October 28, 2018 at https://downloads.erieri.com/pdf/job_analysis_PartI_whitepaper.pdf
[65] Rigler, J. (1984). Connecticut vs. Teal: The Supreme Court's latest exposition of disparate impact analysis. *Notre Dame Law Review,* 59(2): 313-336.
[66] Economic Research Institute (2018). The Position Analysis Questionnaire. Accessed August 9, 2018 at https://www.erieri.com/paq
[67] Villanova, P., Bernardin, H.J., Johnson, D.L., & Dahmus, S.A. (1994). The validity of a measure of job compatibility in the prediction of job performance and turnover of motion picture theatre personnel. *Personnel Psychology,* 47(1): 73-90.
[68] Hackman, J.R. & Oldham, G.R. (1974). The Job Diagnostic Survey: An instrument for the diagnosis of jobs and the evaluation of job design projects. *National Technical Information Service, U.S. Department of Commerce.* Accessed August 9, 2018 at http://www.dtic.mil/dtic/tr/fulltext/u2/779828.pdf
[69] Morgeson, F.P. (2015). The Work Design Questionnaire. Accessed August 7, 2018 athttps://msu.edu/~morgeson/English_WDQ.pdf
[70] Neilson, G.L., Estupinan, J., and Sethi, B. (2015). 10 guiding principles of organizational design. *Forbes Magazine.* April 1. Accessed August 7, 2018 at https://www.forbes.com/sites/strategyand/2015/04/01/10-guiding-principles-of-organization-design/#2116bfd35888
[71] See Landmark: Griggs Versus Duke Power Co. filed 12/14/70. Accessed July 13, 2016 at http://www.naacpldf.org/case/griggs-v-duke-power-co
[72] Presidential Executive Order on Buy American and Hire American. Accessed September 7, 2018 at: https://www.whitehouse.gov/presidential-actions/presidential-executive-order-buy-american-hire-american/
[73] Dan. A. (2012). Kodak failed by asking the wrong marketing question. *Forbes Magazine.* January 23. Accessed September 7, 2018 at: https://www.forbes.com/sites/avidan/2012/01/23/kodak-failed-by-asking-the-wrong-marketing-question/#5cd0ca2e3d47
[74] Anonymous, (2019). India's auto boom goes bust. *Bloomberg Businessweek.* September 16. p. 29.
[75] Ibid.
[76] Anonymous. (2019). 30 under 30 energizers. Get caffeinated with the Forbes 30 under 30, in 30 words or less. *Forbes Magazine.* September 30.
[77] Dunn, E. (2019). Fast-casual chain &Pizza wants to become the most progressive fast-food employer in the U.S. *Bloomberg Businessweek.* September 16.
[78] Ibid.
[79] Ibid.
[80] Ibid.
[81] Balanced Scorecard Institute (2018). Accessed September 7, 2018 at: https://www.balancedscorecard.org/BSC-Basics/About-the-Balanced-Scorecard
[82] Harder, A. (2019). Six tactics you'll want to sharpen up on. Accessed October 13, 2019 at: https://www.hrmorning.com/articles/recruiting-trends-2020/
[83] Petrone, P. (2019). See the industries with the highest turnover rates (and why it's so high). March 19. Accessed October 6, 2019 at: https://learning.linkedin.com/blog/engaging-your-workforce/see-the-industries-with-the-highest-turnover--and-why-it-s-so-hi
[84] SHRM.Org. (2016). Advanced analytics: using data to drive HR excellence. Accessed September 7, 2018 at:

https://www.shrm.org/LearningAndCareer/learning/Documents/SHRM percent20HR percent20Metrics_AA.pdf

[85] Huselid, M.A. (2018). The science and practice of workforce analytics. Introduction to the HRM special issue. *Human Resource Management, 57*(3): 679-684.

[86] Levenson, A. (2018). Using workforce analytics to improve strategy execution. *Human Resource Management, 57*(3): 685-700.

[87] Anonymous. (2017). 2017 Talent Acquisition Benchmarking Report. SHRM. Accessed October 6, 2019 at https://www.shrm.org/hr-today/trends-and-forecasting/research-and-surveys/Documents/2017-Talent-Acquisition-Benchmarking.pdf

[88] Morris, J. R., Cascio, W. F., & Young, C. E. (1999). Downsizing after all these years: Questions and answers about who did it, how many did it, and who benefited from it. *Organizational Dynamics, 27*(3), 78-87. Freeman, S. J., & Cameron, K. S. (1993). Organizational downsizing: A convergence and reorientation framework. Organization Science, 4(1), 10-29.

[89] Pickett, P. (2019). The pros and cons of telecommuting. TheBalanceCareers.com.

[90] Singh, R. (2012). The China Syndrome: recruiting can be tough when there are only a billion people available. Accessed July 18, 2016 at http://www.eremedia.com/ere/the-china-syndrome-recruiting-can-be-tough-when-there-are-only-a-billion-people-available/

[91] Ibid.

[92] Ibid.

[93] Zhang, T. (2015). The unspoken rules of recruitment in China. Accessed July 18, 2016 at http://news.efinancialcareers.com/uk-en/218643/the-unspoken-rules-of-recruitment-in-china

[94] Berthon, P., Ewing, M., & Hah, L.L. (2005). Captivating company: Dimensions of attractiveness in employer branding.

[95] Ibid., p. 151

[96] Herman, R.E. & Gioia, J.L. (2001). Helping your organization become an employer of choice. *Employment Relations Today, Summer (2001)*, 63-78. Higgs, M. (2005). You can pay to be an employer of choice? *Employee Benefits,* 18.

[97] Ungar, R. (2013). Wal-Mart pays employees poorly and sinks while Costco pays employees well and sails – proof that you get what you pay for.*Forbes.* 4/17/2013.

[98] Ibid.

[99] Gasparro, A. & Morath, E. (2015). McDonalds joins the trend in rising pay. *The Wall Street Journal.* 4/1/2015.

[100] Tatley, K. (2015). Zappos – hiring for culture and the bizarre things they do. Recruitloop. Accessed September 19, 2018 at: https://recruitloop.com/blog/zappos-hiring-for-culture-and-the-bizarre-things-they-do/

[101] Ibid.

[102] Aasland, M. S., Skogstad, A., Notelaers, G., Nielsen, M. B., & Einarsen, S. (2010). The prevalence of destructive leadership behaviour. British Journal of Management, 21(2), 438–452; Hogan, R., Raskin, R., & Fazzini, D. (1990). The dark side of charisma. In K. E. Clark (Ed.), Measures of leadership (p. 343–354). West Orange, NJ: Leadership Library of America.

[103] Tepper, B. J. (2007). Abusive supervision in work organizations: Review, synthesis, and research agenda. Journal of Management, 33(3), 261–289. Tepper, B. J. (2000). Consequences of abusive supervision. Academy of Management Journal, 43(2), 178–190. Vredenburgh, D., & Brender, Y. (1998). The hierarchical abuse of power in work organizations. Journal of Business Ethics, 17(12), 1337–1347; Boddy, C.R. (2017). Psychopathic leadership: A case study of a corporate psychopath CEO. *Journal of Business Ethics,* 145: 141-156.

[104] Boddy, C.R. (2017). Psychopathic leadership: A case study of a corporate psychopath

CEO. *Journal of Business Ethics,* 145: 141-156.

[105] Ibid., p. 149.

[106] Jeffrey Skilling. Meet the psychopaths documentary. Accessed March 8, 2018 at https://www.youtube.com/watch?v=VQe1MOv9Z7E

[107] Boddy, C.R. (2017). Psychopathic leadership: A case study of a corporate psychopath CEO. *Journal of Business Ethics,* 145: 141-156.

[108] SHRM. (2015). Avoiding adverse impact in employment practices. Accessed October 12, 2018 at https://www.shrm.org/resourcesandtools/tools-and-samples/toolkits/pages/avoidingadverseimpact.aspx.

[109] Schmidt, F.L. & Hunter, J.E. (1998). The validity and utility of selection methods in personnel psychology: Practical and theoretical implications of 85 years of research findings. *Psychological Bulletin, 124(*2): 262-274.

[110] Legal Information Institute. (2009). Ricci vs. DeStefano (07-1428) Ricci vs. DeStefano (08-328). Accessed October 12, 2018 at https://www.law.cornell.edu/supct/cert/07-1428

[111] Fair Test: The national center for fair and open testing. (2010). Accessed October 12, 2018 at https://www.fairtest.org/nyc-firefighter-test-found-intentionally-discrimin

[112] Costa, Jr., P.T. & McCrae, R.R. (1995). Domains and facets. Hierarchical personality assessment using the Revised NEO Personality Inventory. *Journal of Personality Assessment,* 64(1): 21-50.

[113] Barrick, M.R., Mount, M.K. & Judge, T.A. (2001). Personality and performance at the beginning of the new millennium: what do we know and where do we go? *International Journal of Selection and Assessment,* 9 ½: 9-31.

[114] Schmidt, F.L. & Hunter, J.E. (1998). The validity and utility of selection methods in personnel psychology: Practical and theoretical implications of 85 years of research findings. *Psychological Bulletin, 124(*2): 262-274.

[115] Judge, T.A., Bono, J.E., Ilies, R. and Gerhardt, M.W. (2002). Personality and leadership: A qualitative and quantitative review. *Journal of Applied Psychology,* 87(4): 765-780.

[116] Bennis, W. G. and Nanus, B. (1997), Leaders: The Strategies for Taking Charge, HarperCollins, New York.

[117] Judge, T.A., Heller, D. & Mount, M.K. (2002). Five-factor model of personality and job satisfaction: A meta-analysis. *Journal of Applied Psychology,* 87(3): 530-541.

[118] Judge, T.A., Erez, A., Bono, J.E. & Thoresen, C.J. (2003). The core self-evaluations scale: Development of a measure. *Personnel Psychology,* 56: 303-331.

[119] Ones, D.S., Schmidt, F.L., Viswesvaran, C. & Lykken, D.T. (1996). Controversies over integrity testing: two viewpoints. *Journal of Business and Psychology,* 10(4): 487-509. Fine, S. (2010). Pre-employment integrity testing across multiple industries. *Psychological Reports,* 107(2): 607-610.

[120] Tay, L. (2013). 11 questions every business person should answer to test your integrity. *Business Insider.* October 3. Accessed October 27, 2018 at https://www.businessinsider.com.au/11-questions-every-business-person-should-answer-to-test-your-integrity-2013-10

[121] O'Boyle, Jr., E.H., Forsyth, D.R., Banks, G.C. & McDaniel, M.A. (2012). A meta-analysis of the dark triad and work behavior: A social exchange perspective. *Journal of Applied Psychology,* 97(3): 557-579.

[122] Wertag, A. & Bratko, D. (2019). In search of the pro-social personality: Personality traits as predictors of prosociality and prosocial behavior. *Journal of Individual Differences,* 40(1): 55-62.

[123] O'Boyle, E.H., Forsyth, D.R., Banks, G.C., Story, P.A., and White, C.D. (2015) A Meta-Analytic Test of Redundancy and Relative Importance of the Dark Triad and Five-Factor Model of Personality. *Journal of Personality, 83 (6): 644-666.*

[124] Antes A.L., Brown R.P., Murphy S.T., Waples E.P., Mumford M.D., Connelly S. and Devenport, L.D. (2007) Personality and ethical decision-making in research: The role of perceptions of self and others. *Journal of Empirical Research on Human Research Ethics* 2: 15–34. doi: 10.1525/jer.2007.2.4.15 PMID: 19385805; Nathanson C., Paulhus D.L., Williams K.M. (2006) Predictors of a behavioral measure of scholastic cheating: Personality and competence but not demographics. *Contemporary Educational Psychology, 31*: 97–122. doi: 10.1016/j.cedpsych.2005.03.001;10.1016/j.cedpsych.2005.03.001

[125] Eissa, G., Weiland, R., Lester, S.W. & Gupta, R. (2019). Winning at all costs: An exploration of bottom-line mentality, Machiavellianism, and organizational citizenship behavior. *Human Resource Management Journal, 29:* 469-489.

[126] McKay, D.R. (2018). The Strong Interest Inventory. You need to know about this career assessment. Accessed October 13, 2018 at https://www.thebalancecareers.com/the-strong-interest-inventory-526173

[127] Gilliam, J., & Chatterjee, S. 2011. The Influence of birth order on financial risk tolerance. Journal of Business & Economics Research, 9: 43–50. Campbell, R.J., Jeong, S. & Graffin, S.D. (2019). Born to take risks? The effect of CEO birth order on strategic risk-taking. *Academy of Management Journal, 62(4)*: 1278-1306.

[128] Bertoni, M., & Brunello, G. 2016. Later-borns don't give up: The temporary effects of birth order on European earnings. Demography, 53: 449–470.

[129] Green, B., & Griffiths, E. C. 2014. Birth order and posttraumatic stress disorder. Psychology Health and Medicine, 19: 24–32.

[130] Great Place to Work (2018). How to ensure onboarding is a success. Accessed October 28, 2018 at http://www.greatplacetowork.co.uk/publications-and-events/insights/1071-how-to-ensure-onboarding-is-a-success

[131] John, O.P. & Srivastava, S. (1999) The Big Five Trait Taxonomy: History, Measurement, and Theoretical Perspectives. In: Pervin, L.A. and John, O.P. Eds., Handbook of Personality: Theory and Research, Vol. 2, Guilford Press, New York, 102-138.

[132] Paulhus, D.L. (2013). Dark Triad of Personality (D3-Short). Measurement instrument database for the Social Science. Accessed October 27, 2018 at http://www.midss.org/sites/default/files/d3.pdf

[133] Stanleigh, M. (2018). BIA. Accessed October 17, 2018 at https://bia.ca/coaching-is-the-new-direction-for-performance-management-2/

[134] Aguinis, H. (2009), *Performance Management*. 2nd ed., Pearson Prentice-Hall, Upper Saddle River, NJ., pp. 2

[135] Aguinis, H. and Pierce, C.A. (2008), "Enhancing the relevance of performance management research", *Journal of Organizational Behavior,* Vol. 29 No. 1, pp.140.

[136] Harris, M. M., & Schaubroeck, J. (1988). A meta-analysis of self-supervisor, self-peer, and peer-supervisor ratings. *Personnel Psychology, 41*(1), 43-62.

[137] Bernardin, H.J., Hagan, C., Kane, J.S., and Villanova, P. (1998), "Effective performance management: Precision in management with a focus on customers and situational constraints", In *Performance Appraisal: State-Of-The-Art Methods for Performance Management.* Ed. J Smither, Jossey-Bass, San Francisco, CA. Bernardin, H.J. and Russell, J.E.A. (2013), *Human Resource Management: An Experiential Approach.* 6th ed., McGraw Hill Irwin, New York, NY.

[138] Cascio, W.F. (1991), *Applied Psychology in Personnel Management* (4th ed.), Prentice Hall, Englewood Cliffs, NJ.

[139] Welch, J. with Byrne, J. A. (2001), *Jack: Straight from the gut,* Warner Business Books, New York, NY.
Welch, J. (2013), "Jack Welch: 'Rank and yank.' That's not how it's done. Using

'differentiation' aligns employee performance with an organization's mission and values", *The Wall Street Journal.* November 14th.

[140] Nisen, M. (2015), "Why GE had to kill its annual performance appraisals after three decades." Accessed October 15, 2018 at http://qz.com/428813/ge-performance-review-strategy-shift/

[141] Heneman, R. (1986), "The relationship between supervisory ratings and results-oriented measures of performance: A meta-analysis", *Personnel Psychology,* Vol. 39, pp. 811-826. Nathan, B.R. and Alexander, R.A. (1988), "A comparison of criteria for test validation: A meta-analytic investigation", *Personnel Psychology,* Vol. 41, pp. 517-535.

[142] Tzini, K. & Jain, K. (2018). Unethical behavior under relative performance evaluation. Evidence and remedy. *Human Resource Management, 57*(6): 1399-1414.

[143] Thomason, S.J., Brownlee, A., Harris, A. & Rustogi, H. (2018). Forced distribution systems and attracting top talent. *International Journal of Performance and Productivity Management,* 67(7).

[144] Sahadi, J. (2015), "Amazon workforce raises dread of 'rank and yank' reviews", CNN.Money. Retrieved 6-12-2017 at http://money.cnn.com/2015/08/17/news/amazon-performance-review/

[145] Longanecker, C.O., Gioia, D.A. & Sims, H.P. (1987). Behind the mask: The politics of employee appraisal. *Academy of Management Executive, 1,* 183-193. Jawahar, I., & Williams, C. (1997). Where All the Children Are Above Average: The Performance Appraisal Purpose Effect. Personnel Psychology, 50, 905-925.

[146] Bernardin, H.J., Thomason, S.J., Buckley, M.R. & Kane, J.S. (2016). Rater rating-level bias and accuracy in performance appraisals: the impact of rater personality, performance management competence, and rater accountability. *Human Resource Management, 55*(2): 321-340.

[147] Latham, G.P. & Wexley, K.N. (1980). Increasing productivity through performance appraisal. Reading, PA: Addison-Wesley.

[148] Longanecker, C.O., Gioia, D.A. & Sims, H.P. (1987). Behind the mask: The politics of employee appraisal. *Academy of Management Executive, 1,* 183-193. Jawahar, I., & Williams, C. (1997). Where All the Children Are Above Average: The Performance Appraisal Purpose Effect. Personnel Psychology, 50, 905-925.

[149] Kruger, J., & Dunning, D. (1999). Unskilled and unaware of it: How difficulties in recognizing one's own incompetence lead to inflated self-assessments. *Journal of Personality and Social Psychology, 77*(6), 1121-1134.

[150] Ibid.

[151] Ulrich, D., Brockbank, W., Yeung, A.K. & Lake, D.G. (1995). Human resource competency: An empirical assessment. *Human Resource Management, 34*: 473-495.

[152] Zarya, V. (2015). Performance reviews aren't just annoying - They're biased against minorities and women. *Fortune Magazine.* November 11. Accessed October 28, 2018 at http://fortune.com/2015/11/11/performance-reviews-minorities/

[153] Guillen, L., Mayo, M. & Karelaia, N. (2018). Appearing self-confident and getting credit for it. Why it may be easier for men than women to gain influence at work. *Human Resource Management, 57*(4): 839-854.

[154] 3M (2016). 3M announces new leadership development program. Accessed October 17, 2018 at https://news.3m.com/press-release/company-english/3m-announces-new-leadership-development-program

[155] Forbes HR Council. (2016). Four training and development initiatives to explore at your company. *Forbes.* Accessed October 17, 2018 at https://www.forbes.com/sites/forbeshumanresourcescouncil/2016/07/28/four-training-and-development-initiatives-to-explore-at-your-company/#30103369659b

[156] Association for Talent Development (2018). State of the Industry Report. Accessed

October 17, 2018 at https://www.td.org/research-reports/2017-state-of-the-industry

[157] Coy, P. (2018). Companies give training another try. *Bloomberg Businessweek.* October 29.

[158] Ibid. p. 37.

[159] Kolb, D. A. (1984). *Experiential learning: Experience as the source of learning and development* (Vol. 1). Englewood Cliffs, NJ: Prentice-Hall.

[160] Colquitt, J.A., LePine, J. & Noe, R.A. (2000). Toward an integrative theory of training motivation: A meta-analytic path analysis of 20 years of research. *Journal of Applied Psychology, 85*(5): 678-707. Warr, P. & Bunce, D. (1995). Trainee characteristics and the outcomes of open learning. *Personnel Psychology, 48*(2): 347-375.

[161] Donovan, J. J., & Radosevich, D. J. (1999). A meta-analytic review of the distribution of practice effect: Now you see it, now you don't. *Journal of Applied Psychology, 84*(5), 795-805.

[162] Locke, E.A. & Latham, G.P. (1991). A theory of goal-setting and task performance. *Academy of Management Review, 16*(2): 212-247.

[163] Locke, E.A. (2019). What makes writing about goals work? *Academy of Management Discoveries, 5*(2): 109-110.

[164] Edmonds, S.C. (2017). Are you really onboarding your employees in the best way possible? *Forbes.* Accessed October 17, 2018 at https://www.forbes.com/sites/forbescoachescouncil/2017/07/21/are-you-really-onboarding-your-employees-the-best-way-possible/#64296bd971a7

[165] Jones, R.J., Woods, S.A. & Guillaume, Y.R.F. (2016). The effectiveness of workplace coaching: A meta-analysis of learning and performance outcomes from coaching. *Journal of Occupational and Organizational Psychology, 89*(2): 249-277.

[166] Lemisiou, M.A. (2018). The effectiveness of a person-centered coaching intervention in raising emotional and social intelligence competencies in the workplace. *International Coaching Psychology Review, 13*(2): 6-28.

[167] Kim, S.L. (2019). Enticing high performers to stay and share their knowledge. The importance of trust in a leader. *Human Resource Management, 58*(4): 341-352.

[168] Dirks, K. T., & Ferrin, D. L. (2001). The role of trust in organizational settings. *Organization Science,* 12, 450– 467. van der Werff, L., & Buckley, F. (2017). Getting to know you: A longitudinal examination of trust cues and trust development during socialization. *Journal of Management,* 43(3), 742– 770.

[169] Phalguni, S. (2015). Coach's supply chain and manufacturing model. Market Realist. Accessed July 19, 2016 at http://marketrealist.com/2015/01/coachs-supply-chain-manufacturing-model/.; Coach. Accessed July 19, 2016 at http://www.coach.com/faqs.html

[170] Ibid.

[171] Weise, K. (2018). Amazon to raise minimum wage to $15 for all US workers. *The New York Times.* Accessed October 19, 2018 at https://www.nytimes.com/2018/10/02/business/amazon-minimum-wage.html

[172] Buckley, T. & Patton, L. (2019). I'm loving it. CEO Steve Easterbrook is leading McDonalds into the age of code. *Bloomberg Businessweek.* September 23.

[173] Great Place to Work. (2018) Patagonia. Accessed October 20, 2018 at http://reviews.greatplacetowork.com/patagonia

[174] Gillette, R. (2016). The CEO of Patagonia makes a convincing case for an unorthodox perk. *Business Insider.* August 17th. Accessed at https://www.businessinsider.com/patagonia-ceo-makes-a-convincing-business-case-for-this-unorthodox-perk-2016-8

[175] Schulte, R. (2014). A company that profits as it pampers workers. *The Washington Post.* October 25. Accessed October 20, 2018 at

https://www.washingtonpost.com/business/a-company-that-profits-as-it-pampers-workers/2014/10/22/d3321b34-4818-11e4-b72e-d60a9229cc10_story.html?noredirect=on&utm_term=.652abdd16f32

[176] Ibid.

[177] Nace, T. (2017). After 44 years, Patagonia released its first commercial and it's not about clothing. *Forbes.* August 24. Accessed October 20, 2018 at https://www.forbes.com/sites/trevornace/2017/08/24/44-years-patagonia-released-first-commercial-clothing/#1dfaa57c3c80

[178] World at Work and Vivient Consulting. (2016). Incentive pay practices: Privately held companies. Retrieved from https://www.worldatwork. org/docs/research-and-surveys/survey-briefincentive-pay-practices-survey-privately-heldcompanies-1115.pdf

[179] Johnson, J. (2018). National Compensation Forecast. Economic Research Institute. Accessed October 28, 2018 at https://downloads.erieri.com/pdf/National percent20Comp percent20Forecast percent20July percent202018.pdf

[180] Adams, J. S. (1963) Toward an understanding of inequity. Journal of Abnormal Psychology, 67, 422-436

[181] Greenberg, J. (1990). Employee theft as a reaction to underpayment inequity: The hidden cost of pay cuts. *Journal of Applied Psychology,* 75(5), 561-568.

[182] Cox, L. (2018). Why is pay transparency important? Economic Research Institute. Accessed October 28, 2018 at https://downloads.erieri.com/pdf/Why_Is_Pay_Transparency_Important.pdf

[183] Dhiraj, A.B. (2019). Countries with the highest minimum hourly wages in the world, 2019. *CEO World Biz.* Accessed October 6, 2019 at: https://ceoworld.biz/2019/01/03/countries-with-the-highest-minimum-hourly-wages-in-the-world-2019/

[184] Campion, E.D., Campion, M.C. & Campion, M.A. (2017). Best practices in incentive compensation bonus administration based on research and professional advice. *Compensation and Benefits Review,* 49(3): 123-134.

[185] Dmitrieva, K. (2019). As profits grow, so does inequality. *Bloomberg Businessweek.* October 7. p. 31.

[186] Fottrell, Q. (2018). Fortune 500 CEOs are paid from double to 5,000 times more than their employees. *Forbes.* May 19. Accessed October 20, 2018 at https://www.marketwatch.com/story/fortune-500-ceos-are-paid-from-double-to-5000-times-more-than-their-employees-2018-05-16

[187] Ibid.

[188] Umoh, R. (2018). CEOs make $15.6 million on average – here's how much their pay has increased compared to yours over a year. *CNBC.* Accessed October 20, 2018 at https://www.cnbc.com/2018/01/22/heres-how-much-ceo-pay-has-increased-compared-to-yours-over-the-years.html. https://www.epi.org/files/pdf/130354.pdf; Melin, A. & Lu, W. (2017). CEOs in U.S., India, earn the most compared with average workers. *Bloomberg.* December 28. Accessed October 20, 2018 at https://www.bloomberg.com/news/articles/2017-12-28/ceos-in-u-s-india-earn-the-most-compared-with-average-workers

[189] Jordan, S. (2018). Warren Buffett's $100,000 salary is 1.87 times median pay at Berkshire. *Omaha World-Herald.* March 18. Accessed October 21, 2018 at https://www.omaha.com/money/buffett/warren-buffett-s-salary-is-times-median-pay-at-berkshire/article_caa518b8-77e8-570b-8893-ac1403c12ccf.html

[190] Urbaniec, J. (2018). CEO pay trends in the nonprofit world. Economic Research Institute. Accessed October 28, 2018 at https://downloads.erieri.com/pdf/CEO percent20Pay percent20Trends percent20in percent20the percent20Nonprofit percent20World percent202018.pdf

[191] Ibid.
[192] Fiss, P. (2016). A short history of golden parachutes. *Harvard Business Review.* October 3. Accessed October 19, 2018 at https://hbr.org/2016/10/a-short-history-of-golden-parachutes
[193] Ibid.
[194] Fiss, P., Kennedy, M.T. & Davis, G.F. (2012). How golden parachutes unfolded: Diffusion and variation of a controversial practice. *Organization Science, 23(4):*
[195] Heaps, W. (2010). Ten steps to building a salary structure. *International HR Forum.* July 29. Accessed October 20, 2018 at https://internationalhrforum.com/2010/07/29/ten-steps-for-building-a-salary-structure/
[196] https://www.dol.gov/whd/regs/compliance/whdfs71.htm
[197] Farrell, W. (2005). Exploiting the gender pay gap. *New York Times.* September 5. Accessed October 21, 2018 at https://www.nytimes.com/2005/09/05/opinion/exploiting-the-gender-gap.html
[198] Ghilarducci, T. (2018). Social security does not add to the federal deficit. *Forbes.* October 19. Accessed October 21, 2018 at https://www.forbes.com/sites/teresaghilarducci/2018/10/19/social-security-does-not-add-to-the-federal-deficit/#488093c20815
[199] Haignere, L. (2002). Paychecks: A guide to conducting salary-equity studies for higher education faculty. 2nd ed. Accessed July 18, 2016 at http://www.academic.umn.edu/wfc/Paychecks_ percent20A percent20Guide percent20to percent20Conducting percent20Salary percent20Equity percent20Studies percent20for percent20Higher percent20Education percent20Faculty.pdf
[200] ProCon.org. (2018). Should the federal minimum wage be increased? ProCon. Accessed October 21, 2018 at https://minimum-wage.procon.org/
[201] Campbell, A.F. (2019). Free labor for college athletes may soon come to an end. Vox. Accessed October 4, 2019 at https://www.vox.com/identities/2019/10/3/20896738/california-fair-pay-to-play-act-college-athletes
[202] Ramirez, K. (2018). Another scandal: Wells Fargo alters corporate customers' documents. *Housingwire.* May 17. Accessed October 21, 2018 at https://www.housingwire.com/articles/43401-another-scandal-wells-fargo-alters-corporate-customers-documents
[203] Welbourne, T.M. & Andrews, A.O. (1996). Predicting the performance of IPOs: Should human resource management be in the equation? *Academy of Management Journal, 39(4):* 891-919.
[204] Cable, D.M. & Judge, T.A. (1994). Pay preferences and job search decisions: A person-organization fit perspective. *Personnel Psychology, 47:* 317-348.
[205] Goldman, J.I. (2016). How gainsharing can benefit companies and employees. Goldman and Company: Certified Public Accountants. November 23. Accessed October 21, 2018 at https://goldmanandcompanycpa.com/how-gainsharing-can-benefit-companies-employees/
[206] Bryson, A. & Freeman, R. (2016). Profit-sharing boosts employee productivity and satisfaction. *Harvard Business Review.* December 13. Accessed October 21, 2018 at https://hbr.org/2016/12/profit-sharing-boosts-employee-productivity-and-satisfaction; Blasi, J.R., Freeman, R.B., Mackin, C. & Kruse, D.L. (2008). Creating a bigger pie? The effects of employee ownership, profit-sharing and stock options on workplace performance. *National Bureau of Economic Research.* Accessed October 21, 2018 at https://www.nber.org/papers/w14230.pdf
[207] Blasi, J.R., Freeman, R.B., Mackin, C. & Kruse, D.L. (2008). Creating a bigger pie? The effects of employee ownership, profit-sharing and stock options on workplace

performance. *National Bureau of Economic Research,* pp. 18. Accessed October 21, 2018 at https://www.nber.org/papers/w14230.pdf

[208] Ibid.

[209] Gerhart, B. & Milkovich, G.T. (1990). Organizational differences in managerial compensation and financial performance. *Academy of Management Journal, 33,* 663-691.

[210] Jackson, H.G. (2016). Employee benefits go mainstream. *HR Today.* August 26. Accessed October 22, 2018 at https://www.shrm.org/hr-today/news/hr-magazine/0916/pages/employee-benefits-go-mainstream.aspx

[211] Ibid.

[212] McGrath, M. (2017). Unions are dead? Why competition is paying for America's best workers. *Forbes.* December 12. Accessed October 22, 2018 at https://www.forbes.com/sites/maggiemcgrath/2017/12/12/unions-are-dead-why-competition-is-paying-off-for-americas-best-workers/#5b4d922f578a

[213] Ridic, G., Gleason, S. & Ridic, O. (2012). Comparisons of healthcare systems in the United States, Germany and Canada. *Materia Socio-Medica,* 24(2): 112-120. Accessed October 22, 2018 at https://www.ncbi.nlm.nih.gov/pmc/articles/PMC3633404/

[214] Blundell-Wignall, A.P., Atkinson, P., & Lee, S.H. (2008). The current financial crisis: Causes and policy issues. *Financial Market Trends,* OECD.; Kerr, S. (1995). On the folly of hoping for A, while rewarding B. *Academy of Management Executive,* 9 (1), 7-15.

[215] Dean, M. (2015). Do bonuses work? The pros and cons of employee incentive programmes. Accessed July 13, 2016 at https://peakon.com/guides/lesson/do-bonuses-work-the-pros-and-cons-of-employee-incentive-programmes

[216] Anonymous (1998). Sunbeam girds for fight with ousted chief. June 17th, *Los Angeles Times.*

[217] Editors. (2018). Macron's battle to put France back on track. *Bloomberg BusinessWeek.* April 16.

[218] Dinlersoz, E.M. & Greenwood, J. (2012). The rise and fall of unions in the U.S. Working paper 18079. NBER. Accessed October 22, 2018 at https://www.nber.org/papers/w18079.pdf

[219] Ibid.

[220] Bureau of Labor Statistics (2018). Unions. Accessed October 22, 2018 at https://www.bls.gov/news.release/union2.nr0.htm

[221] Ibid.

[222] Weller, C. (2018). Unions help middle class families save for their future. *Forbes.* August 30. Accessed October 22, 2018 at https://www.forbes.com/sites/christianweller/2018/08/30/unions-help-middle-class-families-save-for-their-future/#3b1c83d31be1; Weller, C.E., Madland, D. & Rowell, A. (2016). Building middle-class wealth through unions. *Center for American Progress Action Fund.* December 1. Accessed October 22, 2018 at https://www.americanprogressaction.org/issues/economy/reports/2016/12/01/164578/building-middle-class-wealth-through-unions/

[223] Weller, C. (2018). Unions help middle class families save for their future. *Forbes.* August 30. Accessed October 22, 2018 at https://www.forbes.com/sites/christianweller/2018/08/30/unions-help-middle-class-families-save-for-their-future/#3b1c83d31be1

[224] National Labor Relations Board (2018). Employee rights. Accessed October 23, 2018 at https://www.nlrb.gov/rights-we-protect/rights/employee-rights

[225] NLRB (2018). The right to strike. Accessed October 24, 2018 at https://www.nlrb.gov/strikes

[226] Office of Public Affairs (2011). Federal judge orders Oakland nursing home to rehire

workers following strike. NLRB. Accessed October 24, 2018 at https://www.nlrb.gov/news-outreach/news-story/federal-judge-orders-oakland-nursing-home-rehire-workers-following-strike

[227] Paul, Hastings, Janofsky & Walker LLP. (2004). An introduction to the Railway Labor Act. Accessed October 28, 2018 at http://apps.americanbar.org/labor/annualconference/2007/materials/data/papers/v2/012.pdf

[228] Taft Hartley Act (2018). NLRB. Accessed October 24, 2018 at https://www.nlrb.gov/who-we-are/our-history/1947-taft-hartley-substantive-provisions

[229] Landrum Griffin Act (2018). UAW. Accessed October 24, 2018 at https://uaw.org/landrum-griffin-act/

[230] Civil Service Reform Act (2018). Union member rights and officer responsibilities under the Civil Service Reform Act. U.S. Department of Labor. Accessed October 24, 2018 at https://www.dol.gov/olms/regs/compliance/CSRAFactSheet.pdf

[231] Labor Relations Institute, Inc. (2018). How to decertify a union. Accessed October 24, 2018 at https://lrionline.com/decertification/

[232] Welch, D. & Gruley, B. (2019). Mary Barra risks it all. *Bloomberg Businessweek.* September 23.

[233] Layne, N. (2015). Walmart to reopen five U.S. stores at center of union complaint. Reuters. Accessed October 24, 2018 at https://www.reuters.com/article/us-wal-mart-stores-workers/wal-mart-to-reopen-five-u-s-stores-at-center-of-union-complaint-idUSKCN0R228820150902

[234] Reuters. (2014). Walmart illegally closed union store, court says. *The New York Times.* June 27. Accessed October 24, 2018 at https://www.nytimes.com/2014/06/28/business/international/walmart-illegally-closed-union-store-court-says.html

[235] Editorial Board. (2019). In brief. *Bloomberg Businessweek.* September 16.

[236] Visser, J. (2006). Union membership statistics in 24 countries. Bureau of Labor Statistics. Accessed July 18, 2016 at http://www.bls.gov/opub/mlr/2006/01/art3full.pdf

[237] ETUC (2016) Accessed July 18, 2016 at https://www.etuc.org/aims-and-priorities

[238] Nilsson, V. (2016). Trade union recipe for a strong economy and workers' rights. Accessed July 18, 2016 at https://www.socialeurope.eu/2016/06/trade-union-recipe-strong-economy-workers-rights/

[239] O'Brien, C.N. (2014). The top ten NLRB cases on Facebook firings and employer social media policies. *Oregon Law Review,* 92(2): 337-370.

[240] National Labor Relations Act (2018). Accessed April 3, 2018 at https://www.nlrb.gov/rights-we-protect/employee-rights

[241] Anonymous. (2015). Substance Abuse Center for Behavioral Health Statistics and Quality. Results from the 2015 National Survey on Drug Use and Health. Detailed Tables. SAMHSA. Accessed May 2, 2018 at https://www.samhsa.gov/data/sites/default/files/NSDUH-DetTabs-2015/NSDUH-DetTabs-2015/NSDUH-DetTabs-2015.pdf

[242] Kounang, N. (2017). Marijuana edging up, survey finds. CNN.com. Accessed May 2, 2018 at https://www.cnn.com/2017/12/14/health/monitoring-the-future-teen-drug-use-2017-survey/index.html

[243] Mehmedic, Z., Chandra, S. Slade, D., Denham, H., Foster, S., Patel, A.S., Ross, S.A., Khan, I.A. & ElSohly, M.A. (2010). Potency trends of ^9-THC and other cannabinoids in confiscated cannabis preparations from 1993 to 2008. *Journal of Forensic Science,* 55(5)" 1209-1217.

[244] Doughterty, T.L. (2016). Marijuana use and its impact on workplace safety and

productivity. Occupational Health and Safety Administration. Accessed May 2, 2018 at https://ohsonline.com/articles/2016/02/01/marijuana-use-and-its-impact-on-workplace-safety-and-productivity.aspx

[245] Meier, M.H., Caspi, A., Ambler, A., Harrington, H., Houts, R., Keefe, R.S.E., McDonald, K., Ward, A., Poulton, R. & Moffitt, T.E. (2012). Persistent cannabis users show neuropsychological decline from childhood to midlife. *Proceedings of the National Academy of the Sciences USA,* 109(40).

[246] Zwerling, C., Ryan, J. & Orev, E.J. (1990). The efficacy of preemployment drug screening for marijuana and cocaine in predicting employment outcome. *Journal of the American Medical Association,* 264(20). 2639-2643.

[247] U.S. Department of Transportation. National Highway Traffic Safety Administration. (2017). Marijuana-impaired driving: A report to congress. July.

[248] Waltemath, J. (2017). Fired medical marijuana user can sue Massachusetts employer for disability discrimination. Wolters Kluwer. Accessed October 3, 2019 at http://www.employmentlawdaily.com/index.php/2017/07/18/fired-medical-marijuana-user-can-sue-massachusetts-employer-for-disability-discrimination/

[249] Milligan, S. (2017). Employees take wellness to a higher level. Society for Human Resource Management. August 21. Accessed October 26, 2018 at https://www.shrm.org/hr-today/news/hr-magazine/0917/pages/employers-take-wellness-to-a-higher-level.aspx

[250] Ibid.

[251] Munna, D.N., Abdullaha, A. & Leeb, O.Y. (2012). Effects of Wellness Programs on Job Satisfaction, Stress and Absenteeism between Two Groups of Employees (Attended and Not Attended). *Procedia, 65:* 479-484.

[252] Rand Health. (2014). Do workplace wellness programs save employers money? Rand Corporation. Accessed October 26, 2018 at https://www.rand.org/content/dam/rand/pubs/research_briefs/RB9700/RB9744/RAND_RB9744.pdf

[253] Ibid.

[254] Aldana, S. (2018). 50 employee wellness program examples for any budget. Accessed October 26, 2018 at https://www.wellsteps.com/blog/2018/01/09/employee-wellness-program-examples-budget/

[255] NCADD. (2018). Drugs and alcohol in the workplace. Accessed October 26, 2018 at https://www.ncadd.org/about-addiction/addiction-update/drugs-and-alcohol-in-the-workplace

[256] Ibid.

[257] Garton, E. (2017). Employee burnout is a problem with the company, not the person. *Harvard Business Review.* April 6. Accessed October 26, 2018 at https://hbr.org/2017/04/employee-burnout-is-a-problem-with-the-company-not-the-person

[258] Salvagioni, D.A.J., Melanda, F.N., Mesas, A.E., Gonzalez, A.D., Gabani, F.L., and de Andrade, S.M. (2017). Physical, psychological, and occupational consequences of job burnout: a systematic review of prospective studies. *PLoS One.* 12(10). Accessed October 26, 2018 at https://www.ncbi.nlm.nih.gov/pmc/articles/PMC5627926/

[259] Ibid.

[260] Ibid.

[261] Deery, S., Rayton, B., Walsh, J. & Kinnie, N. (2017). The costs of exhibiting organization citizenship behavior. *Human Resource Management, 56*(6): 1039-1049.

[262] Kelliher, C., Richardson, J. & Boiarintseva, G. (2019). All of work? All of life? Reconceptualizing work-life balance for the 21st century. *Human Resource Management Journal, 29:* 97-112.

[263] Henry, Z. (2015). 6 companies (including Uber) where it's OK to nap. *Inc.* Sept. 4.

Accessed October 26, 2018 at https://www.inc.com/zoe-henry/google-uber-and-other-companies-where-you-can-nap-at-the-office.html

[264] Gelles, D. (2015). At Aetna, a CEO's management by mantra. *The New York Times.* Accessed October 26, 2018 at https://www.nytimes.com/2015/03/01/business/at-aetna-a-ceos-management-by-mantra.html?_

[265] Bureau of Labor Statistics. (2017). Employer-reported workplace injuries and illnesses. BLS. U.S. Department of Labor. Accessed October 26, 2018 at https://www.bls.gov/news.release/archives/osh_11092017.pdf

[266] U.S. Department of Labor. (2016) Worker falls 22 feet to death, 4 months after OSHA cites employer for failing to protect workers on the same job site. Louisville employer faces $320K in fines for serial disregard of fall protection. *OSHA News Release Area 5.* Accessed October 11, 2019 at: https://www.osha.gov/news/newsreleases/region5/08012016

[267] Ibid.

[268] OSHA. (2018). Know your rights. Occupational Safety and Health Administration. Accessed October 26, 2018 at https://www.osha.gov/workers/index.html

[269] Ibid.

[270] OSHA. (2018). Penalties. Occupational Safety and Health Administration. Accessed October 26, 2018 at https://www.osha.gov/penalties/

[271] Poplin, G.S., Pollack, K.M., Griffin, S., Day-Nash, V., Peate, W.F., Nied, E., Gulotta, J. & Burgess, J.L. (2015). Establishing a proactive safety and health risk management assessment in the fire service. *BMC Public Health,* 15:407.

[272] Ibid

[273] Stebbens, S., Comen, E. & Stockdale, C. (2018). Workplace fatalities: 25 most dangerous jobs in America. 24/7 Wall Street. January 9. Accessed October 27, 2018 at https://www.usatoday.com/story/money/careers/2018/01/09/workplace-fatalities-25-most-dangerous-jobs-america/1002500001/

[274] Arbery, C. & Dougherty, E. (2007). 11th Court: Claims of bank employee shot during robbery rejected. SHRM. 6/1/07.

[275] Deschenaux, J. (2008). Experts: Penalizing overweight workers risky. SHRM.

[276] Charniga, J. (2019). The Anti-Dealer. For Earl Stewart, the customer comes first, but everyone else is catching on. *Automotive News.* October 14.

[277] Ibid.

[278] Ibid.

[279] Dimmitt, R. R. & McQueen, T. (2012). Servant Hearts. USA: Xulon Press.

[280] Bass, B.M. (1985). *Leadership and Performance.* New York: Free Press.

[281] Anonymous. (2019). Developing organizational leaders. SHRM. Accessed October 6, 2019 at: https://www.shrm.org/resourcesandtools/tools-and-samples/toolkits/pages/developingorganizationalleaders.aspx

[282] Anonymous. (2019). America's most innovative leaders. *Forbes Magazine.* September 30.

[283] Greenleaf, R. K. (1977). Servant leadership: A journey into the nature of legitimate power and greatness. New York: Paulist Press.

[284] Greenleaf, R. (1977). Servant leadership: A journey into the nature of legitimate power and greatness. Indianapolis, IN: Paulist Press.

[285] van Dierendonck, D. (2011). Servant leadership: A review and synthesis. *Journal of Management*, 37, 1228–1261

[286] Sendjaya, S. (2015). Personal and organizational excellence through servant leadership: Learning to serve, serving to lead, leading to transform. Switzerland: Springer. p. 4

[287] Eva, N., Robin, M., Sendjaya, S., van Dierendonck, D., & Liden, R.C. (2018). Servant

leadership: A systematic review and call for future research. *The Leadership Quarterly,* in press.

[288] Liden, R.C., Wayne, S.J., Zhao, H. & Henderson, D. (2008). Servant leadership: Development of a multi-dimensional measure and multi-level assessment. *The Leadership Quarterly,* 19: 161-177.

[289] Patterson, K. (2003). Servant leadership: A theoretical model. Accessed April 18, 2018 at
http://www.regent.edu/acad/sls/publications/conference_proceedings/servant_leadership_roundtable/2003pdf/patterson_servant_lead ership.pdf

[290] Ibid.

[291] https://www.modernservantleader.com/servant-leadership/fortunes-best-companies-to-work-for-with-servant-leadership/

[292] The Container Store (2018). Our foundation principles. Accessed October 28, 2018 at http://standfor.containerstore.com/our-foundation-principles/

[293] Schwantes, M. (2017). Here's a top ten list of the world's best CEOs but they lead in a totally unique way. *Inc. Magazine.* March 29. Accessed April 18, 2018 at:
https://www.inc.com/marcel-schwantes/heres-a-top-10-list-of-the-worlds-best-ceos-but-they-lead-in-a-totally-unique-wa.html

[294] Schilpzand, P., Houston, L. & Cho, J. (2018). Not too tired to be proactive: daily empowering leadership spurs next-morning employee proactivity as moderated by nightly sleep quality. *Academy of Management Journal, 61*(6): 2367-2387.

[295] Pink, Daniel (2009). The puzzle of motivation. *Ted Talk.* Accessed April 18, 2018 at:
https://www.ted.com/talks/dan_pink_on_motivation

[296] Peachey, W., Burton, J., Wells, L., Chung, Ryoung, M. (2018). Exploring servant leadership and needs satisfaction in the sport for development and peace context. *Journal of Sport Management,* 32(2): 96-108.

[297] Burton, L.J., Peachey, W., Wells, J. Janelle, E. (2017). The role of servant leadership in developing an ethical climate in sport organizations. *Journal of Sport Management,* 31(3): 229-240.

[298] Linuesa-Langreo, J., Ruiz-Palomino, P., Elche, D., Llull, R. (2016). Servant leadership, empowerment climate, and group creativity: a case study in the hospitality industry. *Journal of Applied Ethics,* 7: 9-36.

[299] Ibid., p. 9.

[300] Reidenbach, R.E. & Robin. D.P. (1990). Toward the development of a multidimensional scale of ethics. *Journal of Business Ethics,* 9(8): 639-653.

[301] Schwartz, S. (2012). An overview of the Schwartz Theory of Basic Values. *Online Readings in Psychology and Culture,* 2(1). Accessed October 27, 2018 at
https://scholarworks.gvsu.edu/cgi/viewcontent.cgi?article=1116&context=orpc

[302] Ibid., p. 17 and p. 15.

[303] Kinnier, R.T., Kernes, J.L. & Dautheribes, T.M. (2000). A short list of universal moral values. *Counseling and Values,* 45: 4-16.

[304] Ibid.

[305] Dahlsgaard, K., Peterson, C. & Seligman, M.E.P. (2005). Shared virtue: The convergence of valued human strengths across culture and history. *Review of General Psychology,* 9(3): 203-213.

[306] Westermarck, E.A. (1906). *The Origin and Development of the Moral Ideas.* London, England: Macmillan.

[307] Haidt, J., & Joseph, C. (2004). Intuitive ethics: How innately prepared intuitions generate culturally variable virtues. *Daedalus: Special Issue on Human Nature, 133*(4), 55–66.

[308] Graham, J., Haidt, J., & Nosek, B.A. (2009). Liberals and conservatives rely on

different sets of moral foundations. *Journal of Personality and Social Psychology, 96* (5), 1029–1046.

[309] Schwartz, M.S. (2005). Universal moral values for corporate codes of ethics. *Journal of Business Ethics,* 59: 27-44, p. 27.

[310] Ibid.

[311] Liden, R.C., Wayne, S.J., Meuser, J.L., Hu, J., Wu, J. & Liao, C. (2008). Servant leadership: Validation of a short form of the SL-28. *Leadership Quarterly,* 26: 254-269.

[312] Tenhiala, A., Giluk, T., Svenkepes, C., Simon, I. & Kim, S. (2014). The research-practice gap in human resource management: A cross-cultural study. *Human Resource Management, 55*(2): 179-200.

Made in the USA
Columbia, SC
25 May 2020